The State and Revolution in the Twentieth Century

The State and Revolution in the Twentieth Century

Major Social Transformations of Our Time

Berch Berberoglu

With James F. Petras and David L. Elliott

ROWMAN & LITTLEFIELD PUBLISHERS, INC.
Lanham • Boulder • New York • Toronto • Plymouth, UK

ROWMAN & LITTLEFIELD PUBLISHERS, INC.

Published in the United States of America
by Rowman & Littlefield Publishers, Inc.
A wholly owned subsidiary of The Rowman & Littlefield Publishing Group, Inc.
4501 Forbes Boulevard, Suite 200, Lanham, Maryland 20706
www.rowmanlittlefield.com

Estover Road
Plymouth PL6 7PY
United Kingdom

British Library Cataloguing in Publication Information Available

Library of Congress Cataloging-in-Publication Data

Berberoglu, Berch.
  The state and revolution in the twentieth century : major social transformations
of our time / Berch Berberoglu.
      p. cm.
  Includes bibliographical references and index.
  ISBN-13: 978-0-7425-3883-2 (cloth : alk. paper)
  ISBN-10: 0-7425-3883-4 (cloth : alk. paper)
  ISBN-13: 978-0-7425-3884-9 (pbk : alk paper)
  ISBN-10: 0-7425-3884-2 (pbk : alk. paper)
 1. Revolutions and socialism. 2. Social change. 3. Revolutions—History—
20th century. I. Title. II. Title: State and revolution in the 20th century.
  HX550.R48B47 2007
  303.6'40904—dc22   2006023270

Printed in the United States of America

©™ The paper used in this publication meets the minimum requirements of
American National Standard for Information Sciences—Permanence of Paper
for Printed Library Materials, ANSI/NISO Z39.48-1992.

Contents

Preface

As we enter the twenty-first century, the state continues to play a central role as the sole authority that maintains its monopoly on the use of force and violence. The capitalist state, as the state of the dominant capitalist class, facilitates the exploitation of labor and the accumulation of capital on a world scale and engages in all sorts of activities to advance the interests of capital to maintain and extend its rule throughout the world.

Today, the advanced capitalist state continues to maintain its global posture as an imperialist state to secure conditions that provide an environment in which transnational capital and the world capitalist system grow and prosper at the expense of the working class and other exploited and oppressed sectors of society on a global scale.

The contradictions of this process, however, are such that the forces that have maintained the rule of capital and repressed labor to prolong the latter's exploitation have at the same time reignited the class struggle against capital and the capitalist state. This struggle is now threatening the very existence of capitalism by revolutions in many countries around the world.

This book provides a historical analysis of the state and revolution in the twentieth century by focusing on the major social transformations of our time. After examining the competing theories of the state and revolution in classical social theory, it analyzes the nature and dynamics of the major socialist revolutions of the past century, including the Russian, Chinese, Vietnamese, Cuban, and Nicaraguan revolutions. The book concludes with a critical analysis of the revolutionary process and the challenges associated with the making and maintaining of the major socialist revolutions of the twentieth century.

It is hoped that a historical analysis of the nature, dynamics, and contradictions of the state and socialist revolutions in a variety of temporal, spatial, and national settings would provide (1) a comparative basis from which we can understand the conditions leading to social change and social transformation and (2) an assessment of the successes and failures of various socialist revolutions that took state power during the course of the twentieth century. This book makes an effort toward achieving that understanding by taking a small step in that direction, arguing that it is the culmination of the experiences of the masses who have taken part in these revolutionary struggles that, in the end, determines the dynamics of the new society and the new social order.

Just as revolution involves the participation of many people, so is the writing of a book on revolution. Such a project is the culmination of cumulative knowledge and its integration into new ways of interpretation and analysis that generates further thinking about the subject matter. In this sense, it is indeed a collective effort. The publication of this book is no exception.

Over the years, there have been numerous influences on my thinking regarding the state and revolution as presented in this book. The impact of these influences has sometimes been immediate but more often than not less obvious but longer lasting, in shaping an entire worldview that I have come to adopt over the course of my intellectual career for the past twenty-nine years. Among these, the strongest and most profound has been that of Albert J. Szymanski—teacher, mentor, activist, and revolutionary intellectual—during the course of my graduate studies at the University of Oregon in the mid- to late 1970s.

Others, some prior to and many after the completion of my advanced graduate studies, have played an important role in shaping my thinking in various ways. Among them are Larry T. Reynolds, Blain Stevenson, and James Petras.

Numerous friends and colleagues have also made important contributions to discussions on the nature of the state and dynamics of revolution and social transformation. I would like to thank Alan Spector, Carla Filosa, Gianfranco Pala, Peter Limqueco, Walda Katz-Fishman, Jerry Lembcke, Martin Orr, David L. Harvey, Johnson Makoba, and David Lott for their valuable input on discussions about the state and revolution.

I thank Blain Stevenson for introducing me to the literature on the Chinese revolution; James Petras for his incisive analyses of the Cuban, Chilean, and Nicaraguan revolutions; and Al Szymanski for his bold analysis of imperialism, the capitalist state, and revolutions around the world, as well as his courageous work on socialism, the Russian revolution, and the former Soviet Union.

I would like to thank my mentor, friend, and colleague James Petras for contributing two chapters to this book—one on twentieth-century socialist revolutions and their class components and another on the Cuban and Nicaraguan revolutions, both of which are reprinted here in slightly condensed form from one of his earlier books, *Class, State, and Power in the Third World*, with permission from Zed Books in London. My thanks also go to my friend and colleague David L. Elliott for contributing a chapter to this book on the Vietnamese revolution, a protracted revolutionary struggle that had a profound effect on all those struggling against imperialism and internal reaction throughout the world.

This work has benefited from numerous trips around the world, including Russia, China, Cuba, Chile, Mexico, Argentina, Bolivia, Ecuador, elsewhere in Latin America, North Africa, South and Southeast Asia, and throughout the Middle East, Central Asia, Western and Eastern Europe, and the former Soviet Union. Colleagues and students at universities in these and other countries across the globe have inspired me to undertake the ambitious task of studying the nature and dynamics of the state and revolution in the twentieth century with a focus on major socialist revolutions of our time.

Finally, I would like to thank my wife Suzan for her support, encouragement, and love for nearly four decades and for her revolutionary spirit stemming from her working-class roots, which has kept my optimism for the future of humanity—a future that will hopefully be a just and egalitarian one, not only for my two sons, Stephen and Michael, but for many others of their generation and generations yet to come.

Introduction

This book deals with a topic that is central to the most important and decisive issues and events of our time—the state and revolution in the twentieth century.

Social scientists have made numerous attempts to understand the causes of revolutions by examining the underlying factors that contribute to revolutionary uprisings. To further these efforts, this book addresses some of the key issues related to this process through both theoretical and empirical inquiry into the nature and dynamics of the state and revolution as a basis for an understanding of the major socialist revolutions of the twentieth century.

This book is not intended to provide a comprehensive overview of all the major theories of the state and revolution and all the major social revolutions of the twentieth century. Instead, it provides a sampling of classical theorists and their work who had a major impact on the study of this topic. Likewise, only a sampling of the major socialist revolutions of the twentieth century are presented here to show the impact of these revolutions on the course of history over the past century. Moreover, the revolutions that I have selected for study were chosen not because of any intent to provide a detailed description of each case but for their historical significance and impact on struggles around the world. Finally, this is not a book about debates on theories of the state and revolution that have preoccupied social scientists over recent decades in both conventional and Marxist discourse. Rather, it is an inquiry into the *nature* and *dynamics* of the state and revolution, so that we can better understand the nature of political power and the process of social transformation to effect change.

The thread that runs through each of the chapters that make up this book, especially in the analysis of the major socialist revolutions that are taken up for study, is the *class nature of the state* and *the class forces involved in the revolutionary process* leading up to the taking of state power, as well as—and more importantly—*the class nature of the forces that have taken power and rule over society* in the postrevolutionary period. Applying class analysis to the study of the state and revolution, I argue, provides us with a clear understanding of *the nature and dynamics of the class struggle* that has been unfolding in societies that have gone through a revolutionary process. Here, of special importance are the *class nature* of the organization of revolutionaries and the *level of class consciousness and political education* of the oppressed and exploited classes, as well as their links to and mobilization by organizations that are fighting for their liberation.

On the other side of the equation in assessing the balance of class forces in the class struggle, one needs to know the nature and degree of cohesion among the dominant class forces, the state's response to the deteriorating social and economic conditions, and the political options the ruling class is prepared to exercise through the state to control the unfolding revolutionary situation. These factors are extremely important in understanding the nature and direction of a revolution in the making, and also in discerning the nature and complexities of the new postrevolutionary regime after the taking of state power. This is especially important in the case of a socialist revolution.

The book begins with a critical analysis of major classical theories of the state and revolution, counterposing the Marxist perspective to conventional theories. Hence, chapter 1 provides an analysis of the works of Hegel, Mosca, Pareto, Michels, and Weber on this question. Common to all of these classical mainstream theories of the state and revolution is their elite-centered, top-down view of society and politics that ignore the role of the masses in history, especially the working class under capitalism. Such an approach often represents the views of the dominant ruling class in society and rationalizes and legitimizes the prevailing social order. In contrast, the classical Marxist perspective, expounded by Marx, Engels, and Lenin and explored in chapter 2, views the state as a tool of the ruling class to advance the interests of this class against that of the oppressed and exploited classes. Hence, in this sense, Marxist theory sides with the masses against the ruling class and its state and sees the working class and its movement as the agent of socialist revolution that would replace capitalism and the rule of the capitalist class.

Against this theoretical background, chapters 3 through 7 provide a series of case studies of the state and socialist revolutions in the twentieth century. Chapter 3 presents an overview of the major twentieth-century socialist revolutions and their class components. This chapter, written by James Petras, examines the nature and dynamics of socialist revolution and traces the origins and evolution of the major socialist revolutions of the past century, integrating a comparative analysis of the Russian, Chinese, Vietnamese, and Cuban revolutions in class terms. Here, Petras focuses on the origins of revolutionary organization, periodization and ideology, class participants in socialist revolution (including intellectuals, rural labor, and urban workers), revolutionary alliance, the revolutionary party and the working class, and the primacy of politics in revolutionary mobilization.

Chapter 4 takes up the October 1917 socialist revolution in Russia as the first successful socialist revolution of the twentieth century. Led by the Bolshevik Party, with Vladimir Lenin at its helm, the victorious proletariat put an end to the tsarist feudal-capitalist state and ushered in proletarian rule that brought the workers and the peasants to power. This chapter traces the various stages of the postrevolutionary period, examining its successes and setbacks brought on by the civil war, imperialist encirclement and invasion, and internal power struggles between rival wings of the Communist Party—a period characteristic of revolutionary transformations that change of power brings about, especially when the change in question is a mass socialist revolution that overthrows an entrenched aristocratic ruling class that has ruled society for centuries. In the years since 1917, workers and peasants have risen up in many lands to throw off the imperialist yoke and free themselves from feudal-capitalist exploitation. In China, Vietnam, Cuba, and many other countries, the victorious laboring masses have, through working-class leadership, set out to build a socialist society.

Chapter 5 takes up the case of the October 1949 Chinese revolution as the first postwar socialist revolution that brought workers and peasants to power by overthrowing a semifeudal, semicapitalist society that was in alliance with imperialism. In China, the mass revolutionary mobilization, led by the Chinese Communist Party with Mao Zedong at its helm, took the workers and peasants to victory through a protracted people's war directed against the landed gentry, the comprador bourgeoisie, and Japanese imperialism, by making the second successful proletarian revolution of the twentieth century. This chapter chronicles the origins and development of the Chinese revolution through its various stages and examines the dynamics of this process by analyzing the policies and practices of the Chinese Communist Party during the second half of the twentieth century and into the twenty-first.

Chapter 6 considers the case of the Vietnamese revolution that succeeded against imperialism and internal reaction in establishing another socialist experiment in East and Southeast Asia. Examining the protracted struggles of the Vietnamese workers and peasants under the leadership of the Communist Party, this chapter, written by David Elliott, provides a political history of the decades-long armed struggle that finally defeated the world's most powerful military force—the United States. Elliott traces key turning points in recent Vietnamese history and highlights the evolution of the Vietnamese national resistance against imperialism and the counterrevolution and the process of socialist construction, culminating in national liberation and the unification of the country.

Chapter 7 takes up the cases of the Cuban and Nicaraguan revolutions in the latter half of the twentieth century. Providing a comparative analysis of the parallels between the two revolutions, this chapter, written by James Petras, highlights the complicated nature of the struggle waged simultaneously on two fronts: against dictatorship propped up by the dominant social classes within the nation and the threat of external imperialist invasion. The battle against "Yankee imperialism" in both cases became the rallying point of the anti-imperialist national liberation struggle that was driven by a popular alliance of the masses led by a radicalized leadership of revolutionary intellectuals sympathetic to socialism. The Cuban and Nicaraguan revolutions, mobilizing broad segments of the population to counter repressive rule of the dominant classes tied to U.S. imperialism, thus came to symbolize the mass struggle against dictatorship and imperialism in Latin America in the latter half of the twentieth century.

Finally, the book concludes with an assessment of some common features of twentieth-century socialist revolutions based on the history of these revolutions and their postrevolutionary experience to the end of the twentieth century.

It is hoped that a study of the origins, nature, and dynamics of socialist revolutions of the twentieth century would contribute to our understanding of revolutions in general and socialist revolutions in particular, thus providing a greater appreciation of the underlying complexities of revolutions and the revolutionary process. Such effort may also provide us with the tools to examine and understand the nature and dynamics of socialist revolutions that are yet to come in the new, twenty-first century.

1

Conventional Theories of the State and Revolution

Classical Statements

Conventional political theories have always served to justify and rationalize the legitimacy of the existing social, economic, and political order. In so doing, they have invariably promoted the interests of the dominant ruling class. This has been the case with the early conservative theorists of the state, such as Niccolò Machiavelli and Thomas Hobbes, who advocated the absolute power of the state, arguing that any means utilized by the state to achieve or maintain power is legitimate.[1]

Jean-Jacques Rousseau, Baron Montesquieu, Georg Wilhelm Friedrich Hegel, Emile Durkheim, and other classical conventional theorists have played a similarly conservative role in defending the existing social conditions and the legitimacy of the prevailing social order by providing a host of theoretical rationalizations that have served to maintain the rule of the dominant class in society.[2]

Classical elite theory, which has viewed the masses as apathetic, incompetent, and unable to govern themselves—and for whom, therefore, elite rule is claimed to be both necessary and desirable—has served the same purpose in no uncertain terms. Moreover, downgrading their intelligence and ability, classical elite theorists have claimed not only that the incompetence of the masses prevents them from taking part in the political process, but that in instances when they do rise up in revolution and take control of the state, their leadership becomes corrupted, and the new ruling class, in turn, comes to dictate its terms over society.

Focusing on classical elite theory and other conventional theorical power, the state, and revolution, this chapter provides a of both the substance and ideological bases of conservative state theory and its reactionary political implications.

We begin our survey with a brief look at Hegel's theory of the state—one that will serve as a basis for an analysis of the classical elite theory of politics and the state.

HEGEL'S THEORY OF THE STATE

Hegel's views on politics and the state were heavily shaped by his idealist philosophy of history and society. In a typical idealist formulation of the problem, Hegel's concept of the state is based not on any existing state but on the *"idea* of the state."[3]

In his rational construction of the concept, Hegel viewed the state as having the task of achieving universality (i.e., as caretaker of the "general will"). In this sense, he counterposed the state's public mission to the private sphere within which civil society functioned. With the state representing the universal community, Hegel assigned to the state the responsibility of combating the harmful effects of civil society based on the individual will. In so doing, he set out to find a moment of mediation between the public and the private spheres to achieve the desired unity.

> The essence of the modern state is that the universal be bound up with the complete freedom of its particular members and with private well being. . . . The universal must be furthered, but subjectivity on the other hand must attain its full and living development. It is only when both of these moments subsist in their strength that the state can be regarded as articulated and genuinely organized.[4]

To obtain this equilibrium and thus to maintain social order and stability in society, the process requires the functional integration of the individual into the prevailing sociopolitical order led by the state.

> The state is absolutely rational inasmuch as it is the actuality of the substantial will which it possesses in the particular self-consciousness once that consciousness has been raised to consciousness of its universality. This substantial unity is an absolute unmoved end in itself, in which freedom comes into its supreme right. On the other hand, this final end has a supreme right against the individual, whose supreme duty is to be a member of the state.[5]

In this context, Frederick Copleston points out that for Hegel, "the State represents the unity of the universal and the particular" such that "in the State self-consciousness has risen to the level of universal self-consciousness."[6] In this sense, Copleston continues, "The individual is conscious of himself as being a member of the totality in such a way that his selfhood is not annulled but fulfilled."[7]

> The State is not an abstract universal standing over against its members: it exists in and through them. At the same time, by participation in the life of the State the members are elevated above their sheer particularity. In other words, the State is an organic unity. It is a concrete universal, existing in and through particulars which are distinct and one at the same time.[8]

Moreover, according to Copleston's further rendering of the Hegelian state, one that highlights its spiritual content, for Hegel, "the State is the actuality of the rational will when this has been raised to the plane of universal self-consciousness. It is thus the highest expression of objective Spirit. And the preceding moments of this sphere are resumed and synthesized in it."[9]

Rationalizing the primacy of the state, Hegel assigned to the state a supreme, all-powerful position that has clearly religious and metaphysical connotations: referring to it as "this actual God,"[10] he viewed the existence of the state as part of a divine plan, one that "embodies the true, the eternal wisdom of the Spirit—of God."[11] His statement along these lines—written in the original German as "Es ist der Gang Gottes in der Welt, dass der Staat ist" and variously translated into English as "The State is the march of God through the world," "The existence of the State is the presence of God on Earth," "The march of God in the world, that is what the state is," or "It is the course of God through the world that constitutes the state"[12]—does, despite the controversy surrounding its precise meaning, convey a link between the state and divine authority that reveals not only its religious or ethically driven character but also its absolute nature, as some critics have accused Hegel to be promoting.[13]

This sacred, religiously defined idealist conceptualization of the state and society is similar to Durkheim's functionalist definition of society as the supreme entity (conceived in similarly religious terms) to which the individual must submit and conform, if the harmony between the individual and the state is to be achieved into a unity—the ideal state.

But for Hegel, the state's role and mission is more than that mandated by God; it is sacred not so much because the state represents God's will but because it involved first and foremost the maintenance of order and harmony in the prevailing feudal society threatened by the rise of private capital (i.e., civil society). "Hegel explains the breakdown of the German state by contrasting the feudal system with the new order of individualist society that succeeded it,"[14] writes Marcuse. "The rise of the latter social order," he adds, "is explained in terms of the development of private property."[15] According to Hegel, "the feudal system proper," Marcuse continues, "integrated the particular interests of the different estates into a true community. The freedom of the group or of the individual was not essentially opposed to the freedom of the whole."[16] But "in modern times," he writes, Hegel believed "exclusive property has completely isolated the particular needs from each other"[17] such that the parts have no relation to the whole. Thus, for Hegel, the only institution that serves to hold society together is the state.

The rationalization and legitimization of the state in these terms, however, serve to justify the continued exploitation of the masses by the dominant ruling class through the harmonizing role of the state over society, notwithstanding the claim that this was done under a divine plan devised by God, when in reality this took place within the context of a feudal social order in which the state was ruled by the landowning class, and the church was among the largest landowners, under the pretext of lifting the people to a higher, spiritual level that would usher in true freedom—one based on the unity of the public and private spheres, through their mutual communion.

Suffice it to say, the Hegelian theory of the state, based, in essence, on an idealist, metaphysical conceptualization, provides us no better than the official propaganda of the dominant classes to legitimize their rule and, in the process, to rationalize the reign of a supreme authority exerting its power over the oppressed and exploited laboring masses.

Moving beyond mythical philosophical statements and rationalizations of the state, an analysis of the class nature of the Hegelian ideal state and its role in society reveals its true nature—a utopian ideal that cannot be achieved in its purest form as projected, on the one hand, and an unconditional support for the state that, however "bad" or "sick" it may be, does represent the entire society, on the other hand. It is this authoritative role that Hegel assigns the state, explained in the abstract and divorced from any fruitful understanding of the class nature of society,[18] which, in the final analysis, reinforces his conservative theory of the state as one that rationalizes and legitimizes the exploitation of the laboring masses and their overall place in society in favor of conformity and law and order, rather than helping them liberate themselves from their misery.

In this context, Hegel did not shy away from making his views known on the affinity between his thinking and that of Machiavelli, when he wrote:

> Profoundly moved by the situation of general distress, hatred, disorder, and blindness, an Italian statesman grasped with cool circumspection the necessary idea of the salvation of Italy through its unification on one state. . . .
>
> Machiavelli's fundamental aim of erecting Italy into a state was misunderstood from the start by the blind who took his work as nothing but a foundation of tyranny or a golden mirror for an ambitious oppressor.[19]

Praising *The Prince* and its author for his brilliant work and its relevance to the nature and tasks of the state, Hegel had this to say about Machiavelli:

You must come to the reading of *The Prince* immediately after being impressed by the history of the centuries before Machiavelli and the history of his own times. Then indeed it will appear as not merely justified but as an extremely great and true conception produced by a genuinely political head with an intellect of the highest and noblest kind.[20]

Aside from his conservative political views and inclinations toward the justification of authoritarian rule—a product of his uncritical acceptance of the prevailing social-economic and political order under both declining feudalism and emerging capitalism, which he accepted as legitimate, including the legitimacy of private property and profit—it took the Young Hegelians, who ended up rebelling against him, to liberate Hegel from the shackles of his own metaphysics and to set his theory free from the influence of conditions so well cultivated by the church and the dominant ruling classes that Hegel himself could not (or did not want to) see for what they were. For, doing so otherwise may have forced Hegel to pick up the banner of revolution (as did Marx, Engels, and Lenin) and effect change by smashing the state, not glorifying it, as Hegel did, toward its ideal perfection.

This, of course, had to wait until the mature Marx, like the Young Hegelians before him, was able to turn everything Hegelian, including Hegel himself, on its head and provide us with a materialist theory of history and the state—one that I will take up in chapter 2.

For now, however, I shall look at the theories of several other classical conservative political theorists who, directly and without any pretense, have advocated a conception of the state and society that has lent support to the justification and legitimization of elite rule—theories that were instrumental in giving rise to and were the rationalization of a series of authoritarian fascist dictatorships in Europe in the early twentieth century. I am, of course, referring to classical elite theory.

CLASSICAL ELITE THEORY ON POLITICS AND THE STATE

Classical (aristocratic) elite theory is best exemplified by the works of Gaetano Mosca, Vilfredo Pareto, and Robert Michels. Together, their work on elite formation and oligarchic rule constitutes the core of the classical bureaucratic elite theory of politics and the state.

Classical elite theory maintains that all societies are ruled by elites and that the state is the political instrument by which the vast majority is ruled. This is so, according to this view, because the masses are inherently incapable of governing themselves; therefore, society must be led by a small number of individuals (the elite) who rule on behalf of the masses.

An understanding of the historical context in which Mosca, Pareto, and Michels developed their theories is important and instructive, for they formulated their approach in reaction to socialist currents in Europe at the end of the nineteenth century and beginning of the twentieth.

Mosca on the Political Elite and the State

"In the world in which we are living," wrote Mosca quite bluntly, "socialism will be arrested only if a realistic political science succeeds in demolishing the metaphysical and optimistic methods that prevail at present in social studies."[21] Targeting in particular Karl Marx and his theory of historical materialism, Mosca argued that his book *The Ruling Class* "is a refutation of it."[22]

> Now one of the doctrines that are widely popular today, and are making a correct view of the world difficult, is the doctrine commonly called "historical materialism." . . . The greatest danger that lies in the wide acceptance of the theory, and in the great intellectual and moral influence which it exerts, lies on the modicum of truth that it contains. . . .
>
> The conclusion of the second assumption of historical materialism, and indeed of the doctrine as a whole, seems to us utterly fantastic—namely, that once collectivism is established, it will be the beginning of an era of universal equality and justice, during which the state will no longer be the organ of a class and the exploiter and the exploited will be no more. We shall not stop to refute that utopia once again. *This whole work* [The Ruling Class] *is a refutation of it.*[23]

The "realistic science" that Mosca wanted to develop was in fact primarily intended to refute Marx's theory of power on two essential points:

> First, to show that the Marxist conception of a "ruling *class*" is erroneous, by demonstrating the continual circulation of elites, which prevents in most societies, and especially in modern industrial societies, the formation of a stable and closed ruling class; and secondly, to show that a classless society is impossible, since in every society there is, and must be, a minority which actually rules.[24]

Let us take a closer look at the substance of Mosca's theory and attempt to understand it against this background and in relation to Pareto's and Michels's views on politics, the state, and revolution.

Mosca's main objective in his major work *The Ruling Class* was to develop a *political* theory of power. He divided people in all societies into two distinct groups: "the ruling class" (the political elite) and "the class that is ruled" (the masses). The political elite always enjoy a monopoly of power over the masses and directs society according to its own interests.

In all societies . . . two classes of people appear—a class that rules and a class that is ruled. The first class, always the less numerous, performs all political functions, monopolizes power and enjoys the advantages that power brings, whereas the second, the more numerous class is directed and controlled by the first, in a manner that is now more or less legal, now more or less arbitrary and violent.[25]

Mosca attempted to establish "the real superiority of the concept of the ruling, or political, class," to show that "the varying structure of ruling classes has a preponderant importance in determining the political type, and also the level of civilization, of the different peoples."[26] Hence, for Mosca, it is the political apparatus of a given society and an organized minority (i.e., the political elite) that controls this apparatus—not the class structure—that determines the nature of the state and its transformation.[27]

Claiming that the political elite is usually composed of "superior individuals" and that this superiority serves to further the legitimization of elite rule, Mosca writes:

Ruling minorities are usually so constituted that the individuals who make them up are distinguished from the mass of the governed by qualities that give them a certain material, intellectual or even moral superiority; or else they are the heirs of individuals who possessed such qualities. In other words, members of a ruling minority regularly have some attribute, real or apparent, which is highly esteemed and very influential in the society in which they live.[28]

At one point, Mosca entertains the possibility that "the discontent of the masses might succeed in deposing a ruling class," but he immediately adds, "inevitably . . . there would have to be another organized minority within the masses themselves to discharge the functions of a ruling class."[29] Hence, for Mosca, it is pointless to make a revolution since every revolution will bring to power a minority (an elite) that will become the new ruling class and exercise its power over the masses.

Pareto on the Circulation of Elites

Although there are similarities between the arguments presented by Mosca and Pareto, the latter's theoretical formulation of "the governing elite" and his conceptualization of elite rule need to be clarified: "So let us make a class of the people who have the highest indices in their branch of activity, and to that class give the name of *elite*."[30] By the term *elite*, Pareto meant to stress the superior (psychological) qualities of the ruling minority.

Further elaborating on the internal composition of this group, he divided the elite into two (political and social) segments:

> A *governing élite*, comprising individuals who directly or indirectly play some considerable part in government, and a *non-governing élite*, comprising the rest. . . .
>   So we get two strata in a population: (1) a lower stratum, the *non-élite*, with whose possible influence on government we are not just here concerned; then (2) a higher stratum, *the élite*, which is divided into two: *(a)* a governing *élite*, *(b)* a non-governing *élite*.[31]

Within this framework, the fundamental idea set forth and developed by Pareto was that of the "circulation of elites." By this, he meant two diverse processes operative in the perpetual continuity of elite rule: (1) the process in which *individuals* circulate between the elite and the nonelite and (2) the process in which a *whole elite* is replaced by a new one.

The main point of Pareto's concept of the circulation of elites is that the ongoing process of replenishment of the governing elite by superior individuals from the lower classes is a critical element securing the continuation of elite rule. "The governing class is restored not only in numbers, but—and that is the more important thing—in quality, by families rising from the lower classes and bringing with them the vigor and the proportions of residues necessary for keeping themselves in power."[32]

A breakdown in this process of circulation of elites, however, leads to such serious instability in the social equilibrium that "the governing class crashes to ruin and often sweeps the whole of a nation along with it."[33]

In Pareto's reasoning, a "potent cause of disturbance in the equilibrium is the accumulation of superior elements in the lower classes and, conversely, of inferior elements in the higher classes."[34] Hence, "every *élite* that is not ready to fight to defend its position is in full decadence; there remains nothing for it to do but to vacate its place for another *élite* having the virile qualities which it lacks."[35]

Thus, Pareto reaches an inescapable conclusion in his four-volume study: "Aristocracies do not last. Whatever the causes, it is an incontestable fact that after a certain length of time they pass away. History is a graveyard of aristocracies."[36] According to Pareto, the dynamics of societal development are such that they eventually lead to total social transformation, and no elite is immune to this law of history.

"Revolutions," Pareto writes,

> come about through accumulations in the higher strata of society . . . of decadent elements no longer possessing the residues suitable for keeping them in power, and shrinking from the use of force; while meantime in the lower strata of society elements of superior quality are coming to the fore, possessing

residues suitable for exercising the functions of government and willing enough to use force.[37]

Pareto's explanation of the nature and dynamics of elite rule and their circulation, therefore, rests in large part on the personal qualities of individuals in both elite and nonelite segments of society and their willingness or failure to use force to acquire and retain political power.

Pareto's concern with the decline in legitimacy of the existing order in Italy in the early decades of the twentieth century, together with the rising popularity of Marxism, which he opposed, drove him to fascism. "Fascism, for Pareto," writes Irving Zeitlin,

> seemed not only to confirm his theories but also to hold out hope for a "new era." That he identified with the new order is borne out by the fact that on March 23, 1923, he accepted an appointment as senator—a position he had declined to accept in the pre-fascist government. In a letter to an acquaintance at the time of acceptance, he wrote: "I am happy to see that you are favorably disposed to the new regime, which, in my opinion, is the only one capable of saving Italy from innumerable evils." And, in the same vein, "France will save herself only if she finds her own Mussolini."[38]

"In general," Zeitlin continues, "Pareto's attitude seems to have been that since the pre-fascist regime did not, or could not, save the country from 'anarchy' by legal means, fascism had to do it by force."[39] Such an attitude is similar to Hegel's, which, as we have seen earlier in our discussion, led him to develop a similar admiration of Machiavelli and his role in history.

Pareto's affinity with fascism goes well with his conservative theory of elite rule that despises the masses for their incompetency, a view that is consistent with a reactionary world view characteristic of conservative conventional theories of the state and revolution.

Michels on Bureaucratic Organization and the State

Robert Michels, the third influential classical elite theorist, stressed that the source of the problem of elite rule lies in the nature and structure of bureaucratic organization.[40] He argued that the bureaucratic organization itself, irrespective of the intentions of bureaucrats, results in the formation of an elite-dominated society. Thus, regardless of ideological ends, organizational means would inevitably lead to oligarchic rule: "It is organization which gives birth to the domination of the elected over the electors, of the mandataries over the mandators, of the delegates over the delegators. Who says organization, says oligarchy."[41]

At the heart of Michels's theoretical model lie the three basic principles of elite formation that take place within the bureaucratic structure of political organization: (1) the need for specialized staff, facilities, and, above all, leaders; (2) the utilization of such specialized facilities by leaders within these organizations; and (3) the psychological attributes of the leaders.

Michels argued that the bureaucratic structure of modern political parties or organizations, as well as the state, gives rise to specific conditions that corrupt the leaders and bureaucrats. These leaders, in turn, consolidate power and set themselves apart from the masses.

"Even the purest of idealists who attains to power for a few years," he wrote, "is unable to escape the corruption which the exercise of power carries in its train."[42] For Michels, this pointed to the conservative basis of (any) organization, since the *organizational form* as such was the basis of the conservatism, and this conservatism was the inevitable outcome of power attained through political organization. Hence, "political organization leads to power, but power is always conservative."[43]

Based on this reasoning, one might think that Michels was an anarchist. He was not. He insisted that *any* organization, *including those of the anarchists,* was subject to the "iron law":

> Anarchism, a movement on behalf of liberty, founded on the inalienable right of the human being over his own person, succumbs, no less than the Socialist Party, to the law of authoritarianism as soon as it abandons the region of pure thought and as soon as its adherents unite to form associations aiming at any sort of political activity.[44]

This same phenomenon of elitism/authoritarianism, argued Michels, also occurs at the individual level. Hence, to close the various gaps in his theory, he resorted to human nature-based tautological arguments: Once a person ascends to the leadership level, he or she becomes a part of the new social milieu to the extent that the person would resist ever leaving that position. The argument here is that the leader consolidates power around the newly acquired condition and uses that power to serve his or her own interests by preserving the maintenance of that power. To avoid this and eliminate authoritarianism, which comes about in "associations aiming at any sort of political activity," one must not "abandon the region of pure thought." Herein lay the self-serving conservatism of Michels, who in the latter part of his life turned, like Pareto before him, to the cause of Italian fascism.

In his introduction to a recent edition of Michels's book *Political Parties*, Seymour Martin Lipset writes, "Michels, who had been barred from academic appointment in Germany for many years, . . . left his position at the University of Basle to accept a chair at the University of Perugia offered to him personally by Benito Mussolini in 1928."[45] Lipset goes on to point out that "Michels found his charismatic leader in Benito Mussolini. For him, Il Duce translated 'in a naked and brilliant form the aims of the multitude.'"[46] Finally, he adds, Michels "died as a supporter of fascist rule in Italy."[47]

The three major proponents of classical elite theory—Mosca, Pareto, and Michels—have provided a political theory of elites that they believed explains the nature and dynamics of power in modern society. Best exemplified in Mosca's characterization of the ruling class as the governing elite of full-time politicians in charge of the state apparatus and society in general, classical elite theory has argued in favor of a theory based on a conceptualization centered in bureaucratic organization, particularly in the sphere of politics, such that power, according to their view, resides in government and the governing elite.

Given its contempt for the masses and its acceptance of elite rule over them as an inevitable outcome of bureaucratic organization prevalent in modern politics, classical elite theory lends itself to antipopular, reactionary conclusions that have important political implications diametrically opposed to the prospects for change and social transformation in favor of the masses.

Weber's Theory of Bureaucracy, Power, and the State

Although Max Weber is generally not included among classical elite theorists of the state, his analysis of bureaucracy and political power lends itself to an affinity with elite theory (especially with Michels's "iron law of oligarchy") as he assigns a *quasi*-autonomous role to the state wherein the bureaucrats appear to be serving their own interests, and the bureaucracy appears to be a power unto itself, with more and more permanent features.[48] "Bureaucracy," writes Weber, "is a power instrument of the first order," adding that "where the bureaucratization of administration has been completely carried through, a form of power relation is established that is practically unshatterable."[49]

"Bureaucratic organizations, or the holders of power who make use of them," Weber points out, "have the tendency to increase their power still further by the knowledge growing out of experience in the service."[50] But "expertise alone does not explain the power of bureaucracy"; equally important is the bureaucrats' possession of "official information" to which they and they alone have direct access—something that Weber sees as the "supreme power instrument" of the bureaucracy.[51]

In Weber's view, bureaucracies are large-scale, impersonal organizations in which power relations are organized in a top-down hierarchical manner for purposes of efficiently attaining centrally defined goals. Thus, bureaucratic discipline "is nothing but the consistently rationalized, methodically prepared and exact execution of the received order, in which all personal criticism is unconditionally suspended and the actor is unswervingly and exclusively set for carrying out the command."[52]

The bureaucratic form of social organization, Weber argues, thus lends itself to control and domination of society and the individuals within it and generates as a by-product a social alienation that puts managers and workers, bureaucrats and citizens, in opposite camps, thus leading to conflict between those who control and govern and those who are controlled and governed at all levels of society.

Given their logic and organizational structure, bureaucracies, Weber believed, often take on lives of their own, which are often beyond the control of individual bureaucrats who take part in their daily operation. Thus, according to Weber, once a bureaucracy is firmly in place, it becomes a political force that can very seldom be successfully dismantled or eliminated.

> The individual bureaucrat cannot squirm out of the apparatus into which he has been harnessed. . . . In the great majority of cases he is only a small cog in a ceaselessly moving mechanism which prescribes to him an essentially fixed route of march. . . .
>   The ruled, for their part, cannot dispense with or replace the bureaucratic apparatus once it exists. . . . Increasingly the material fate of the masses depends upon the continuous and correct functioning of the ever more bureaucratic organizations of private capitalism, and the idea of eliminating them becomes more and more utopian.[53]

The key question then becomes one of determining *who* controls and directs the complex bureaucratic machine. Unlike Michels, however, Weber does *not* believe that bureaucracy is, in essence, an autonomous power unto itself; rather, it is a tool or instrument *of* power.

> The bureaucratic structure goes hand in hand with the concentration of the material means of management in the hands of the master. This concentration occurs, for instance, in a well-known and typical fashion in the development of big capitalist enterprises, which find their essential characteristics in this process. A corresponding process occurs in public organizations.[54]

Thus, "the consequences of bureaucracy," Weber concludes, "depend therefore upon the direction which *the powers using the apparatus* give to it."[55]

Weber's statement here could be interpreted in two possible ways: one that assigns primacy to the *political* process and grants a special role to the bureaucrats—as individuals and as a group—who manage the day-to-day affairs of the political apparatus, and another where the source of power is located outside the narrow confines of the political institutions in which individual bureaucrats and the bureaucracy as a whole operate—that is, the economy and class structure of society.

It is not surprising that most contemporary Weberians have separated Weber's analysis of bureaucracy from his generalized theory of class and power in society and thus have managed to give a conservative twist to his otherwise controversial analysis. Viewed within a broader societal context, however, it becomes clear that bureaucracy and political power to Weber are the manifestations of the real social forces that dominate the social-economic structure of modern society. Thus, to give primacy to the analytic strength of these secondary political concepts would mean one is dealing with surface phenomena.

This is clearly evident, for example, in the works of most contemporary theorists of complex organizations, where power is consistently located within the structure of specific bureaucratic organizations, while bureaucracies are given a logic of their own and are conceived in terms of their special power and dynamics. But, to Weber, to understand more fully the logic of bureaucracy and political control one must examine the nature of property, income, status, and other dimensions of class relations, in society. It is here, in his differential conceptualization of class, status, and power based on market relations that one finds a uniquely Weberian approach to bureaucracy, power, and the state.

CONCLUSION

Despite the differences between various classical theorists of the conventional mode on the nature of the state, bureaucracy, and the political sphere of public life examined in this chapter, one prevalent issue that is of special concern is the problem of bureaucracy. And as we shall see throughout our analysis, the relationship of class struggle, the state, and revolution has been mediated through the all-powerful force of the state bureaucracy in different societal settings and has yielded varied results in determining the success or failure of various revolutions after a movement has captured state power. After studying the various cases of social revolution considered in this book, I will provide an assessment of the role of bureaucracy and the bureaucratic apparatuses of the state in the postrevolutionary context and draw some lessons on the nature and dynamics of power in society.

Counterposed to the varieties of conventional political theories examined in this chapter in their classical context, I take up in the next chapter the classical Marxist theory of the state and revolution as an alternative to the conservative theorizing on the nature and dynamics of the state, society, and social transformation.

NOTES

1. See Niccolò Machiavelli, *The Prince* (1513); Thomas Hobbes, *Leviathan* (1651).

2. Jean-Jacques Rousseau, *The Social Contract* (1762); Baron Montesquieu, *The Spirit of Laws* (1748); Georg Wilhelm Friedrich Hegel, *Philosophy of Right* (1821); Emile Durkheim, *The Division of Labor in Society* (1893).

3. G. W. F. Hegel, *Philosophy of Right* (Oxford: Knox, 1942), 258.

4. Hegel, *Philosophy of Right*, 260.

5. Hegel, *Philosophy of Right*, 258.

6. Frederick Copleston, *A History of Philosophy*, Vol. 7 (New York: Doubleday Image, 1994), 212.

7. Copleston, *A History of Philosophy*.

8. Copleston, *A History of Philosophy*.

9. Copleston, *A History of Philosophy*.

10. Hegel, *Philosophy of Right*, 213.

11. Irving M. Zeitlin, *Ideology and the Development of Sociological Theory*, 6th ed. (Upper Saddle River, N.J.: Prentice Hall, 1997), 52.

12. These series of translations correspond to the following sources, respectively: Hegel, *Selections*, ed. J. Loewenberg (New York: n.p., 1929), 443; E. F. Carritt, "Hegel and Prussianism," in *Hegel's Political Philosophy*, ed. Walter Kaufmann (New York: Atherton, 1970), 36; Hegel, *Philosophy of Right*, 279; C. J. Friedrich, ed., *The Philosophy of Hegel* (New York: Modern Library, 1953), 283.

13. Karl R. Popper, *The Open Society and Its Enemies* (Princeton, N.J.: Princeton University Press, 1950).

14. Herbert Marcuse, *Reason and Revolution: Hegel and the Rise of Social Theory* (New York: Oxford University Press, 1941), 53.

15. Marcuse, *Reason and Revolution*.

16. Marcuse, *Reason and Revolution*.

17. Hegel quoted in Marcuse, *Reason and Revolution*, 53.

18. Hegel's rudimentary class model identifies three general classes in society: the agricultural class (which includes landlords and peasants alike), the commercial class (which includes the business class), and the "universal" class (made up of civil servants in the bureaucracy). Workers in this model are completely left out of the picture—they are not part of any class! See, for example, Shlomo Avineri, *Hegel's Theory of the Modern State* (Cambridge: Cambridge University Press, 1972), 98–109.

19. Hegel, *Political Writings*, 219–20.

20. Hegel, *Political Writings*.

21. Gaetano Mosca, *The Ruling Class* (New York: McGraw-Hill, 1939), 327.

22. Mosca, *The Ruling Class*, 447.

23. Mosca, *The Ruling Class*, 439, 447; emphasis added.

24. T. B. Bottomore, *Elites and Society* (Baltimore: Penguin, 1966).

25. Mosca, *The Ruling Class*, 50.

26. Mosca, *The Ruling Class*, 51.

27. Mosca, *The Ruling Class*, 329.

28. Mosca, *The Ruling Class*, 53.

29. Mosca, *The Ruling Class*, 51.

30. Vilfredo Pareto, "Elites and Their Circulation," in *Structured Social Inequality,* ed. C. S. Heller (New York: Macmillan, 1969), 35.

31. Pareto, "Elites and Their Circulation," 1423–24; italics in the original.

32. Pareto, "Elites and Their Circulation," 1430–31.

33. Pareto, "Elites and Their Circulation," 1431.

34. Pareto, "Elites and Their Circulation."

35. Pareto, "Elites and Their Circulation," vol. 1:40.

36. Pareto, "Elites and Their Circulation," vol. 3:1430.

37. Pareto, "Elites and Their Circulation."

38. Zeitlin, *Ideology,* 194.

39. Zeitlin, *Ideology.*

40. Robert Michels, *Political Parties* (New York: Free Press, 1968).

41. Michels, *Political Parties,* 365.

42. Michels, *Political Parties,* 355.

43. Michels, *Political Parties,* 333.

44. Michels, *Political Parties,* 327–28.

45. Seymour Martin Lipset, "Introduction," in Michels, *Political Parties,* 33.

46. Lipset, "Introduction," 32.

47. Lipset, "Introduction," 38.

48. Max Weber, *From Max Weber: Essays in Sociology,* trans., ed., and with an intro. by H. H. Gerth and C. Wright Mills (New York: Oxford University Press, 1967).

49. Weber, *From Max Weber,* vol. 1:228.

50. Weber, *From Max Weber,* vol. 1:225.

51. Weber, *From Max Weber,* vol. 3:1418.

52. Max Weber, *Economy and Society,* 3 vols., ed. Guenther Roth and Claus Wittich (New York: Bedminster, 1968), vol. 3:1149.

53. Weber, *Economy and Society,* 987–88.

54. Weber, *Economy and Society,* 980.

55. Weber, *From Max Weber,* 230; emphasis added.

2

The Marxist Theory
of the State and Revolution

The Classics

In contrast to conventional theories of the state and revolution that provide conservative views on the nature of the state, politics, and society, this chapter offers an alternative, Marxist perspective that differs from its conventional counterparts in some very important ways. The central component of this divergence is an analysis of the class nature of the state and politics, and the class character of revolutionary movements vying for state power, as well as the nature and role of the state that assumes power following a social revolution.

Situating the problem in class context, I argue that society and the state are products of social forces that struggle to maintain or transform class relations. Class relations are thus a product of the balance of class forces that are always anchored in class struggles. In these struggles, it is always the case that the dominant ruling class strives to maintain law and order in order to prolong its rule over society, whereas the oppressed class(es) attempt(s) to rise up and overthrow the state in order to capture state power and establish its rule over society.

This chapter analyzes the dynamics of this process and addresses the central problem within the conceptual and analytical framework of classical Marxist theory. Thus, the writings of Marx, Engels, Lenin, and other Marxist theorists play a prominent role in the presentation of the theoretical issues that define the parameters of the Marxist theory of the state and revolution in the twentieth century.

THE CLASS NATURE OF THE STATE

The state is the most powerful and most pervasive social and political institution in the world, as it holds its sway over vast territories populated by millions of people and does so in proportion to its size and strength relative to other states that claim the same rights in their respective spheres of control and influence around the world.

The state is the only institution that exercises a monopoly on the use of force and violence through legally sanctioned behavior that allow it to raise armies; declare war; maintain police powers; preside over the legal system; print money; collect taxes; arrest, try, and imprison people, including the imposition of the death penalty; and exercise other forms of official control in governing and regulating society through a vast network of a political bureaucracy where no other societal power supercedes its authority. It is for these reasons that the state, regardless of regime, is both feared and revered by the citizens of a given society who have come to accept the rule of the state over their lives and sanction the legitimacy of that rule under "normal" conditions.

While the dominant ruling class controls and uses the state as an instrument to advance its class interests, rival groups and classes struggle to wrest power from the ruling class. However, the legitimacy of the state's rule is seldom questioned, and the powers that control the state are much less scrutinized, except when the state's authority is called into question during crisis periods when it fails to resolve the fundamental social, political, and economic problems of society. A period of decline in legitimacy of the state, and of the ruling class that controls it, follows on the heels of crisis—a period of great turmoil that sometimes leads to social revolution. Such revolutions have occurred in the past, and will continue to occur in the future, in direct relation to the state's failure to meet the needs of the people and to represent their will. It is in this sense that the state has become the scene of class struggle where rival class forces have fought over control of this vital political organ.

The great social revolutions of the twentieth century, and of previous centuries, have always been fought for the overthrow of the dominant ruling class and the prevailing social order by capturing state power to effect change in a new direction in line with the interests of the victorious forces that have succeeded in coming to power.

The rise to power of the despotic rulers of past empires, the emergence of a slave-owning class and its reign over the state and the people under the slave system, the rule of the landed nobility over the serfs under feudalism, and the triumph of the capitalist class over the landlords and its subsequent reign over wage labor, as well as the victory of the proletariat against the landlords and the capitalists, have all occurred through revolutions waged against the dominant classes and the state throughout the course of human history.

THE STATE AND CLASS STRUGGLE

The classical Marxist theory of the state, based on the writings of Karl Marx, Frederick Engels, and V. I. Lenin, focuses on the class basis of politics as the major determinant of political phenomena. It explains the nature of the superstructure (including, first and foremost, the state) as a reflection of the *mode of production*, which embodies in it social *relations of production* (or property-based class relations). Once fully developed and matured, these class relations result in open class struggles and struggles for *state power*.

In all class-divided societies throughout history, write Marx and Engels, "political power is merely the organized power of one class for oppressing another."[1] Political power, they point out, grows out of economic (class) power driven by money and wealth, but to maintain and secure their wealth, dominant classes of society establish and control political institutions to hold down the masses and assure their continued domination. The supreme superstructural institution that historically has emerged to carry out this task is the state.

In class society, writes Lenin, the state has always been "an organ or instrument of violence exercised by one class against another."[2] Thus, as Engels has also noted, "the more it [the state] becomes the organ of a particular class, the more it directly enforces the supremacy of that class,"[3] such that "the fight of the oppressed class against the ruling class becomes necessarily a political fight, a fight first of all against the political dominance of this class."[4]

The centrality of the state as an instrument of *class rule*, then, takes on an added importance in the analysis of social class and class struggles, for political power contested by the warring classes takes on its real meaning in securing the rule of the victorious class when that power is ultimately exercised through the instrumentality of the state.

The emergence of the state coincided with the emergence of social classes and class struggles in the transition from the primitive communal mode to more advanced modes of production when an economic surplus was first generated. Ensuing struggles over control of this surplus led to the development of the state; once captured by the dominant classes in society, the state became an instrument of force to maintain the rule of wealth and privilege against the laboring masses, to maintain exploitation and domination by the few over the many. Without the development of such a powerful instrument of force, there could be no assurance of protection of the privileges of a ruling class, who clearly lived off the labor of the masses. The newly wealthy propertied classes needed a mechanism, writes Engels, that

> would not only safeguard the newly-acquired property of private individuals against the communistic traditions of the gentile order, would not only sanctify private property, formerly held in such light esteem, and pronounce this sanctification the highest purpose of human society, but would also stamp the gradually developing new forms of acquiring property, and consequently, of constantly accelerating increase in wealth, with the seal of general public recognition; an institution that would perpetuate, not only the newly-rising class division of society, but also the right of the possessing class to exploit the nonpossessing classes and the rule of the former over the latter.
>
> And this institution arrived. The *state* was invented.[5]

Throughout history, class divisions and class struggles have shaped the structure of society and social relations. And the struggle between rival class forces to take state power through the overthrow of the state has been the central driving force of history.

Historically, a number of conditions have set the stage and led to the emergence of capitalism and the capitalist state in Western Europe and elsewhere. These include the availability of free laborers, the generation of moneyed wealth, a sufficient level of skills and technology, markets, and the protection provided by the state. In general, these conditions were the foundations on which feudal society became transformed into a capitalist one.[6]

With the principal relations of production being that between wage labor and capital, capitalism established itself as a mode of production based on the exploitation of workers by capitalists, whose power and authority in society derived from their ownership and control of the means of production legally sanctioned by the capitalist state. Lacking ownership of the means necessary to gain a living, the workers were forced to sell their labor power to the capitalists in order to live. As a result, the surplus value produced by labor was appropriated by the capitalists in the form of profit. The appropriation of surplus value from the workers over the course of capitalist production in time led to the accumulation of capital so that the capitalists came to amass an ever-growing profit and wealth. Thus, private profit, generated through the exploitation of labor, became the motive force of capitalism.

The contradictions embedded in such antagonistic social relations in time led to the radicalization of workers and the formation of trade unions and other labor organizations that were to play an important role in the struggle between labor and capital. The history of the labor movement in Europe, the United States, and elsewhere in the world is replete with bloody confrontations between labor and capital and the latter's repressive arm, the capitalist state. From the early battles of workers in Britain and on the Continent in the late eighteenth and early nineteenth centuries to the decisive role played by French workers in the uprising of 1848–1851 to the Paris Commune in 1871 to the Haymarket massacre and the heroic struggle of the Wobblies in the United States in the early twentieth century, the working class put up a determined struggle in its fight against capital on both sides of the Atlantic—a struggle spanning over two centuries.

THE NATURE AND ROLE OF THE CAPITALIST STATE

The central task of the early capitalist state in Europe and the United States was that of disciplining the labor force. Union activity, strikes, demonstrations, agitation, and propaganda initiated by workers against the employers and the system were systematically repressed.

The capitalist state became heavily involved in the conflict between labor and capital on behalf of the capitalist class, bringing to bear its repressive apparatus on labor and its allies who threatened the capitalist order. Law and order enforced by the capitalist state served to protect and preserve the capitalist system and prevent its transformation. In this sense, the state came to see itself as a legitimizing agency of the new social order and identified its survival directly with the capitalists who controlled it.

Established to protect and advance the interests of the capitalist class, the early capitalist state thus assumed a pivotal role that assured the class rule of capitalists over society and became an institution of legitimization and brute force to maintain law and order in favor of capitalism. Sanctioning and enforcing laws to protect the rights of the new property owners and disciplining labor to maintain a wage system that generated profits for the wealthy few, the capitalist state became the instrument of capital and its political rule over society. This led Marx and Engels to observe that the state in capitalist society serves as a political organ of the bourgeoisie for the "guarantee of their property and interests."[7] Hence, "the bourgeoisie has . . . conquered for itself, in the modern representative State, exclusive political sway. The executive of the modern State is but a committee for managing the common affairs of the whole bourgeoisie."[8]

In our epoch, writes Lenin, "every state in which private ownership of the land and means of production exists, in which capital dominates, however democratic it may be, is a capitalist state, a machine used by the capitalists to keep the working class and the poor peasants in subjection."[9]

Democracy in capitalist society, Lenin points out, is always bound by "the narrow limits set by capitalist exploitation, and consequently always remains, in effect, a democracy for the minority, only for the propertied classes, only for the rich."[10] In this sense, "Freedom in capitalist society always remains about the same as it was in the ancient Greek republics: freedom for the slave-owners."[11]

Owing to the conditions of capitalist exploitation, the modern wage slaves are so crushed by want and poverty that "they cannot be bothered with democracy," "cannot be bothered with politics"; in the ordinary, peaceful course of events, the majority of the population is debarred from participation in public and political life. . . .

Democracy for an insignificant minority, democracy for the rich—that is the democracy of capitalist society.[12]

"Marx grasped this *essence* of capitalist democracy splendidly," Lenin continues, "when, in analyzing the experience of the Commune, he said that the oppressed are allowed once every few years to decide which particular representatives of the oppressing class shall represent and repress them in parliament!"[13]

"People always have been the foolish victims of deception and self-deception in politics," Lenin writes elsewhere, "and they always will be until they have learnt to seek out the *interests* of some class or other behind all moral, religious, political and social phrases, declarations and promises."[14]

In an important passage in *The State and Revolution*, Lenin points out that the state in capitalist society is not only the political organ of the capitalist class; it is structured in such a way that it guarantees the class rule of the capitalists and, short of a revolutionary rupture, its entrenched power is practically unshakable: "A democratic republic is the best possible political shell for capitalism," Lenin writes, "and, therefore, once capital has gained possession of this very best shell . . . it establishes its power so securely, so firmly, that *no* change of persons, institutions or parties in the bourgeois-democratic republic can shake it."[15] But the dialectics of this process is such that the contradictions and conflicts embedded in capitalist society propel the workers into action against the capitalists and the capitalist state. Such a move on the part of the workers culminates, in its highest political expression, in an anticapitalist, socialist revolution.

THE CAPITALIST STATE, CLASS STRUGGLE, AND REVOLUTION

Writing in August 1917, on the eve of the Great October Socialist Revolution in Russia, Lenin considers in *The State and Revolution* both the class nature of the state *and*, more important, the necessity of its revolutionary overthrow. "If the state is the product of the irreconcilability of class antagonisms," he writes, and

if it is a power standing *above* society and "*alienating* itself *more and more* from it," it is clear that the liberation of the oppressed class is impossible not only without a violent revolution, *but also without the destruction* of the apparatus of state power which was created by the ruling class and which is the embodiment of this "alienation."[16]

Thus, the transformation of capitalist society, Lenin points out, involves a revolutionary process in which a class-conscious working class, led by a disciplined workers' party, comes to adopt a radical solution to its continued exploitation and oppression under the yoke of capital and exerts its organized political force in a revolutionary rupture to take state power.

The victory of the working class through a socialist revolution leads to the establishment of a socialist (workers') state. The socialist state constitutes a new kind of state ruled by the working class and the laboring masses. The cornerstone of a socialist state, emerging out of capitalism, is the abolition of private property in the major means of production and an end to the exploitation of labor for private profit.

"The theory of the class struggle, applied by Marx to the question of the state and the socialist revolution," writes Lenin,

> leads as a matter of course to the recognition of the *political rule* of the proletariat, of its dictatorship, i.e., of undivided power directly backed by the armed force of the people. The overthrow of the bourgeoisie can be achieved only by the proletariat becoming the *ruling class*, capable of crushing the inevitable and desperate resistance of the bourgeoisie, and of organizing *all* the working and exploited people for the new economic system.[17]

The establishment of a revolutionary dictatorship of the proletariat (as against the dictatorship of capital) is what distinguishes the socialist state from its capitalist counterpart. Marx pointed out in *Critique of the Gotha Program* that the dictatorship of the proletariat (i.e., the class rule of the working class) is a transitional phase between capitalism and communism. "Between capitalist and communist society," Marx wrote, "lies the period of the revolutionary transformation of the one into the other. Corresponding to this is also a political transition period in which the state can be nothing but *the revolutionary dictatorship of the proletariat*."[18]

During this period, the state represents and defends the interests of the working class against capital and all other vestiges of reactionary exploiting classes, which, overthrown and dislodged from power, attempt in a multitude of ways to recapture the state through a counterrevolution. Thus, once in power, the proletarian state has a dual role to play: to break the resistance of its class enemies (the exploiting classes) and to protect the revolution and begin the process of socialist construction.

The class character of the new state under the dictatorship of the proletariat takes on a new form and content, according to Lenin: "During this period the state must inevitably be a state that is democratic *in a new way* (for the proletariat and the propertyless in general) and dictatorial *in a new way* (against the bourgeoisie)."[19] Thus, *"simultaneously* with an immense expansion of democracy, which *for the first time* becomes democracy for the poor, democracy for the people, and not democracy for the money-bags, the dictatorship of the proletariat imposes a series of restrictions on the freedom of the oppressors, the exploiters, the capitalists."[20] Lenin stresses the necessity of suppressing the capitalist class and its allies to deny them the freedom to foment a counterrevolution, barring them from politics and isolating and defeating efforts to undermine the new worker's state.

Used primarily to suppress these forces and build the material base of a classless, egalitarian society, the socialist state begins to wither away once there is no longer any need for it. As Engels points out:

> The first act in which the state really comes forward as the representative of society as a whole—the taking possession of the means of production in the name of society—is at the same time its last independent act as a state. The interference of the state power in social relations becomes superfluous in one sphere after another, and then ceases of itself. The government of persons is replaced by the administration of things and the direction of the processes of production. The state is not "abolished," *it withers away.*[21]

In this sense, the state no longer exists in the fully matured communist stage, for there is no longer the need in a classless society for an institution that is, by definition, an instrument of class rule through force and violence. Lenin writes:

> Only in communist society, when the resistance of the capitalists has been completely crushed, when the capitalists have disappeared, when there are no classes (i.e., when there is no distinctions between the members of society as regards their relation to the social means of production), *only* then "the state . . . ceases to exist," and *"it becomes possible to speak of freedom."* Only then will a truly complete democracy become possible and be realized, a democracy without any exceptions whatever.[22]

It is in this broader, transitional context that the class nature and tasks of the state in socialist society must be understood and evaluated, according to the Marxist classics.

Thus, for Marx, Engels, and Lenin, the period of transition to communist society is a period exhibiting an infinitely higher form of democracy than that found in capitalist society, for democracy under capitalism is democracy for the few, democracy for the rich capitalists, whereas under socialism democracy is for the masses, democracy for the great majority of the laboring people working together to build an egalitarian, classless society.

While the transition from socialism to communism takes place under conditions of advanced socialism, when the rule of the working class is on a firm footing and when the democratization of social life among the workers has reached a high point, the Marxist classics, above all Lenin, were very concerned with the initial period of transition from capitalism to socialism in the immediate postrevolutionary period. This concern centered around two key problems that would have to be guarded against to prevent the degeneration of the workers' revolution: (1) the ever-present danger of counterrevolution and the necessity of constant vigilance against the overthrown ruling class(es) who, anxious to return to power, resort to all sorts of schemes to foment a counterrevolution in order to regain their lost power; and (2) the danger of bureaucratization among the leadership of the revolution once the revolutionary power becomes established. Lenin went out of his way to stress the urgency of the fight against these two ominous threats to the survival of the proletarian revolution during the transition to socialism.

As we shall see in our analysis of various cases of socialist revolution around the world, these dangers were an ongoing concern of the leadership of these revolutions and became very much real, and, at least in some cases, as in the former Soviet Union, they succeeded in either derailing the revolution or ultimately overthrowing it through a counterrevolution.

Let us now examine the experiences of the major socialist revolutions of the twentieth century through an analysis of the class forces that propelled movements to take state power.

NOTES

1. Karl Marx and Frederick Engels, "Manifesto of the Communist Party," in Marx and Engels, *Selected Works* (New York: International Publishers, 1972), 53.

2. V. I. Lenin, *The State and Revolution*, in V. I. Lenin, *Selected Works in Three Volumes*, vol. 2 (Moscow: Progress, 1975), 374.

3. Frederick Engels, "Ludwig Feuerbach and the End of Classical German Philosophy," in Marx and Engels, *Selected Works*, 627.

4. Engels, "Ludwig Feuerbach."

5. Frederick Engels, *The Origin of the Family, Private Property and the State* (New York: International Publishers, 1972), 263.

6. Karl Marx, *Pre-Capitalist Economic Formations* (New York: International Publishers, 1965).

7. Marx and Engels, *The German Ideology*, 59.

8. Marx and Engels, "Manifesto of the Communist Party," 37.

9. V. I. Lenin, *The State*, in Karl Marx, Frederick Engels, and V. I. Lenin, *On Historical Materialism* (New York: International Publishers, 1974), 641.

10. Lenin, *The State and Revolution*, 301.

11. Lenin, *The State and Revolution*.

12. Lenin, *The State and Revolution*.

13. Lenin, *The State and Revolution*, 301–2.

14. V. I. Lenin, "The Three Sources and Three Component Parts of Marxism," in V. I. Lenin, *Selected Works in One Volume* (New York: International Publishers, 1971), 24.

15. Lenin, *The State and Revolution*, 247.

16. Lenin, *The State and Revolution*, 242; emphasis in the original.

17. Lenin, *The State and Revolution*, 255; emphasis in the original.

18. Karl Marx, *Critique of the Gotha Programme*, in Karl Marx and Frederick Engels, *Selected Works* (New York: International Publishers, 1972), 331; emphasis in the original. For an extended discussion on the concept of the "dictatorship of the proletariat," see Etienne Balibar, *On the Dictatorship of the Proletariat* (London: New Left Books, 1977).

19. Lenin, *The State and Revolution*, 262; emphasis in the original.

20. Lenin, *The State and Revolution*, 302; emphasis in the original.

21. Frederick Engels, *Anti-Duhring* (New York: International Publishers, 1976), 307.

22. Lenin, *The State and Revolution*, 302–3; emphasis in the original.

3

Twentieth-Century Socialist Revolutions and Their Class Components

James F. Petras

Any attempt to theorize socialist revolution must start at the point where conditions of exploitation are converted into the practice of class struggle. Socialist revolutions in the twentieth century unfolded as complex processes decisively dependent on the emergence and growth of a revolutionary political organization. The central political organization (party or movement) passes through several crucial interrelated phases, *each* of which provides a unique contribution to the ultimate success of the whole enterprise. The sequence leading to the revolutionary transformation begins with the formative period, involving the organization and ideology of the party. This is followed by class and political struggles, in which forces are accumulated, roots are put down among the masses, a mass membership is won, and, finally, power is seized. Subsequently, the socialist revolutionary process includes the establishment of a government, reorganization of the state, and efforts to transform social relations.

THE ORIGINS OF REVOLUTIONARY ORGANIZATION

While later influences play an important part in shaping the form and content of the revolutionary process, the origins and initial organization of the revolutionary party play perhaps the key role. Critical to an understanding of the embryonic revolutionary organization is the political culture in which it is embedded—the degree to which class struggle and social mobilization have occurred. The insertion of the embryonic revolutionary party into an ascending mass movement or within a politicized population is crucial in the creation of the collective experiences within which the cadres will frame their revolutionary programs. The cadres are the distillation of class struggles and the bridges between past struggles and the future revolution. As carriers of the early formative class experiences, they play a decisive role in determining the ultimate direction of the revolutionary process and in weaving its specific organizational forms, leadership, and ideology. But the cadres themselves, and the struggles they lead, are reflections of broader historic conflicts that provide the parameters within which particular actions and movements occur.

In Russia, the events of 1905—the uprising of the working class and the formation of Soviets—propelled the Bolshevik Party forward, strengthening the socialist component in its ideological armory, creating cadres, and providing a historical reference for the social transformation in October 1917. In China, the early workers' struggle provided the organizational and ideological direction that sustained the Communist Party on a socialist path, despite the shift of activity toward rural petty-commodity producers. The continuity of the revolutionary movement in China must be stressed against all those who attempt to submerge China's socialist revolution in a host of special features and events related to China's rebellious peasantry, the strategic wisdom of Mao, the nature of guerrilla war, the Japanese invasion (peasant nationalism)—all of which fail to explain *the particular moment* of revolutionary mobilization or the *substantive changes* that took place after the revolution. China's socialist revolution did not take place during centuries of rebellious peasant movements; nor did it occur during more than a half century of imperialist invasions and guerrilla warfare; nor was the socialist orientation a product of Mao Zedong alone. The peasantry moved toward socialist revolution only after the worker-based Communist Party inserted itself in the country and after the peasants uprooted by Japanese imperial capital found an ideological and organizational expression in the Communist Party—and in no other party or army. Finally, Mao's own strategic orientation toward the class struggle road to socialism, and even his fundamental tactical commitment toward maintaining an autonomous army/party, were products of the experiences of the 1921–1927 period (although drawing lessons from the negative experiences of subordination to the Kuomintang [KMT]).

If we conceptualize the revolution as a protracted and complex process, we capture the historical importance of the formative period: the qualitative ideological and organizational factors that enabled the party to gain the allegiance of the great mass of exploited Chinese and ultimately to succeed in revolutionary combat. Any periodization of the revolution that focuses exclusively on the "Yenan period" (Mark Selden), the Japanese invasion (Chalmers Johnson), or the postwar disintegration of the KMT fails to explain the politics of each period.[1] For each account presents particular features of an environmental setting (rural areas, peasantry; war-induced conditions, nationalism) as the basic determinants of the policy and direction of the revolutionary struggle. Yet these features affected all tendencies and political groupings within the political system, while only one—the Communist Party—was able to fashion a program and accumulate forces capable of taking it to ultimate success. The basis of this success was not conjunctural but the result of a painstaking and continuous effort to create the human political resources needed to formulate tactics, strategies, and organizational structures through each conjuncture.

The central notions of class struggle, combining social and democratic revolution, derived from Marx and Lenin and embodied in the Chinese Communist cadre, contributed immensely to establishing a revolutionary strategic direction. The adaptations and nuances of application in the surrounding agrarian areas by Mao and his colleagues were innovations at the level of applied theory. The particular forms that armed struggle took—efforts to destroy the state—were based on classical Marxist-Leninist notions of the class character of the state. The same can be said concerning the politics of the revolutionary forces vis-à-vis the national bourgeoisie, although here Mao's analysis at times ran counter to his organizational practice: While arguing that such classes existed, he never allowed the party to become enmeshed in a subordinated alliance.

The party, founded on the principles of class struggle, baptized in the fire of mass urban struggles, proceeded to the countryside and reeducated a whole generation of rural laborers, petty-commodity producers, and their uprooted brethren in the ideology of class struggle and class politics. The fundamental politics of Yenan originated in the 1920s, as did the anti-imperialism that brought forth the anti-Japanese alliance. Without the basic cadre formed in the earlier phase, the mighty waves of peasant masses might have broken before the onslaught of the organized Japanese or KMT forces, leaving little long-term, large-scale change in the society. Thus, the study of revolution as a process requires that the continuity and interrelatedness of each period be emphasized. Particular events mark historical moments, with particular configurations of forces. But without an understanding of the preceding sequence, the molecular processes of accumulation of forces, the end product of successful revolution, cannot be grasped. Each differential moment in the revolutionary process contributes to the understanding of the whole. The issue, in determining the final outcome, is to understand the relationship between each sequence.

PERIODIZATION AND IDEOLOGY

The second basic requirement for a theory of socialist revolution is to differentiate correctly the periods in which different classes enter the revolutionary process. In periods of profound societal crises, classes enter into political and social combat unevenly, and in many cases political parties are not present to provide the organizational mechanisms through which they can act. Moreover, the moment of entry of a class—especially during a massive and tumultuous eruption—can bend the direction and orientation of the revolutionary movement. For example, in the case of the Cuban revolution, the petite bourgeoisie and bourgeoisie entered the revolutionary movement in the late 1950s—that is, after the early founders of the July 26th Movement, but before the mass of workers and peasants who joined early in 1959. Thus, these bourgeois, antisocialist forces neither held the organizational leadership nor had ties with newly awakened rural and urban workers. The prior presence of the Castro leadership—shaped ideologically by the earlier workers' struggles of the 1930s—ensured that the key posts and measures would not be controlled by bourgeois forces. The subsequent entry of the working class into the revolutionary movement, facilitating (and reflecting) the transformation in state power, undermined the position of bourgeois representatives in the government. The urban/rural workers became the dominant force in the revolutionary process after the uprising that overthrew Batista. The latter was merely one moment in the revolutionary struggle, whose crucial significance was that it facilitated the massive *arming of the working class,* which in turn was the critical factor permitting the overthrow of class relations.

The importance of periodizing the entry of different classes into the revolutionary process is highlighted by the fact that many writers, in seeking to identify the class character of a party, adopt an excessively numerical approach, which downplays the determination by specific social forces. In the case of China, for example, many scholars write off the relative importance of the working class because of the rural setting of much of the fighting and the fact that the revolutionary movement was predominantly composed of peasants. In the case of Cuba, the same writers emphasize the presence of middle-class participants in the mid- to late 1950s as the central characteristic in defining the nature of the revolution, but they overlook both the earlier working-class struggles, which established a popular, anticapitalist political culture, and the later massive entry of rural and urban workers into the political movement.

While the revolutionary process encompasses a variety of social forces—and the timing of entry of these forces varies from situation to situation—it is important not only to count heads but to identify the qualitative position (power) of each social force within the movement. Early or late entry of the working class can be the decisive factor in propelling a revolutionary party or movement toward overthrowing capitalism and collectivizing the means of production. In Russia, the working class was the central force initiating and sustaining the revolution; in China, it initiated the struggle and the organization of the party; in Vietnam, it initiated the struggle and sustained activity on a secondary plane; in Cuba, it created a revolutionary culture that was vital for the formation of the Castro leadership and subsequently played a central role in the decisive social struggles after the political regime was transformed. In all cases, the revolution had a socialist character because working-class struggles profoundly influenced the ideas and practices of the revolutionary organization.

The third necessary element in theorizing socialist revolution is a differentiation of the levels at which various social forces participate in the revolutionary process. We can note six levels of organization: leaders, cadres, militants, fighters, sympathizers, and supporters. The ideology and formative experience of participants at each level reflect the particular moment in which they entered the struggle. This qualitative distinction is crucial, insofar as revolutions in the course of their successful trajectory attract a variety of social forces and thus may appear to be polyclass in character, or in some cases they may appear to have no working-class content. This was especially the case in China, where the great mass of militants and fighters were uprooted peasants and largely grounded in rural struggles. That the leaders and many of the cadres were directly or indirectly influenced by the workers' struggle and its ideology has been obscured in many accounts, which have focused on one level of the party organization and its "empirical" rather than its "historical" base. The long-term direction of the revolutionary process was primarily influenced by the historic base in the working class, not in the peasantry: The seizure of power led to the collectivization of production, not to the proliferation of petty-commodity production.

In the case of Cuba, the bulk of the leaders and cadres were increasingly committed to building a mass party centered in the working class, even though a substantial number of sympathizers and supporters and even fighters came from bourgeois and petit bourgeois strata. Because socialist leaders controlled key posts, despite a substantial number of antisocialist supporters at one (the preinsurrectional) phase, the revolutionary movement could shift gears and expand support among rural and urban workers, creating a mass base of militants and fighters among them. Because the central core of the organization was composed of committed socialist revolutionary forces, the accumulation of petit bourgeois support did not adversely affect the revolutionary trajectory of the movement. Located primarily in the subcadre levels of the revolutionary movement, the nonrevolutionary forces provided fighters or economic support but were not decisive for the historical content of the revolutionary struggle.

The fourth element in the theorization of socialist revolution concerns the central concepts and ideas that influence and shape the ideology of the revolutionary movement. The ideas are of two types: (1) the core notions that express the motivating forces and historic goals and methods of the revolution and (2) the tactical/strategic ideas that express the conjunctural struggles and immediate needs of particular strata and organizations and reflect efforts to accumulate forces around the central party cadre. The key notions of twentieth-century revolutionary socialist movements revolve around class struggle, imperialism, the class nature of the state, and the collectivization of the means of production. The tactical-strategic ideas vary from conjuncture to conjuncture, from one class and stratum to another. Tactical-strategic ideas are essentially directed toward a discrete problem area, for instance, a reform or set of reforms as a means of creating political alliances or fronts. Thus, the tactics of a revolutionary socialist party may, at a certain moment, give the appearance of an agrarian-peasant movement, as in China during the 1930s, or of a democratic populism, as in Cuba in the 1950s, or of a nationalist movement, as in Vietnam in the 1950s and 1960s. The shifting terrain of revolutionary struggle requires tactical shifts and an accompanying ideological flexibility. Nevertheless, these changes are informed by core ideas that are largely the product of the historic forces of socialist transformation embodied in the working class and distilled in its organizational expression.

CLASS PARTICIPANTS IN SOCIALIST REVOLUTION

Three social forces have played a decisive role in twentieth-century socialist revolutions: the intellectuals, rural labor, and the urban working class. Each has contributed to the organizational, ideological, and military efforts necessary for a successful transformation. Yet the social characteristics that enabled them to take an active and specific part in the revolutionary process, which fundamentally remade their societies, have rarely been adequately identified. These basic characteristics have instead been obscured by an emphasis on social psychological and/or vulgar economistic attributes. However, the long-term commitments and large-scale presence of these social forces, through the worst adversities and changing circumstances, cannot be explained in terms of simple individual experience or immediate economic interest. The great personal sacrifices and social suffering that have accompanied the prolonged revolutionary struggles of a country require structural explanations and a broader grasp of the societal crises that engendered the historic alliance that has and continues to transform society.

Most efforts to characterize revolutionary processes have nevertheless relied, in one form or another, on identifying the social characteristics of political participants. One of the most commonplace notions is that these have a class identity that can be readily deduced by noting the family background of individuals. The experiences of class and class struggle, however, are transmitted from one generation to another directly through the family only if parents and offspring continue to inhabit the same situation, affected by the same sets of operative forces. But in the twentieth century, forces of world-historical proportions have intervened in social processes, disrupting the regular reproduction of classes. Imperial wars, colonial conquests, and massive flows of capital have produced severe disjunctions between family and class and the position of individuals within the class structure. The role of imperial force in jarring individuals loose from their class matrix has been a recurrent phenomenon in both European and third world countries. Visibility in social background may even become a hindrance to understanding the dynamic interplay between political commitment and class position, when class position itself is subject to sudden and massive disruption. The impact of historical forces on the class structure thus has decisive importance in determining whether individuals will conform to the class practices of their forbearers.[2]

THE SOCIAL IDENTITY OF THE INTELLECTUALS

Intellectual strata are, of course, particularly affected by the tremors that are set off when war, capitalist crisis, or class struggle upsets the equilibrium of exploitative society. Hence, although many revolutionary intellectuals have middle-class backgrounds, this has less significance in determining their social orientation than the worldwide struggles that impinge upon a social formation.

The growth of a revolutionary socialist intelligentsia in Russia and China occurred during a prolonged period of class conflict, in which the economic position of the intellectuals was less important in shaping a political vocation than the class struggles emerging in the society as a whole. The problematic of the revolutionary socialist intellectual cannot be reduced to a determination by declassed forces on the fringes of society. For lack of anchorage, resulting from large-scale disruptions, is not the main element in determining his or her specific ideological commitments. Rather, for us, the primary force providing a social identity for such intellectuals is their political membership in the working-class movement. Their social identity is a product of the influence, ideas, and activities of an ascending class—which even before it transforms society modifies the conditions in which society produces and reproduces itself. Their incorporation into the mass movement and the process through which this is achieved—class struggle, national wars—provide the basic ingredients for determining the class loyalty of the intellectuals. Insofar as their class situation is in flux, the primary determinants are not to be found in their economic roles, but in the political role they play in the class struggle.

RURAL LABOR AND SOCIALIST REVOLUTION

The relationship of landlord and peasant has been characterized by relatively long periods of stability, punctuated by periods of rebellion and protest. In the classic cases of peasant revolt the land-hungry peasants attack the symbols and substance of landlord domination but are incapable of reordering society in their own image. The twentieth century witnessed the rise of imperial capital, which appropriates means of production and surplus from the peasantry but accumulates outside the particular social economy. The separation of the process of exploitation from the locus of accumulation has led to profound dislocation of the rural labor force. For massive numbers of peasants are stripped of their means of production while being divorced geographically from employment in the locus of accumulation, in centers of industrial production. Rural labor that was drawn into twentieth-century socialist revolutions is not the same peasantry exploited for centuries by landlords. On the contrary, the features of rural existence and the forces acting on it, leading to socialist revolution, are unique to the twentieth century and account for the distinct path that "peasant" revolts have taken.

The crucial elements in the internal development of the countryside are found in the uprooting of the peasantry, the proletarianization of the labor force, and the incorporation of part of this displaced and proletarianized rural labor force in forms of disciplined revolutionary organization. The immediate effect of imperial domination has been to accentuate the uprootedness of the rural labor force. The decomposition of the village through force, commercial relations, and/or corporate expansion has been a central feature of prerevolutionary societies. The process of differentiation that capitalism has fomented through the extension of investment from centers of capital to the countryside has been accompanied by large-scale military-political movements, which have dominated and blocked the emergence of indigenous capitalist forces capable of exercising hegemony. The rural labor force, concerned with the occupation of the countryside, is no longer the peasant oppressed by the landlord. The impersonal forces of imperial capital penetration obliterate traces of particularistic domination and establish conditions of generalized exploitation and uprootedness.

Socialist revolution has nowhere been based on an undifferentiated mass peasantry. Rather, it is the dispossessed former peasant, uprooted by the combined political-military-economic efforts of imperial powers, who has set in motion the movement of peasants toward political action. The dissolution of local ties to the land facilitates participation in revolutionary socialist activity. As the revolution enters into conflict with capitalist or precapitalist relations of production, its reliance on rural labor (which approximates the conditions of the classical proletariat) increases. And although smallholders—or even kulaks—may enter into the revolutionary struggle under conditions of imperial appropriation, despite the cost of dispossession, it nevertheless remains the case that as the revolutionary movement takes on more clearly socialist objectives, landless laborers and uprooted former peasants increasingly become the fulcrum for political action. It is neither middle peasants nor undifferentiated oppressed peasants that are the instruments of a socialist transformation, but the depeasantized rural labor force caught in the maelstrom of urban-led mass struggles.

In addition, as imperialist forces (capital and military) have acted on the countryside, the massive transformations evidenced throughout rural society have provided fertile ground for rural revolutionary movements. The efforts of imperial capital to transform society in accordance with its needs have led to the large-scale intrusion of military technology, without any accompanying alternative form of socioeconomic organization capable of massive integration of the labor force in productive labor. The intervention of imperialist forces on a scale commensurate with the subjugation of whole populations has homogenized or leveled opposition and has provided a common target for quite disparate class forces. The clue to the massive nature of rural participation in twentieth-century revolutions is to be found in common collective experiences resulting from the pervasive impact of imperialism on the countryside. Furthermore, the specific changes wrought in the labor force by the impact of world capitalism—in the form both of colonial and imperial wars and of market investment forces—undermine the notion that "the peasantry" as such has been a revolutionary force. It is rather the case that this peasantry has been transformed and its class situation altered—and that any turn toward socialist solutions is thus a direct response to the new forces impinging upon society, the modern organizational forms of imperial armies and capital. Indeed, this transformation of the peasantry is clearly the reason that rural labor has been so prominent in all successful socialist revolutions to date.

The critical issue, however, is not simply to recognize the immense revolutionary possibilities inherent in rural labor but to locate precisely the latter's role in the revolutionary process. Specifically, has the mass character of rural labor's participation enabled it to *direct* the process of transformation? Given what has already been said about the vital part played by uprooted former peasants incorporated into the revolutionary organization, is it not possible to view them as the directing force in the confrontation with imperialism, in much the same way as earlier Marxists conceived of the proletariat as the hegemonic class in the revolutionary bloc of forces?[3] The problem with this conception is that it drastically exaggerates the degree to which *socioeconomic changes* and *military experience* are in themselves *sufficient* to shape and create a new socialist consciousness among former peasants.

Close to the recent past, in which petty-commodity relations predominated, ever embedded in a rural matrix containing peasants anchored
in productive relations, the rural labor force has never completely severed
its ties with the society out of which it emerged. The struggle against the uprootedness generated by imperialism *weakens* these ties; but the ex-peasant
never loses sight of the past. There is a continuing tension within the mass
consciousness of the revolutionary rural labor force between, on the one
hand, a break with the past (incorporation in a socialist movement) and,
on the other, a continuity with that past expressed in the tendency, if left to
their own devices, to return to petty-commodity production. It is this tension, this ambiguity, and the lack of a formulated collectivist conception
that the rural labor force can execute *on its own* that limits the latter's role to
that of an *influential base*—and *not a revolutionary vanguard.*

Thus, to envision the involvement of rural labor en masse in revolutionary
activity as a self-generating process is to overlook the centuries of ties and relationships engendered within the countryside. It was, rather, the degree to
which rural labor was uprooted by imperialism that determined its extent of
participation in a collectivist enterprise oriented and organized by the
worker-rooted central party cadre. In the Soviet Union, where peasant revolts
were directed essentially against the landlords, the peasants remained wed-
ded to petty-commodity production and showed few inclinations toward
collectivist agriculture. Even the millions of uprooted peasants—conscripted
for the army or victims of Western military occupation—remained under the
hegemony of the core of peasants who remained in petty-commodity production, in the absence of any mass Bolshevik political organization capable
of reorganizing production on the land.

In China, by contrast, the revolutionary armies were recruited mainly
from the uprooted rural masses and, in turn, provided a discipline and social organization within which peasant agriculture could develop; they thus
came to represent an alternative source of hegemony over those displaced
and uprooted by wars and class conflict. In Vietnam, the process was similar: Collectivism was implanted through the mass integration of uprooted
peasants into socialist revolutionary organizations; U.S. bombers, in addition to murdering millions, cleared the fields of centuries of precapitalist or
decades of capitalist social relations, providing a carte blanche for the
wholesale restructuring of the countryside under the undisputed hegemony
of the worker-rooted Communist Party. The case of Cuba reflects a different
set of imperialist forces: largely, massive flows of imperial capital into agriculture, which had the equivalent effect of uprooting the peasantry. Moreover, the transformation of the peasantry reached the most advanced state,
going beyond uprootedness and actually creating a substantial rural proletariat in factories and in the fields. The more thorough change effected by
the impersonal economic forms of imperialism—in contrast with more bla-

tant military-cum-economic depredations—accounts for the more rapid collectivization of agriculture in Cuba than in Russia, China, or Vietnam.

While Cuban rural labor was in a more advanced socioeconomic position to initiate the process of collectivization, the leadership of the revolution did not possess, at least initially, the same direct ties to the rural workers' struggle as the Chinese or Vietnamese Communists. For the degree, extent, and duration of the rural class struggle, independent of the level of the productive forces, can be viewed as a crucial variable in shaping the organization of postrevolutionary social and political institutions in the countryside. In China and Vietnam (unlike in Russia or Cuba), the uprooted rural masses achieved strategic positions at middle-cadre levels as a result of the prolonged and mass rural character of the war; this presence gave them influence over the top leadership and shaped the particular collectivist measures that were instituted. The influence of rural labor in both cases, however, was not a function of its mere numerical strength but of its position in the party organization.

RURAL LABOR AND POLITICAL ORGANIZATION

The position of rural labor within the revolutionary movement varied from one revolutionary experience to another. In the Soviet Union it was always a marginal force, largely an unintegrated mass operating outside the organized movement—although acting on the latter and in turn being acted upon. In Cuba, rural labor was incorporated into the mass movement, especially the people's militias and the Committees for the Defense of the Revolution (Comites de Defensa de la Revolución). These bodies played a decisive role in carrying out the struggles that culminated in collectivization of the economy. Nevertheless, because they were not essentially and directly political organs that made decisions within productive units, these mass-based organizations did not become organs of political rule. At best, they served as a reminder to the leadership of the specific social and economic interests of rural labor and thus set limits to the types of concession that might be granted to opposing strata.

The effectiveness of rural labor's role in safeguarding its social interests through the mass organizations can be seen in the thoroughness with which their enemies were expropriated, the short shrift given to agrocapitalists, and the care given to legislation benefiting rural labor. Meanwhile, the process of revolutionary struggle in China and Vietnam saw a massive incorporation of rural labor into the political-military structures, with many former peasants rising to substantial positions of influence, after varying periods of resocialization into the ideas and norms of collectivism. The combined influence of early working-class struggles and ideas

on long-term leaders and of confrontation and struggles with imperialist
forces on the uprooted rural labor force produced an influential militarized
rural cadre. Their presence within the party at upper and middle levels, as
well as at the base, was a product of their entry into the party during the
middle years of the revolution.

In the Russian case, the peasants as a mass never played a major role
within the organized movement (although they did play a substantial political role informally and provided decisive military support at the base);
hence, they were unable to influence and shape rural policy. This is part of
the explanation for the manner in which collectivization was ultimately
imposed on the peasants from above. The case of Cuba is closer to that of
China or Vietnam, insofar as rural labor was incorporated into the last but
decisive stages of the socialist transformation and, as such, remained to
play a role in *indirectly* shaping regime priorities and the allocation of resources. However, the late involvement of the Cuban rural labor force ensured that its position in the strictly organizational structures of the revolutionary movement would remain peripheral. For the earlier rural labor
enters the revolutionary struggle, the more influential its role is in political decision making, as well as in military operations. At the same time, it
is not sheer numbers alone that determine what say rural labor will have
in the revolutionary process. Cuba, for example, had less than 50 percent
of its labor force in agriculture—a smaller proportion than in Russia—yet
its influence on the revolutionary process was greater. Likewise, in China
and Vietnam, rural labor was just as numerous in the 1920s and early
1930s as it was later, yet it became influential only when its numerical
strength was embodied in party and military organizations that exercised
control over productive units.

The early involvement of rural labor in the revolutionary movement depends above all on the elaboration by the party of an appropriate program
and its application to the concrete struggles emerging in the countryside.
In Russia the prior existence of widespread commercial agriculture and a
preexisting petty-commodity structure inhibited the Bolsheviks from developing organic ties to the rural labor force—fearing, as they might, their
ideological influence on the party. The different character of the peasantry
in Russia and the different development of the class struggle led the Bolsheviks to formulate programs that relegated the peasantry to a supportive
role, outside the political organization—thus ensuring that they would
continue to follow the view of the petty-commodity producer. Hence, even
when the peasants were drafted en masse into the army during World War
I, they retained a peasant rather than a proletarian consciousness. In China
and Vietnam, by contrast, the prolonged struggles fought and the organic
ties forged in rural areas prior to the revolution were accompanied by an

early formulation and application of an agrarian program as one of the centerpieces of party policy.

However, that the revolutionary leaderships in China, Cuba, and Vietnam developed a conception of the peasantry as a proto-proletarian mass was itself a reflection of the uprootedness and relative proletarianization that accompanied imperialist penetration in those countries. Thus, it was not merely a program that created a political unity between displaced urban cadres and rural labor: It was ultimately the common bonds of uncertainty and uprootedness generated by imperialist penetration that enabled the two to merge in a common organization. While the early presence of a party agrarian program *facilitated* the early entry of rural labor into the party, it was the development of imperialism on a world scale that uprooted and radicalized rural labor en masse and precipitated the conflicts that led to its disciplining and integration into a revolutionary movement.

In this way, the attempt by world capitalism to overcome its historic crisis through external expansion proved, in the specific conditions of its military-economic intervention in Vietnam, China, and Cuba, to carry within it the seeds of capitalism's own destruction: For it catalyzed a rural labor force, uprooted and without the chains of age-old oppression, but with a newly forged revolutionary socialist leadership. Thus, the program and ideology of the revolutionary struggle did not express internally generated productive forces, but those resulting from the advanced social formations of the imperial world. A collectivist consciousness developed within rural labor not because of past landlord abuses but as a direct product of the new forces of destruction and production, operating on a world scale, that originated in the imperialist countries. Therefore, it is not subjective will or local backwardness that generates revolutionary action among rural labor. There is no inverse relationship between rural radicalization and development of the productive forces. Nor are rural movements for socialist revolution premature, because the productive forces have not been developed within the social formation itself. For from a world-historic perspective, as the most developed forces operated within the backward formations to precipitate revolutionary socialist action, they provided ample testimony to the ripeness of the social situation.

THE ROLE OF URBAN WORKERS

Conventional sociology has often downplayed the role of the urban working class in socialist revolutions. A number of attributes imputed to the working class are alleged to have prevented it from making any decisive contribution to the overall success. Not infrequently, the thinly disguised purpose has been to deny the centrality of class struggle in the making of history and to refute Marxism as a science: Revolutions have been explained by conjunctural causes (wars, crises), social psychological phenomena (power drives of intellectuals), and/or the collapse of precapitalist societies.

One fundamental error is the notion that class consciousness is an attribute possessed by an individual, which can be measured outside of the class struggle. The attitude studies, the opinion surveys, the interviews that purport to measure class consciousness—all abstract the individual from the class, the class from the class struggle, the class struggle from the historical process. Yet the essential relationships established prior to the individual's response, the social and political organizations within which he or she acts, the struggles in which he or she is involved, and the global relations between conflicting classes and the state are in fact the crucial determinants of class consciousness. Class consciousness has its basis in the class struggle, and the class struggle is rooted in class consciousness. The study of class consciousness requires the study of classes acting in history. It is a dimension of a historical process, not a static, psychological attribute derived from interpersonal encounters.

When conventional sociology studies consciousness, it tends to isolate the individual and, in the context of immediate circumstances, record responses registering what is most urgent, obvious, and obtainable for the individual. Hence, most close-up studies of consciousness have discovered over and over again that workers subject to the constraints of local circumstances and pressing needs respond with preferences for immediate economic rewards. From this limited vantage point, the conventional anti-Marxists argue that the working class—conceived of as an aggregate of static individualized responses—is economistic and lacking in revolutionary will. If workers take part in revolutionary movements, it is basically because clever leaders (intellectuals) have manipulated their immediate needs to serve the alien larger ends. This approach denies the reality of larger movements existing in their own right, providing a new reality, existing as a social force capable of increasing the power of individuals insofar as they stand together behind a common set of demands that subsume immediate needs and define new historical projects. It cannot comprehend that the economic interests of isolated individuals are, through the action of the class, converted into collective class demands. The movement of a class that has elaborated on the demands of each member is no longer speaking merely the economistic language of the individual worker.

In reality, that economic issues may initially be felt to be important by isolated individuals does not at all preclude the elaboration of a general class political program. Merely to ascertain the economic stance of the individual worker is to scratch the surface of social reality, leaving unexplored the sociopolitical matrix that constrains or facilitates further elaboration of political and social demands. In the course of the socialist revolutions that occurred in the twentieth century, there certainly were many instances in which workers raised economist demands; and these, at a certain point, may have embodied the sentiments of the bulk of the class. Nonetheless, the historic process of working-class struggle soon led to an incorporation of economic with political demands. The greater the scope and intensity of the class struggle, the more closely economic and political, or immediate and historic, demands became merged: wages and redistribution, working conditions and control, repressive laws and state power. And it was in the whole complex of demands and in the struggles, over time, to win them— not in the one-dimensional, immediate wants of individual workers—that the class consciousness of the working class was expressed.

At the same time, history makes clear that class consciousness can continue to exist in a latent form even when repression has enforced an apparent surcease of the class war. For example, in the 1920s the Chinese urban labor movement was clearly spearheading a social and political movement of substantial dimensions. That movement was savagely repressed. Throughout the 1930s and up to the mid-1940s, workers, we are often told, became nonrevolutionary and economistic. Yet with the overthrow of the KMT, the workers became integral elements in the process of social transformation. Similar cycles appear in the cases of Russia, Cuba, and Vietnam. In Russia, the revolutionary mobilization of the working class in 1905 was followed by an economistic slide until 1917, when revolutionary struggles and organization reemerged in much the same form (Soviets) as before. In Cuba, militancy in the 1930s was followed by repression in the 1940s, then by an urban proletarian resurgence in the anticapitalist, anti-imperialist struggles of the early 1960s. Similarly, Vietnamese workers, active in the mass upsurge of the 1930s and 1940s, were relatively less active in the 1950s; the Tet Offensive, however, gave a fresh indication of worker consciousness, and the postliberation reconstruction of industry has witnessed a massive incorporation of the working class within the revolutionary process. Clearly, therefore, the decline or even disappearance of revolutionary working-class activity in a particular period, whether as the result of repression or, more generally, as a reflection of the possibilities inherent in those specific conditions with that specific state regime, does not mean that the workers have become economistic in any essential historical sense— that they have given up their historic interest in social transformation. It is rather the case that conjunctural circumstances may force revolutionary consciousness to become latent, subject to a change in state relations.

A second (and related) characteristic error of non-Marxist sociology is the mechanistic counterposition of reform to revolution. It is assumed that the presence of reformist demands within the workers' movement ipso facto excludes the possibility that workers will carry the struggle through to a revolutionary outcome. When workers, at a particular moment, put forward a set of discrete demands, the conclusion is drawn that these demands define the nature of the movement. The unspoken assumption is that workers are by nature reformist and incapable of transcending their immediate surroundings. It is ironic indeed that a corollary thesis to this patronizing view of the working class should present the revolutionary party as fundamentally elitist—an outside presence, imposing its values and political beliefs on the class.

In reality, the relation of reform to revolution is by no means so simple. The knowledge the working class obtains of the social system is a function of the scope and depth of the class struggle. Some segments of the class historically arrive at an understanding of the nature of society and its contending forces before others. This uneven process results in differential degrees of political organization and combativity. The class, as a whole, becomes fully involved only at certain key conjunctural moments, thereby signaling a social crisis or even a prerevolutionary situation of dual power. At other times, the process of working-class struggle involves merely segments of the class and partial demands (reforms). But it is the overall trajectory of the movement that determines whether these are mere reforms or the building blocks for the mobilization of the whole class toward a systematic confrontation.

To argue that the working class is inherently reformist because, in a particular historical conjuncture, only part of it is involved in class struggle, or because the class as a whole is demanding only partial changes, is to reduce historical movement to the changing circumstances of the moment. In a word, working-class support for reforms does not make the working class *reformist.* On the contrary, all profound revolutionary changes have had their immediate origins in limited demands for reforms. But what is crucial in the ensuing struggles is the speed and extent to which these immediate issues lead to revolutionary struggles for power, challenging state authority and the dominance of existing ruling classes. In all socialist revolutions, the workers' movement has integrated struggles for reform with wider demands for revolutionary change.

THE MYTH OF WORKING-CLASS PRIVILEGE

A third common misconception (in which Fanonism rubs shoulders with functionalism) sees the working class throughout the third world as, by and large, incorporated into existing society, its relatively higher wages and greater privileges (by comparison with the rural masses) having been purchased at the price of its subordination to the dominant classes. Once again, this view sees the working class as fundamentally economistic, its consciousness determined in the last resort by its wage levels, whether absolute or relative. However, a consideration, first, of the significance of differential wages within the working class itself and, second, of the relations between workers and peasants will clearly show the spurious nature of this conception.

In the first place, the overwhelming participation of relatively better-paid workers (relative to peasants) in revolutionary mass organizations in Russia both before and after 1917, in China during the 1920s and after 1949, in Cuba during the 1930s and in the late 1950s and early 1960s, and in Vietnam during the 1930s and 1940s and again in 1968 and after liberation suggests that class consciousness is not reducible to salary payments. The class nature of society is brought home to workers constantly, in extremely material forms: a repressive state, fluctuations of the economy and of state economic policy, oppressive social relations of production, and so on. Thus, the broader sociopolitical context of class society and the exploitative relationships embodied in it have often proved to be more fundamental determinants of class consciousness than wage levels. Moreover, the degree to which certain segments of the working class are paid higher wages may precisely be a function of their greater militancy, and it may reinforce their political allegiance to a revolutionary party. Hence, the notion that workers, or even better-paid workers, are in essence privileged strata, incapable of participating in revolutionary struggles, is both historically and logically incorrect. The notion of a privileged working class assumes that higher wages are derived from exploiting others. Yet in reality the workers neither employ labor nor appropriate surplus. Rather, usually located in highly productive imperialist enterprises, they are themselves producers of surplus value and, in fact, are technically subject to greater exploitation (i.e., produce greater surplus value). By not increasing their share of the value that is produced, they would not lessen the exploitation in society or improve the condition of other toilers; rather, they would simply heighten the concentration of wealth in the hands of the capitalist class.

The degree of solidarity in action of the working class, of course, varies with the issue being contested. Structural differentiation is obvious and extensive. Yet in Russia, China, Cuba, and Vietnam, issues arose that made clear the common situation and evoked a class solidarity, despite any historic differences in wage levels. In Russia, the war and the exceptional cost it imposed on the working class blurred over internal differences and hastened the formation of Soviets, incorporating all segments of the class. In China, the common demands of all urban labor for improved minimum conditions of payment, hours, and political rights evoked a massive and turbulent mobilization. In Cuba, the corrupt and repressive character of the Batista regime, and the generalized insecurity of employment under U.S. dominance, triggered a massive unified working-class movement. In Vietnam, the colonial situation combined with state repression of labor struggles forced miners, plantation workers, and municipal employees to unite behind revolutionary socialist forces. Thus internal differentiation of the working class has not historically proved to be an insurmountable obstacle to the unity of high- and low-wage workers in mass revolutionary struggle.

Perhaps more weighty arguments have been adduced in an attempt to establish an incompatibility and even fundamental antagonism between urban and rural labor. These have pointed to disparities in income, standard of living, and social relations and to all the very real inequalities that subsist between countryside and city. The notion has been popularized that the highly organized, better-paid workers are unwilling to support peasant struggles; that the workers' movement is simply another particularistic interest group, intent only on satisfying its immediate demands by negotiating with the state and employers for better terms. For Fanon, the workers are part of colonial society; for others, they form an aristocracy of labor divorced from the revolutionary class struggles waged by the peasants. In addition, it is true that relations between workers' parties and peasant movements have not always been optimal, conducive to the forging of a revolutionary alliance. However, in reality, there is no structural reason why an alliance between workers and peasants cannot be brought about; moreover, the historical experience of the four socialist revolutions we have considered has shown this conclusively. The revolutionary alliance was achieved in each, despite the disparities, and was to prove sufficiently strong to lead to a fundamental transformation of the entire social structure and economic system. In each revolution, the role of the working class and its party was to provide moral, political, and material direction for, and support to, the peasant struggles.

THE REVOLUTIONARY ALLIANCE

In China, the Communist Party, which became the leading revolutionary force in the countryside, was formed in and by urban workers' struggles. Throughout the 1920s, the workers' movement supported agrarian reform demands and frequently provided material support. Later, after the suppression of the mass workers' movement in 1926–1928, thousands of cadres shaped and influenced by those urban struggles turned to the rural masses, organizing and directing revolutionary activity in the countryside. The overthrow of the KMT set the stage subsequently for the full integration of rural and urban labor in the task of collectivizing the economy and transforming social relations. The apparent break in the emerging alliance of urban and rural labor after the 1926–1928 urban repression occurred only at the level of *mass* movements. For the Communist Party carried proletarian ideology, embodied in its cadres, to the peasants. Basing itself on past work-ing-class experience, and anticipating the future reassertion of the alliance, the Communist Party during the 1930s and 1940s became the link between the working class and the peasantry.[4] The proof lies in the post-1949 over-throw of capitalist relations of production, which was the expression not merely of peasant forces, but of combined elements from both the working class and the peasantry. Had the working class been completely eclipsed, had only the peasants counted, the subsequent act of alliance in collec-tivization would be a gratuitous act, an inexplicable occurrence because of fortuitous circumstances. This is hardly convincing.

In Cuba, the disintegration of petty-commodity production and the con-struction of sugar mills in the countryside created a rural proletariat able and willing to politicize and radicalize the remaining peasantry. The differ-ences between urban and rural labor became obliterated: both were wage workers employed by corporate capital, both were organized in trade unions and engaged in class struggle, and both provided a base for the Communist Party. As the dominant social force in the countryside, rural wage labor thus served as a bridge between urban wage labor and rural petty-commodity production. The struggles of the 1930s and the subse-quent revolutionary movement of the 1950s and 1960s saw a convergence in action. And the rural laborers and urban workers, who provided the cen-tral core of forces pressing through the elimination of capitalist relations of production, also guaranteed the continued existence of petty producers, making them, in effect, into an auxiliary support group for the revolution.[5]

In Vietnam the semiproletarian rural labor force (part-time petty-commodity and subsistence peasants, part-time migratory laborers), which mingled with wage workers in the mines and plantations, was or-ganized and engaged in class-struggle politics under the leadership of the Communist Party and thereby became linked to the urban working class. The heightened repression in the late 1930s and the subsequent emergence of a Communist-led rural guerrilla movement facilitated the transfer of urban working-class-influenced cadres to the countryside and the communication of ideas and spread of organizations among petty-commodity producers and semiproletarians.

During the 1960s, the massive U.S. invasion of Vietnam and the ensuing uprooting of millions of peasants hastened the flow of ex-peasants simul-taneously into the guerrilla movement and into the festering slums of Saigon. The forced marches, concentration camps, and terror bombing freed the peasants from their land and from petty-commodity production and facilitated their recruitment by the Communist Party. The synthesis of forcibly uprooted peasants and a revolutionary vanguard party, grounded in past proletarian struggles and ideology, provided the driving force for a mass movement that would be not merely anti-imperialist but socialist.

In the case of the Russian Revolution, the worker–peasant alliance was less the product of large-scale movements of capital, uprooting, and transforming peasants into rural proletarians than was the case in Cuba; nor were the military incursions of imperialism sufficient to erode the organization of petty-commodity production, as was the case in Vietnam and China. On the contrary, by devastating the cities and the marketing system, imperialist intervention positively encouraged a return to small self-sustaining agriculture. Moreover, huge areas of Russia were without any working-class presence whatsoever, which made the task of extending proletarian hegemony and sustaining the alliance with the peasants more difficult. Thus, some of the basic historic forces that facilitated and cemented the worker-peasant alliance in China, Cuba, and Vietnam were absent—or operated in the opposite direction—in Russia. And the alliance, although it was decisive in establishing a workers' state, could not be maintained over time.[6]

We can now summarize the forces that have acted to forge the revolutionary alliance of workers and peasants. Uprooting and proletarianization of the peasantry have reduced some of the crucial structural differences between rural and urban labor. While these processes have not brought about a clean break with the past, they have nevertheless served to sever the primordial ties to local authority, custom, and tradition (what Marx called village idiocy). Stripped of his means of production, the ex-peasant has become more open to proletarian ideology and worker-founded parties. The social and geographic proximity of centers of capitalist production, in the economic enclaves established by imperialism, has helped to spread the organizational skills and ideology of working-class struggle throughout the countryside, incorporating strata only partially linked to the capitalist mode of production. Revolutionary armies and militia have served as mechanisms for the diffusion of socialist ideas and cadres, as transmission belts for the revolutionary party. Paradoxically, the defeat of geographically anchored and concentrated proletarian movements in earlier periods resulted in a greater mobility of revolutionary collectivist ideas and organization throughout the countryside, whereas victorious capital became entrenched and inflexible in limited areas of influence and dominance.

The transmission of revolutionary ideas and organization to the countryside, via productive and political-military apparatuses, has thus converged with structural changes within the countryside to create a dynamic toward worker–peasant alliance. The crucial subjective force acting on this objective dynamic to realize the alliance in practice has been the revolutionary party. It is the party that incorporates the experience of class struggle in the cities; forms the cadres in the fields, mines, and armies; and organizes the diffusion of collectivist ideology and practice throughout the countryside, analyzing the basic coordinates of the situation and intervening in the crucial political, economic, and military structures to detonate revolutionary struggles. The alliance between the working class and the peasantry is a historic product of the unfolding of capitalist and imperialist development, insofar as this brings the two classes into a common set of exploitative relations. But this objective convergence only becomes a political force and reality if a revolutionary party formulates a program and devises a strategy capable of channeling the energies of both classes toward common goals and against common enemies. Without such a party, the objective situation of common oppression can be dissipated into a thousand secondary struggles involving communal, ethnic, or sectoral interests—struggles that, incidentally, provide the favorite terrain for conventional bourgeois sociologists intent on refuting Marxist class analysis.

THE REVOLUTIONARY PARTY AND THE WORKING CLASS

But what is the relationship of the party leading the struggle for socialist revolution to the working class itself?[7] It has often been argued that such parties, made up of professional revolutionaries, mainly intellectuals and other non-working-class elements, are distinct and apart from the class and pursue policies that the workers themselves would not elaborate. The party *of* the working class is in reality the party *over* the working class. Moreover, elitist in composition, it is also elitist in its methods; it acts from "outside," "manipulating" the interests of the workers to serve the power drives and the interests of the intellectual elite that runs the party. In the arena of social struggles, the workers' economic interests are "sacrificed" to the political aims of the party, which stands to gain from its accession to power. The ground is thus prepared for the new exploitative society that will emerge when this proto-class takes power and begins to reorganize society to serve its own as opposed to the workers' interests. Such a view of the party seeks to minimize the extent of working-class participation in the revolutionary struggle; or, if it is clear that masses of workers are active, it seeks to differentiate party involvement from that of workers in general; or, if the two cannot be separated, it argues that the common orientation is merely conjunctural and that the long-term conflict of interests will become manifest over time. A related line of argument presents the party as basically oriented toward "modernization" and "industrialization," while the workers are allegedly concerned only with immediate problems.

Although this way of presenting the relationship between party and class is misconceived, a certain material basis for it does exist in the nature of postrevolutionary developments in a number of countries. "Elites" have emerged and have restratified society; industrial plans have been imposed rather than debated by workers' councils; gaps have appeared between the concrete interests of the workers and the demands of the planners; above all, decision making has been the prerogative of the party, or rather of the party leadership, and the workers have consequently often expressed their interests in narrowly economic terms.[8] Moreover, these real divergences of interest after the revolution have not merely been pointed to by anti-Marxists as evidence of a universal and inherent contradiction between party and class; they have also been endowed with a similarly universal value from the other side, by the postrevolutionary regimes and their apologists. Liberal scholars discover that all subsequent distortions were inscribed in the process, party, and ideology of socialist revolution. Quotations out of context from Lenin, vacuous sociological generalizations about party structures and class/party relations, social psychological hypotheses about the motives of political and social leaders—all serve as a substitute for concrete analysis of the historical process. Propagandists for the postrevolutionary regimes, for their part, follow an essentially similar procedure, although from a sympathetic rather than a hostile vantage point: once again, out-of-context citations from Lenin, a one-sided emphasis on the role of the party and its leaders, and a claim for absolute continuity between the period of revolutionary change and postrevolutionary policies. The only difference is that the authoritarianism, economic developmentalism, and bureaucratic domination associated with the postrevolutionary period are presented as necessary and positive accompanying features of the revolution, whereas the liberals present them as elements of a new exploitative society.

In fact, however, the problem of relations between the working class and the revolutionary party, and of the role of the working class in the socialist revolutions that have occurred to date and in the societies created by them, is both more complex and dialectical and more historically specific than such simplistic theses suggest. The essential point here is that postrevolutionary undermining of the working classes' power is no reason to omit, distort, or downplay the historic role of the working class in providing the impetus to revolution. And to get at the real relationship between party and class during the revolutionary process itself, it is necessary to clear the field of the two mirror-opposite views described earlier.

First, the founding of a party does not necessarily reflect the activities of the class it will ultimately represent. Usually, parties are founded by small groups of people from diverse backgrounds, drawn together by a common set of ideas or a common project. Thus, the founding meetings of the Communist parties of Russia, China, and Vietnam included substantial numbers of intellectuals, who had as yet little direct connection with the burgeoning social struggles of the period. The small initial organization could hardly be said to "represent" the class. But in a sense, this goes without saying. The crucial test, however, is the capacity of a party to move from a primarily intellectual position outside the working class and to integrate itself into the mass movement, winning new members and trans-

forming itself from a party of the "elite" into a party representing a substantial segment of the working class.

The early history of the Russian, Chinese, or Vietnamese parties shows
an evolving relationship with the working class, in the course of which
they were progressively transformed into parties increasingly composed of
workers. This was achieved by a direct and growing participation in class
struggles, and subsequently through the establishment of mass organizations. "Overlap" of membership between party and mass organization,
mass organization and working class, is the prime index for the true relationship of party to class. The quantitative growth in working-class membership of the party and the extension of party-affiliated or influenced
mass organizations suggest a progressive *integration* of the party in the
class, a convergence of political and economic interests. The capacity of
the party to sustain its working-class membership and affiliates, to augment the level of struggles, and to extend its influence on the basis of more
elaborate programmatic statements (going beyond immediate economic-
political interests, in the direction of a full socialist program), suggests that
its integration within the class was not conjunctural but reflects its own
historic nature as a working-class party.

A second strand in the argument that the revolutionary party is something alien to the working class concerns the explicit central role of "professional revolutionaries." Since workers work all day, the argument goes,
the possibility for them to play any substantial role in the "vanguard party"
is necessarily limited. Hence, the party of professional revolutionaries acts
on the class, not vice versa. But this confuses a number of issues. First, the
notion of professional revolutionaries should not be taken to mean foot-
loose intellectuals dissociated from the workplace. Rather, it refers to workers who are *primarily political activists*, precisely *in work* as well as *after work*.
The capacity to act effectively as a serious, committed ("professional") revolutionary presupposes insertion within a network of solidarity and joint
activity, at the point of production or within a mass front. The capacity of
the Bolshevik Party to enroll tens of thousands of members in the few
months after February 1917, or of the Chinese Communist Party to grow by
leaps and bounds in the 1924–1927 period, was based on the prior recruitment of working-class cadres, who were in a position to insert themselves in the mass upsurge when this erupted. The party could not have created such cadres when the struggle erupted, any more than it could have
"imposed" its line or leaders upon the mass movement from outside. After
all, there were other organized political forces fighting for hegemony over
that movement, some of which could draw on the power of the state (however weakened this may have been).

It is also true, of course, that the revolutionary party has nowhere embodied all of the working class. In the cases we have been considering, not

only were there competing political groups with influence in the working class, but many workers were not organizationally committed to any party. The point is that a substantial part of the party was in each case made up of workers, and these in turn acted within the broad working-class movement to provide political direction and leadership, transmitting to the class programmatic demands for transforming society. At the same time, the course of party activity, to the extent it has succeeded, has reflected the capacity of the workers' movement not merely to assimilate but to modify the party's program and orientation. It is not merely the party that has shaped the workers' struggle but the workers' struggle that has influenced and formed the members of the party. The whole growth of party–class integration is a dialectical process. And, of course, successful policies of the party at moments of class upsurge have resulted in a new influx of members, while severe defeats have resulted in mass exodus.

THE PRIMACY OF POLITICS

The central issue raised by the massive entry of workers into a revolutionary party is that of *representation* of the class and *articulation* of its historic interests. There is no reason to take up the highly politicized and demanding existence of a party militant, unless there is some prior commitment to transforming the *political* role of the working class in society. To enter a revolutionary socialist party presumes recognition of the inadequacy of existing forms of political representation and, more important, of existing social relations of production—central targets of party program and activity. The positive act of joining the party and the affirmation of its program through party-directed activity reflect a primary concern not for economic issues (whether consumption or production) but rather for political and social ones: political freedom, embodied in direct forms of workers' representation and power, and the replacement of exploitative social relations of production by collective ownership and self-management.

In each successful revolutionary experience, the outcome depended on the fusion of significant segments of the working class with the revolutionary party and the incorporation of representative demands of the class into the activity of the party. In the Russian revolution, the central slogan of the Bolsheviks was a *political* demand to concentrate power in the hands of the most representative institutions of workers' struggle: "All power to the soviets." This was the high point of the revolution, the *culmination* of foregoing economic and social struggles; it reflected the intense interaction between the Bolshevik working-class cadre and the class as a whole. In China, the massive upsurge of the working class was cut short by the savage repression in 1926–1928; nevertheless, the notion of mass representative councils (soviets), popular militia, and other forms of mass representation in the state remained in the forefront of the rural struggle throughout the prerevolutionary period. That the idea of mass representation, derived from the workers' experiences, should have persisted through the radical-agrarian and antifascist periods—in fact, right up to the seizure of state power—suggests that while socioeconomic demands could be downplayed for conjunctural reasons, the issue of representation could not.

In Vietnam, the shift from urban class struggle to guerrilla war and national liberation struggle was sustained through the elaboration of a variety of institutions of representation. In liberated villages, parallel committees were formed; in factories, clandestine councils were established. Everywhere, demands for freedom from bourgeois rule predominated, even while economic and social demands were watered down to accommodate petit bourgeois and other forces. Political representation and the organizational articulation of worker and peasant interests played a central role in orienting and directing the protracted struggle; this accounts for the relative ease with which the Vietnamese were able to administer the war-devastated country, after the defeat and the departure of the United States and their clients.[9]

In Cuba, the revolutionary process emphasized the elimination of class differences to the point where all private businesses, even the most petty, were expropriated during the Great Revolutionary Offensive of 1968. An end to exploitation, and the social relations based on it, was a central priority of the revolution for at least the first decade. The elaboration of representative organs found expression especially in military-security units—the popular militia, the People's Courts, the local Committees for the Defense of the Revolution. This form of representation was confined to acting *against* enemies of the revolution—a key task in the early years, when imperialist intervention was a real and constant threat. Nevertheless, it became increasingly obvious that this was an inadequate form for articulating the workers' demands and interests. The attrition of the trade unions as organs of representation, and the failure to replace them with new institutions, has led to a crisis of consciousness. Confronted with an absence of political channels and with demands for economic performance, workers inevitably tend to revert to economistic demands.

Thus, the central importance of the dialectical relationship between the revolutionary party and the working class needs no further emphasis. No twentieth-century socialist revolution occurred without the establishment of such a relationship. The party experience and the class struggles that resulted from the integration of party and class interests were essential in forging the ideology and cadre that made the revolution possible. And that integration was based on political demands—for freedom, representation, and an end to exploitation.

CONCLUSION

We have seen the many ways in which non-Marxist sociology has miscon-
strued or distorted working-class activity and consciousness: the counterposition of reforms to revolution; the separation of economic issues from
political; the attempt to derive consciousness from a particular set of immediate demands or attitudes or directly from wage levels, extrapolating from
the wider social and political context of class struggle and state; the imputa-
tion of fundamental political cleavages between industrial workers and rural labor, on the basis of cultural or conjunctural differences; and so on. We
have noted that these conceptions fail to grasp the real historic processes involved in twentieth-century socialist revolutions. Throughout the century, in
major social transformations involving Europe, Asia, and Latin America, the
workers' movement played an essential role. In Russia, China, Cuba, and
Vietnam, it was the large-scale entry of the working class onto the center
stage of political struggle that transformed a process aimed at political reform into one leading to a combined political and social revolution. In Russia, it was the workers' parties that moved beyond demands for the overthrow of the autocracy toward a social transformation. In China, it was with
the large-scale urban and rural movements organized by the working-class-
centered Communist Party that the national struggle of the 1920s became
also a struggle over land ownership and against class exploitation. In Cuba,
the extension of the revolutionary process beyond the anti-Batista struggle
to the expropriation of land and U.S. enterprises was accompanied by a
massive entry of urban and rural labor into the political arena.

Far from being inherently economistic, workers are stimulated by the
adoption of broader political and social demands, while their activity in
turn radicalizes social and political struggle in general. Thus, the development of those working-class movements that have led to social revolutions
has been accompanied by an integral interplay between widening working-
class participation and an ever-greater combination of political and economic demands. In no sense are immediate demands eliminated, but they
become linked to a broader struggle for basic changes in regime and property ownership. Individual demands for land become linked to the expropriation of the landlord class. It thus makes no sense to seek to measure
consciousness through observation of individual attitudes; what alone
makes sense is to study the political and social organizations that mobilized rural and urban labor and that formulated the goals and found the
means to realize them.

Working-class consciousness is not the product of some essential "condition" but rather of all the collective associations and struggles within which
an individual worker is correctly located. Hence, in the case of Russia,
China, Cuba, and Vietnam, the presence of better-paid as well as lower-paid

workers within the same revolutionary organizational matrix was a function of their common exploitation by imperialist capital, warlords, or local capitalists. No matter how great the income disparities, savage encounters with the state and constant efforts by employers to raise the level of exploitation forced "aristocrats" and "coolies" into the same general struggle. What is crucial is not the differential gains that may have accrued to different segments of the working class, but the *method of struggle* adopted to win these. High- and low-paid workers alike engaged in class struggle under the leadership of the Communist Party, which acted to unify the disparate forces and provide a central political focus.

The common methods, political organizations, and programs that embraced high- and low-paid workers thus overrode the internal differentiation of the class. Confronted by a set of overarching problems and adversaries, income differences were subordinated to the common struggle. In Cuba, for example, skilled and semiskilled urban workers and cane cutters united to furnish the backbone of the popular militias that defeated U.S.-backed military incursions, guerrilla attacks, and urban sabotage. A shared experience of class struggle created common bonds between different segments of the working class, and these sustained the revolutionary movement and formed the cadres that eventually succeeded in transforming society. In the absence of revolutionary perspectives and organization, day-to-day economic struggles have reflected the internal differentiation of the working class, taking the form of a whole series of disparate conflicts and demands. But to the degree to which the party has extended its membership and influence in the working class, to the degree to which the entire activity of the class has thus become party oriented, even the most apparently "economistic" struggles have served as a basis for the large-scale, long-term changes, evidenced in subsequent, societal confrontations. Individual subjectivity has become subsumed within movements-in-struggle, and it is these movements that have defined the level of consciousness of the working class.

The strategic importance of the working class in the development of these revolutions derived, above all, from its qualitatively greater capacity to pose socialist goals. No other class possessed the same degree of cohesiveness and organization, linked to a socialist purpose. For while masses of peasants supported agrarian demands, and dispossessed peasants moved toward collectivist solutions, it was the proletarian forces—clearly separated from the means of production—that initially supported the formulation of a collectivist program. And the disparate strata of intellectuals, petty-commodity producers, shopkeepers, or civil servants were incapable even of themselves uniting as coherent, organized forces, let alone of formulating a program envisioning the socialization of production. The fact that individuals from these strata came over to the working class, and even played a major role within the working-class movement in formulating such a program, does not change the fundamental nature of the strata themselves. Such individuals were *won over* to the revolutionary movement, as a result of the prior existence of an organized revolutionary pole rooted in the working class.

Since the twentieth-century revolutions in which the workers' movement played such an important role occurred in mainly rural societies, it is clear that the numerical size of the working class was less important than its strategic position. Tied to urban industrial centers, largely exploited by imperialist capital, organized in class-based unions, the collective experience of propertylessness and class struggle permeated its political experience and facilitated its mobilization behind socialist objectives. The centers of capitalist production gave birth to the key ideas, organization, and cadres that were to provide leadership and an orientation for the vast, amorphous rural masses. And the strategic role of the proletariat was further made manifest in the outcome of those primarily rural-based revolutions: the means of production, including land, were collectivized, not fragmented into the peasant ideal of small property.

The historic role of the working class as "initiator" and "definer" of the revolutionary process made possible only by the adoption en masse of socialist goals. In Russia, China, Vietnam, and Cuba alike, it was the idea of an end to exploitative relations, to class and class privilege that detonated the assault on property holders and their instruments of domination. Economic demands became, as it were, only pretexts. Arguments about inadequate economic performance (important in winning over petit bourgeois strata) rationalized an attack on the existing regime, whose real motives were far more fundamental. The emotional energy and the political drive behind the mobilization of the masses in the course of these revolutions derived from the thousand indignities they suffered daily at the hands of the authorities—the industrialists, merchants, generals, and police chiefs—with their absolute power concentrated in the state. The appeal of socialism was rooted in this latent class hatred, and the revolutionary movement removed social inhibitions at the same time as it provided a focus for political expression. After the assumption of state power, the working-class character of the postrevolutionary state was in each case consolidated and made manifest in the transformation of property relations (despite programs that, in the Chinese, Cuban, and Vietnamese cases, had before the seizure of power not posed this as an objective). In each case, this was crucial in ensuring the survival of the workers' state, in a world still dominated economically (and, at least until recently, also militarily) by imperialism. Further advance in the direction of socialism, moreover, requires the establishment of forms of *working-class* democracy and power, which alone are capable of transcending the nationally limited, bureaucratic structures of the postrevolutionary regimes.

NOTES

1. Mark Selden, *The Yenan Way in Revolutionary China* (Cambridge, Mass.: Harvard University Press, 1974); Chalmers Johnson, *Peasant Nationalism and Communist Power* (Stanford, Calif.: Stanford University Press, 1962). See also Benjamin Schwartz, *Chinese Communism and the Rise of Mao* (Cambridge, Mass.: Harvard University Press, 1971), and Edgar Snow, *Red Star over China* (New York: Modern Library, 1944).

2. In a complementary study, the author investigates the highly disruptive effects of imperialism and war on a global scale. See James Petras, "Toward a Theory of Twentieth Century Socialist Revolutions," *Journal of Contemporary Asia* 3 (1978). But see also Gabriel Kolko, *The Politics of War* (New York: Random House, 1968); Gabriel and Joyce Kolko, *The Limits of Power* (New York: Harper & Row, 1976); Fernando Claudin, *The Communist Movement: From Comintern to Cominform* (New York: Monthly Review Press, 1975); Ernest Mandel, *Late Capitalism* (London: New Left Books, 1975), especially chaps. 2 and 11; and Andre Gunder Frank, *Capitalism and Underdevelopment in Latin America* (New York: Monthly Review Press, 1969).

3. See, for example, Eric Wolf, *Peasant Wars of the Twentieth Century* (New York: Harper & Row, 1969); Norman Miller and Roderick Aya, *National Liberation: Revolution in the Third World* (New York: Free Press, 1971); Frantz Fanon, *The Wretched of the Earth* (New York: Grove, 1963).

4. For social forces in the Chinese revolutionary process, see, in particular, Jean Chesneaux, *The Chinese Labor Movement 1919–1927* (Stanford, Calif.: Stanford University Press, 1968); Harold Isaacs, *The Tragedy of the Chinese Revolution* (Stanford, Calif.: Stanford University Press, 1961); Lucien Bianco, *The Origins of the Chinese Revolution, 1915–1949* (Stanford, Calif.: Stanford University Press, 1971); Jean Chesneaux, *Peasant Revolts in China, 1840–1947* (New York: Norton, 1973); Nym Wales, *The Chinese Labor Movement* (New York: Day, 1945); and Jack Belden, *China Shakes the World* (New York: Harper, 1949). The underlying element of political continuity from the 1920s to the 1940s and beyond is discussed in Isaac Deutscher, "Maoism: Its Origins and Outlook," in *Revolution and Class Struggle*, ed. Robin Blackburn (Atlantic Highlands, N.J.: Humanities Press, 1977).

5. For social forces in twentieth-century Cuba, see, in particular, *Pensamiento Critico* 39 (April 1970) (Havana), a special issue on the struggles of the 1920s and 1930s; Lowry Nelson, *Rural Cuba* (Minneapolis: University of Minnesota Press, 1950); Luis Aguilar, *Cuba 1933: Prologue to Revolution* (Ithaca, N.Y.: Cornell University Press, 1972); Leo Huberman and Paul Sweezy, *Cuba: Anatomy of a Revolution* (New York: Monthly Review Press, 1961); Che Guevara, *Episodes of the Revolutionary War* (Havana: Book Institute, 1966); Maurice Zeitlin, *Revolutionary Politics and the Cuban Working Class* (Princeton, N.J.: Princeton University Press, 1967); Martin Kenner and James Petras, eds., *Fidel Castro Speaks* (London: Lane, 1970); and Vania Bambirra, *La Revolución Cubana* (Mexico City: Nuestro Tiempo, 1978).

6. The popular basis of the Russian revolution, and the exceptional vitality and initiative displayed by the working class during the period of the conquest of power, is well conveyed in Alexander Rabinowitch, *The Bolsheviks Come to Power* (New York: Norton, 1976). But see also Leon Trotsky, *The History of the Russian Revolution*, 3 vols. (New York: Simon & Schuster, 1932); E. H. Carr, *The Bolshevik Revolution, 1917–1923*

(New York: Norton, 1950), vols. 1 and 2; Isaac Deutscher, *Stalin: A Political Biography* (New York: Oxford University Press, 1949); James Bunyan and H. H. Fisher, *The Bolshevik Revolution 1917–1918* (Stanford, Calif.: Stanford University Press, 1974); Marcel Liebman, *Leninism under Lenin* (London: Cape, 1975); and Moshe Lewin, *Russian Peasants and Soviet Power* (New York: Norton, 1968).

7. While a great deal of attention has been paid recently by Marxists to the relative autonomy of the state, and correlatively to the extent of its institutionalization, there has been less discussion of the relative autonomy of political organizations. But see Antonio Gramsci, *Prison Notebooks* (New York: International Publishers, 1971); Lucio Magri, "Problems of the Marxist Theory of the Revolutionary Party," *New Left Review* 60 (March–April 1970); Ernest Mandel, "The Leninist Theory of Organization," in *Revolution and Class Struggle*, ed. Robin Blackburn (Atlantic Highlands, N.J.: Humanities Press, 1977); Louis Althusser, "What Must Change in the Party," *New Left Review* 109 (May–June 1978).

8. On postrevolutionary developments in the Soviet Union and China, with special reference to the relationship between bureaucracy and the working class, see E. H. Carr, *Socialism in One Country*, vols. 1 and 2 (London: Macmillan, 1958 and 1959); Isaac Deutscher, *Stalin*, and *The Prophet Unarmed* (London: Oxford University Press, 1959); Moshe Lewin, *Lenin's Last Struggle* (New York: Monthly Review Press, 1969); Roy Medvedev, *Let History Judge* (New York: Knopf, 1971); Lucio Colletti, "The Question of Stalin," in *Revolution and Class Struggle*; and Livio Maitan, *Party, Army, and Masses in China* (Atlantic Highlands, N.J.: Humanities Press, 1976).

9. For social forces in the Vietnamese revolutionary struggles, see, in particular, Ho Chi Minh, *Selected Writings* (Hanoi: Foreign Languages Publishing House, 1977); Phang Thang Son, "Le Movement ouvrier vietnamien de 1920 à 1930," in *Tradition et révolution au Vietnam*, ed. Jean Chesneaux, Georges Boudarel, and Daniel Hémery (Paris: Anthropos, 1971); John T. McAlister, *Vietnam: The Origins of Revolution* (New York: Knopf, 1969); Joseph Buttinger, *A Dragon Defiant* (New York: Praeger, 1972); Anonymous, *Brief History of the Vietnam Workers' Party 1930–1975* (Hanoi: n.p., 1976); Pierre Rousset, *Le Parti Communiste vietnamien* (Paris: Maspero, 1975); William Duiker, *The Rise of Nationalism in Vietnam, 1900–1941* (Ithaca, N.Y.: Cornell University Press, 1976); Van Tien Dung, *Our Great Spring Victory* (New York: Monthly Review Press, 1977); Ti-ziano Terzani, *Giai Phong: The Fall and Liberation of Saigon* (New York: St. Martin's, 1976); Daniel Hémery, *Revolutionnaires vietnamiens et pouvoir colonial en Indochine* (Paris: Maspero, 1975); I. Milton Sacks, "Communism and Nationalism in Vietnam," Ph.D. diss., Yale University, n.d.; Ta Thu Yhau, "Indochina: The Construction of the Revolutionary Party," *Fourth International* (November/December 1938); and Hoang Quoc Viet, *Short History of the Vietnamese Workers' and Trade Union Movement* (Hanoi: Foreign Languages Publishing House, 1960).

4

The Russian Revolution

The Proletariat Takes State Power

The Great October Socialist Revolution in Russia in 1917 marked the first successful proletarian revolution of the twentieth century that brought workers to state power. The socialist revolution in Russia, led by the Bolshevik Party under the leadership of Vladimir I. Lenin, was the most fundamental social upheaval of modern times. It brought about a complete social transformation of Russian society from a semifeudal/semicapitalist state to a socialist one, stretching across a vast territory from Europe in the West through Central Asia to the Pacific Ocean in the East. It swept away Tsar Nicolas II's reign over the Russian Empire and thus brought to an end some three hundred years of the Romanov Dynasty. The October 1917 socialist revolution marked the victory of the Russian proletariat and set the stage for a new era of social transformation ushered in by this first socialist revolution of the twentieth century.

HISTORICAL BACKGROUND

Russia in the early twentieth century was a semifeudal/semicapitalist society with strong roots in an agrarian economy based on the labor of peasants, who accounted for upward of 80 percent of the population. While serfdom was officially abolished in 1861, the condition of the peasantry did not improve in any real sense, and they continued to struggle to hold onto what little they possessed. Most of them lived in extreme poverty and were under the whims of the dominant semifeudal tsarist state. With little to show for in material wealth, they were also repressed by the authoritarian state tied to the wealthy landowners, who kept them in their place. However, this unbearable situation generated a high level of discontent among the peasantry and played a key role in the revolutionary turmoil that subsequently developed.[1]

The situation in the urban areas was not much better. While there was substantial development in commercial and industrial activity to move Russia along the capitalist path, the level of economic development was still quite low, and the condition of the relatively small working class was no more than a notch above the impoverished peasantry. Workers were paid very low wages, had little protection in the factories and mines, and were under the constant watch of the repressive state and its police apparatus, especially in the repression of any trade union and organizing activity that would challenge the authority of the tsarist state.

While the formation of political parties was illegal up through the end of the nineteenth century, a few managed to rally the support of workers and peasants into a strong political organization that became the driving force of the proletarian movement that later toppled the tsarist state. The Russian Social Democratic Party—which in 1903 had split into the Bolshevik and Menshevik wings over strategy and tactics of the movement, its leadership, and views of the transition to a socialist society—played a central role in the developing revolutionary situation that moved Russia through the events of the first two decades of the twentieth century, most notably the political revolution of 1905 and the February and October revolutions of 1917.

The critical event that precipitated the developments surrounding the rebellion in 1905 occurred early in the year. On January 9, 1905, remembered in Russian history as Bloody Sunday, some fifty to sixty thousand workers marched to the Winter Palace to deliver a petition to Tsar Nicholas II, listing grievances regarding working conditions.[2] However, rather than meeting with the workers to address their grievances, "the tsar had his soldiers fire on the workers, killing thousands. This led to strikes and peasant protests throughout Russia."[3] Moreover, "[T]he tsar sent the army into areas where rebellion was still occurring and had thousands of people shot; thousands of others were deported from the country."[4]

The period following the events of 1905 and the subsequent reforms, which failed to produce any lasting changes (in fact, most of these reforms were subverted by the government to prolong autocratic rule), can be characterized as a period of increasing political instability and crisis:

> Between 1905 and 1917, Russia remained a deeply divided and extremely contentious society. Unrest continued, as did revolutionary activism. Indeed, both intensified. In February of 1917 there were large-scale strikes by industrial workers in many cities. Troops were dispatched to Petrograd (formerly St.

Petersburg) to disperse the large crowd that had assembled there, but the majority of soldiers refused to fire on the protesters, and, indeed, many joined forces with them. Lacking the military support it needed, the tsar's regime, already severely weakened through its involvement in World War I, lost its capacity to rule. Nicolas was forced to abdicate on March 16 and was put under house arrest.[5]

The Provisional Government that followed was made up of dominant class forces and could not reverse the deteriorating political situation. Led by Alexandr Kerensky, the Provisional Government failed to gain the legitimacy it needed to stay in power and thus was rejected by broad segments of the laboring population. In contrast, the Bolsheviks, led by Lenin, became more and more the key political organ that challenged Kerensky's bourgeois regime:

> Lenin opposed the Provisional Government and agreed with the slogan "All Power to the Soviets!" He saw the Provisional Government as representing the interests of the bourgeoisie and argued that another revolution was needed, a true Marxian proletarian revolution. In the months to follow, he was successful at pushing his fellow Bolsheviks into an increasingly hard-line position. Moreover, the Bolsheviks were attracting followers at an extraordinary rate. From at best 24,000 Bolsheviks at the time of the February Revolution, their numbers increased to over 100,000 by the end of April and to approximately 350,000 by October.[6]

"Marxism spread widely among Russian workers," writes Tim McDaniel: "Marxism taught them that workers were at the forefront of social progress and that to fulfill this responsibility the working class must fight for political rights in an organized way. For workers, the alternatives were clear: either a worker [state] or a tsarist state."[7] Thus, with the decline in the ability of the Provisional Government to remain in control of the developing revolutionary situation, on one hand, and the increasing ranks of the Bolsheviks who succeeded in building a mass base to wage an all-out war to take state power, on the other, the fate of Russia was becoming more and more evident in the period leading to the impending events that were yet to come a few months later. "July was an especially tumultuous month," writes Stephen K. Sanderson:

> Mass demonstrations and popular disorder erupted in Petrograd and lasted for three days. The demonstrators, who may have numbered half a million, consisted of sailors, soldiers, and workers. The Provisional Government blamed the Bolsheviks . . . and responded by arresting a number of Bolshevik leaders, including Trotsky. An order was made for the arrest of Lenin, but he escaped to Finland.[8]

"By the end of September," continues Sanderson, "the Bolsheviks had become a majority in the soviets of both Petrograd and Moscow, helping Lenin to reach the conclusion that it was time for the Bolsheviks to overthrow the Provisional Government and seize power themselves."[9]

"Throughout 1917, confronted with deteriorating economic conditions and the continuation of the war," writes McDaniel, "the urban working class increasingly came to regard class conflict irreconcilable. . . . By October, in their overwhelming majority they were willing to support the only party, the Bolsheviks, that advocated a workers' government to rule in their interests."[10]

On the evening of October 24, a group of soldiers, sailors, and workers followed the order of Trotsky—who had recently been released from prison and became the leader of the Bolsheviks in the absence of Lenin—to take control of several transportation and communication centers, as well as the Winter Palace of the tsar. The insurrectionaries occupied the telegraph offices and railway stations, and set up roadblocks on bridges. There was little resistance by military personnel, few of whom continued to recognize the legitimate authority of the Provisional Government, and thus little bloodshed. The Provisional Government was toppled by the next day, and its head, Kerensky, fled.[11]

A revolution had thus taken place and the proletariat, and its political organ the Bolshevik Party had taken state power to usher in the rule of the working class under communist leadership, a development that was to set the stage for postrevolutionary transformation of Russian society, but not before a three-year-long bloody civil war.

THE DEVELOPMENT OF THE SOCIALIST STATE

Following the Great October Socialist Revolution in 1917, Russia went through several important stages in its political and economic development. First came War Communism (mid-1918–1921), followed by the New Economic Policy (1921–1928), and finally the Five-Year Development Plans and the consolidation of socialism after 1928. Moreover, Soviet policy since the mid-1950s became a controversial one, alternating between liberalization and consolidation of the gains of socialism achieved during the twentieth century, only to see the demise of the Soviet state by century's end.

October 1917 to June 1918

In the months immediately following the revolution, no sweeping measures of confiscation or nationalization were proposed. This initial, transitional period, which Lenin called "state capitalism," was "characterized by control over private trade and industry rather than by extensive socialization . . . [and] an immediate transition to a socialist economy was not on the agenda in the early months of the new Soviet regime."[12] Lenin, in his *The Principal Tasks of Our Day*, spoke of state capitalism as a "gigantic step forward" and emphasized that the "period of transition between Capitalism and Socialism" would be mixed.[13] State capitalism was thus seen as a mechanism utilized by the proletarian state that would generate rapid economic growth and at the same time prepare the conditions for the transition to a socialist economy. In such circumstances, writes Maurice Dobb, "It was urgently necessary both to study and copy the State Capitalism of the wartime countries of Central and Western Europe."[14]

By the summer of 1918, two decisive factors brought the policies of the initial period to a close. The first was directly tied to the workplace; the revolution had matured, and the consciousness of the workers had elevated to a level where the workers challenged the underlying relations of production of the mixed economy. They pressed the state to transfer the administrative process of the factories into their hands and completely nationalize the means of production. The second decisive factor was the outbreak of civil war, supported by the armed intervention of foreign powers, led by German imperialism.

War Communism (June 1918–1921)

Under these conditions, the Soviet state made a move to introduce a decree for the wide-based nationalization of major industries that were still in private hands.

> At the end of June (1918) a governmental measure was precipitately adopted which closed one chapter of policy and opened another. This was the Decree of General Nationalization of June 28th, which applied nationalization by a stroke of the pen to practically all large-scale enterprises without distinction. It applied to all companies with more than a million roubles of capital . . . in mining, metal, textiles, glass, leather, cement, and the timber and electrical trades. . . . And in the next six or nine months a series of particular decrees followed, nationalizing whole groups of enterprises or sections of an industry. By the end of the year the nationalized concerns reached the figure of 1000, and by the autumn of 1919 some 3000 or 4000.[15]

The decree on nationalization of June 28, 1918, was the prelude to War Communism. For the next two years, the Soviet state was fighting a war for survival against both domestic and foreign enemies.[16]

> The drift toward nationalized control of industry, centralized allocation of supplies and centralized collection and distribution of products was to be rapid.

What came to be known as the period of "War Communism" had been launched: a product of the forcing house of a mortal struggle of the new regime against extinction, when military necessity ruled all and problems of industry were virtually identified with the problem of military supplies.[17]

War Communism, as most Soviet leaders—including Lenin—agreed, was a temporary measure, not a normal economic policy. It was historically and economically inevitable under the conditions in which the state found itself. There was the civil war on the one hand, and external invasion on the other. Hence the measures adopted by the Soviet state were precisely to deal with concrete, historically created conditions over which the state had little or no control. In his pamphlet *The Tax in Kind* (April 1921), Lenin said quite explicitly that "War Communism was forced on us by war and ruin. It was not, and could not be, a policy that corresponded to the economic tasks of the proletariat."[18] Indeed, the measures adopted during this period (1918–1921) were emergency measures under stress of war.

In the midst of the continuing crisis faced by the Soviet state, there was no choice but to abandon War Communism. "The switch of trains we made in the spring of 1921," wrote Lenin, "was dictated by circumstances which were so overpowering and convincing that there were no debates and no differences of opinions among us."[19] The new policy, which Lenin introduced to the Tenth Congress and which was subsequently adopted to replace War Communism, was the New Economic Policy (NEP).

New Economic Policy (1921–1928)

The adoption of the NEP meant a return to the "state capitalism" experimented with during the period immediately following the October Revolution. The central measure of the NEP

> was the granting to the peasantry of the right to trade in the open market in whatever produce they had left, after a certain specified amount had been turned over to the government. This decision meant the return of the profit motive and exchange relationships to an important sector of the economy. In the field of industry the government retreated to the "commanding heights" of control over banking, transportation, and certain large industries, permitting private enterprise to take over the rest.[20]

For Lenin, the key for rapid progress toward socialism was not in the state control of the entire economy and the overall socialization of the means of production, all at once, as the state was forced into in 1918. Rather, it was the political control of the state machinery by proletarian leadership, through which the state, coupled with its control of large-scale industry, would direct the national economy as a whole toward the realization of socialist goals. Hence, during the period of the New Economic Policy, most retail and wholesale trade and small business firms were returned to private hands. This not only was to accelerate trade and exchange between industry and agriculture but to serve a political purpose as well: the consolidation of the peasant masses, as Lenin put it, "in such a way that the entire mass will actually move forward with us."[21]

On the question of private capital under the NEP, Bukharin, in agreement with Lenin, stated, "By using the economic initiative of peasants, small producers, and even bourgeois, by tolerating subsequently private accumulation, we are putting them objectively to the service of the socialist state industry and of the economy as a whole: this is what the meaning of NEP consists in."[22]

Although Lenin's economic program under the NEP meant a retreat from the policies adopted under War Communism, the success of the NEP was so overwhelming that it carried the Soviet economy beyond the range in which its immediate survival was at stake.

The output of large-scale industry which had plummeted to 14 percent of its pre-war level by 1920 rose to 46 percent in 1924 and to 75 percent in the following year. The marketable output of agriculture climbed by 64 percent from 1922 to 1925. Last but not least, the year 1924 saw the sum total of gross investment for the first time since 1917 exceed annual depreciation.[23]

And by 1927, the overall performance of the economy had reached the 1913 level.[24] This pronounced progress in all the major areas of economic activity set the stage and provided the impetus for the emergence of new ideas for accelerated growth and for the expansion of the economic base to a point where it would elevate the Soviet Union to the rank of a major industrial power in the world.

Five-Year Development Plans of the Stalin Era

With the introduction of the First Five-Year Plan in 1928, tremendous progress began to take place under centralized state control of industry. "All of the country's resources were concentrated on certain objectives and their dissipation on other objectives, not conductive to rapid industrialization, was avoided."[25] This was clearly stated by Stalin himself, who said that

it was necessary to accept sacrifices, and to impose the severest economy in everything. It was necessary to economize on food, on schools, on manufactured goods so as to accumulate the indispensable means for the creation of industry. This was the only way for overcoming the famine with regard to technical equipment.[26]

Thus, the main target during the First and Second Five-Year Plans was the development and expansion of heavy industry, with particular emphasis on the production of capital goods.

For the rapid development of industry, however, a concurrent and equally rapid development of the agricultural sector was imperative. The introduction of large-scale farming on cooperative lines was the cornerstone of the industrialization program: "This transformation of the age-old basis of Russian agriculture was adopted," writes Maurice Dobb, "as the 'missing answer' for which the country was seeking: as the only solution to the riddle of how to industrialize on the basis of NEP."[27]

The collectivization of Soviet agriculture was at first initiated by Stalin on the principle of voluntary participation of small peasant farms into large farms, organized around collective units. In his report to the Fifteenth Congress of the CPSU, in which this policy was enunciated, Stalin spoke as follows:

> The way out is to turn the small and scattered peasant farms into large united farms based on the common cultivation of the soil, to introduce collective cultivation of the soil on the basis of new and higher technique. The way out is to unite the small and dwarf peasant farms gradually and surely, not by pressure but by example and persuasion, into large farms based on common, cooperative cultivation of the soil, with the use of agriculture. There is no way out.[28]

But as resistance grew, mainly among the *kulaks* (rich peasants), against the state's collectivization efforts, the state found it necessary to exert force to overcome the obstacles to the advancement of socialist industrialization. For, as Paul Baran points out, "The collectivization of agriculture in Russia . . . was the only possible approach to a broad avenue of economic, social, and cultural progress."[29] And as the material performance of the agricultural sector was later to prove, "Collectivization was a tremendous, and, indeed, an indispensable step toward economic and social advancement";

> in the final year of the Second Five-Year Plan, the grain harvest reached an all-time record, while the output of so-called technical crops (flax-fiber, cotton, sugar beet) more than doubled by comparison with 1928.
>
> Thus was solved not only the food problem, both in the collectivized village and the rapidly expanding city, but consumer's goods industries obtained the raw materials base indispensable for their growth, and the government came into a position of accumulating substantial food reserves for possible emergencies. . . . What is equally important is that the increased agricultural production was accompanied by a release of over 20 million people from agriculture—a migration from village to city that was indispensable for the growth of indus-

try. It reflected a per capita increase of productivity in agriculture of as much as 60 percent between 1928 and the end of the 1930s. And this in turn was the result of a "proffer of social assistance" to agriculture on a tremendous scale. Having received in the course of the First Five-Year Plan nearly quarter of a million tractors, and almost twice as many by the end of the Second Five-Year Plan, Russian agriculture, [quoting Baylov] "previously one of the most backward . . . [was able] to accumulate in the space of a few years an enormous production capital—in agricultural machinery and buildings—and to mechanize the main branches of cultivation to a much greater extent than other countries have done in the course of a long period of history."[30]

In sum, the collectivization drive in Soviet agriculture achieved its major economic objective in serving as the *basis* for industrialization. And the tremendous growth of industrial production (over 18 percent per year from the beginning of the industrialization campaign in 1928, and an increase of approximately 16 percent per year in aggregate output during the same period) was an exceptional achievement. This is confirmed by the well-known developmentalist Alexander Gerschenkron's Rand Corporation study, which reports average annual rates of growth in Soviet heavy industry between 1928–1929 and 1937 of 18.9 percent for machinery, 18.5 percent for iron and steel, 14.6 percent for coal, 11.7 percent for petroleum products, 22.8 percent for electric power, and 17.8 percent for all heavy industry.[31] Thus, as Dobb points out:

> Such a rate of growth represents a doubling each quinquennium, and is nearly twice as great as that found during exceptional boom periods in the capitalist world, such as the United States in the second half of the 1880s (8.6 percent), Russia in the 1890s (8 percent), or Japan between 1907 and 1913 (8.6 percent). With this may be compared a 5 percent rate of growth for manufacturing production in the United States between 1899 and 1929 and 3 percent in Britain between 1885 and 1913.[32]

Moreover, this unprecedented achievement in all the major fields of economic activity began gradually to improve the standard of living of the Soviet people: "By the end of the First Five-Year Plan," writes Baran, "the worst 'squeezing' of the consumer was over, by 1935 rationing could be abolished."[33] "While the rise in living standards was interrupted by the threat of war, and in particular by the war itself, the postwar decade witnessed their rapid and consistent improvement. By the end of 1954 they were approximately 75 percent above those of the last year before the war."[34]

These achievements in the Soviet economy and society were made possible by the integration of both agriculture and industry into the mainstream of the Soviet economy. It was done by the socialization and collectivization of the means of production under state supervision and control, and the promotion of a major industrialization drive during the Stalin era.

The Post-Stalin Era to the Present

After Stalin's death in 1953, the Soviet Union embarked on a cyclical path of centralized versus liberalized forms of economic organization and political rule—from Khrushchev and the Kosygin reforms to the centralist Brezhnev era to Gorbachev's reforms of perestroika and glasnost, and finally to Yeltsin's market reforms and subsequent turn to capitalist forms under Putin.

The coming to power of Khrushchev and the liberal technocratic forces signaled a shift toward greater managerial control of the production process and led to the reorganization of work at the point of production, thus providing the impetus for local control, on one hand, and weakening the grip of the Communist Party over the structure of production at various levels, on the other. The power struggle that led to the ascendance of the technocratic forces under Khrushchev at the same time brought about a split within the international communist movement and led to a rupture in relations with the People's Republic of China. The full-scale ramifications of the strained Soviet-Chinese relations did not become evident until the launching by Mao of the Great Proletarian Cultural Revolution in 1967, which, while domestic in nature, nevertheless was initiated to prevent developments in China similar to those under way in the Soviet Union at the time.

The interpretation of changes in the Soviet Union since Stalin's death and the rise to power of the technocratic forces have taken many twists and turns—sometimes guided by a genuine materialist analysis, but often through the dictates of the prevailing party line devised more for its propaganda value than for a clear understanding of the unfolding situation. Such was the case, for example, of the Chinese characterization of the Soviet state during the 1960s and 1970s as a "monopoly capitalist state of the fascist type," or the elevation of the Soviet Union to the level of a "superpower" that is "more dangerous" than the United States. The concept of "social imperialism" was thus devised during this period, corresponding to what the dominant forces within the Chinese Communist Party viewed as allegedly taking place within the Soviet Union—that is, a capitalist counterrevolution. Hence, the struggle against "capitalist roaders" within the Chinese Communist Party became the priority of the day.

Despite the dogmatic nature of the attacks on the Soviet state by ultraleftist forces within the Chinese Communist Party for the former's "deviation" from the principles of Marxism-Leninism, it is true that in the 1960s, structural shifts did take place in the Soviet economy that can be construed as moving the country in a "capitalist direction" (i.e., shifts resulting from reforms initiated to increase efficiency and productivity). Although factional struggles within the Communist Party have historically shifted the base of power in the Soviet Union through the 1980s, these changes represented variations in policy within the framework of a developing socialist state. However, the changes that took place during this period facilitated the spread of capitalist practices that worked to eventually undermine the further development of socialism in the Soviet Union in the subsequent period, resulting in the reforms that took place in the 1980s and early 1990s.

Developments in the former Soviet Union and Eastern Europe during the 1990s did indicate a movement toward a market-oriented economy, where capitalist elements became integrated into a socialist base within the framework of multiparty politics. In Poland and Hungary, such changes became institutionalized through a process of reform that preempted a mass uprising that later swept across Eastern Europe in 1989. But elsewhere, as in the German Democratic Republic, Bulgaria, and, most violently, Romania, mass protests and movements directed at the governments in power in these countries accelerated the pace of change, in some cases unleashing the forces of counterrevolution that came to power following a violent confrontation between the army and the security forces, as in Romania. In contrast, the reform movement in the former Soviet Union came from within the Communist Party.

The monumental social, economic, and political transformations that took place in Russia under the Yeltsin regime, as well as in other former Soviet republics, in the period following the collapse of the Soviet Union in the early 1990s, do indicate a counterrevolutionary development that has had a major impact on Russia and many of the other former Soviet republics. Whether the transformations that are now taking place throughout the former Soviet Union and Eastern Europe will lead to the restoration of capitalism there is still difficult to say, especially since the greatest portion of productive resources, land, and capital continues to remain in the hands of the state. Although such a situation can easily lead to the establishment of a form of bureaucratic state capitalism that does not require the widespread conversion of state property into private capital, this has not yet developed to the extent that it would pose a threat to the prevailing social system.

Whether the market-oriented reforms introduced under the Yeltsin and Putin regimes will lead Russia to a new era of capitalist democracy as the West hopes, or continue to sink the country deeper into the malaise of a deformed Mafia capitalism, only time will tell. It is clear, however, that at least as of this writing in late 2006, the dynamics of Russian society are moving that nation in the latter direction. Whatever the momentary detractions and reversals that Russia and the other former Soviet republics continue to face today, the dialectics of the class contradictions that are maturing under conditions of deformed capitalism in these countries, are bound to lead to further struggles for power among the contending class forces and open up new arenas of mass struggle that go beyond criticisms of exploitation and economic deprivation, and toward collective action to gain state power and effect change in favor of the working class and the laboring masses.

CONCLUSION

We have seen that the experience of the Soviet Union in socialist construction was the result of social and historical conditions that set the boundaries in which the development process was to proceed. The circumstances that shaped the policies set forth and implemented by the state in the former Soviet state were beyond the control of any individual(s); they required the concerted effort of the working class allied with the laboring masses and led by a vanguard political organ, the Communist Party, which assured its control and domination of the state and formulation of state policy favorable to the working class.

Throughout the postrevolutionary period, the Soviet state took numerous measures to offset any negative effects on the socialist order. These measures, such as the ones taken during the 1920s under the New Economic Policy, affected the course of socialist development in a big way, sometimes arresting its progress and even forcing tactical retreats. Nevertheless, it can be argued that the policies implemented in Russia during the early stages of postrevolutionary construction were seen as necessary for the survival of the socialist state. No amount of high-sounding pronouncements would have corrected the situation in favor of the proletariat when the balance of class forces, domestically and internationally, was stacked decisively against it. Clearly, it was the relentless efforts of a committed revolutionary leadership imbedded in the struggles of the time that made it possible to safeguard, defend, and advance the interests of the proletarian state, in spite of the concessions they were forced to make to the enemies of the revolution and of the socialist state.

In retrospect, it should be pointed out that while it is easy to wish for a smooth and linear progression of socialist construction following a proletarian revolution, the realities of the capitalist-dominated world economy force us to see that the transition from capitalism to communism is anything but a smooth and linear process. It is, in fact, a conflicting and contradictory process of development that the Soviet Union went through to safeguard socialism in the various stages of socialist construction that it initiated to promote its socialist development during the course of the twentieth century.

NOTES

1. Stephen K. Sanderson, *Revolutions: A Worldwide Introduction to Political and Social Change* (Boulder, Colo.: Paradigm, 2005), 26–27.
2. Tim McDaniel, "The Russian Revolution of 1917: Autocracy and Modernization," in *Revolutions: Theoretical, Historical, and Comparative Studies,* ed. Jack A. Goldstone, 3rd ed. (Belmont, Calif.: Wadsworth/Thomson Learning, 2003), 187.

3. Sanderson, *Revolutions*, 29.

4. Sanderson, *Revolutions*, 30.

5. Sanderson, *Revolutions*, 30.

6. Sanderson, *Revolutions*, 31.

7. McDaniel, "The Russian Revolution of 1917," 188.

8. Sanderson, *Revolutions*, 32.

9. Sanderson, *Revolutions*, 32.

10. McDaniel, "The Russian Revolution of 1917," 188.

11. Sanderson, *Revolutions*, 32.

12. Maurice Dobb, *Soviet Economic Development since 1917* (London: Routledge & Kegan Paul, 1948), 88, 92.

13. V. I. Lenin, *Selected Works in Three Volumes*, vol. 2 (Moscow: Progress, 1975), 634.

14. Dobb, *Soviet Economic Development*, 93.

15. Dobb, *Soviet Economic Development*, 95–96.

16. See Barrington Moore Jr., *Soviet Politics: The Dilemma of Power* (Cambridge, Mass.: Harvard University Press, 1950); E. H. Carr, *History of Soviet Russia*, vol. 2 (New York: Macmillan, 1952); Dobb, *Soviet Economic Development*.

17. Dobb, *Soviet Economic Development*, 96.

18. Lenin, *Selected Works*, 3, 537.

19. Quoted in Alexander Erlich, *The Soviet Industrialization Debate* (Cambridge, Mass.: Harvard University Press, 1960), 3.

20. Moore, *Soviet Politics*, 93.

21. Quoted in Erlich, *Soviet Industrialization*, 6.

22. Erlich, *Soviet Industrialization*, 10.

23. Erlich, *Soviet Industrialization*, xvi–xvii.

24. Carr, *History of Soviet Russia*.

25. Charles K. Wilber, *The Soviet Model and Underdeveloped Countries* (Chapel Hill: University of North Carolina Press, 1969), 59.

26. J. V. Stalin, *Questions of Leninism* (Moscow: Foreign Languages Publishing House, 1939), 487.

27. Dobb, *Soviet Economic Development*, 222.

28. Stalin, quoted in Dobb, *Soviet Economic Development*, 222.

29. Paul Baran, *The Political Economy of Growth* (New York: Monthly Review Press, 1957), 297.

30. Baran, *Political Economy of Growth*, 280.

31. Alexander Gerschenkron, *A Dollar Index of Soviet Machinery Output, 1927–28 to 1937* (Los Angeles: Rand Corporation, 1951); and Alexander Gerschenkron, *Economic Backwardness in Historical Perspective* (Cambridge, Mass.: Belknap Press of Harvard University Press, 1962), 247.

32. Maurice Dobb, "The Soviet Economy: Fact and Fiction," *Science and Society* (Spring 1954).

33. Baran, *Political Economy of Growth*, 282.

34. Baran, *Political Economy of Growth*, 282.

5

The Chinese Revolution

Workers and Peasants Rise Up
in the Long March to Power

The Chinese Revolution of October 1949, under the leadership of Mao Zedong and the Chinese Communist Party, was one of the major political events of the post–World War II period that came to define the nature and direction of revolutions that challenged capitalism, imperialism, and neocolonialism throughout the third world during the second half of the twentieth century. The mobilization of millions of peasants and workers through a long and arduous process of organizing that took many years across the Chinese countryside, as well as major cities, resulted in the march to victory that brought to power the Chinese masses led by a dedicated communist cadre who succeeded in waging a protracted struggle against external imperialist aggression and internal neocolonial reaction to secure final victory.

HISTORICAL BACKGROUND

For hundreds of years, under various dynasties, the workers and peasants of China lived in abject poverty. First under the despotic empires and later under the rule of the landed gentry, the Chinese masses came to endure severe oppression and exploitation through long periods of extreme hardship, famine, and hunger—conditions that ultimately led to worker–peasant uprisings throughout the course of recent Chinese history, especially during the late nineteenth and early twentieth centuries.

Until the early twentieth century, notes Mark Selden, "China had been ruled for more than two thousand years by an imperial bureaucracy, in alliance with powerful landowners who wielded enormous local influence."[1]

> In the eighteenth century, Imperial China was at the center of an East Asian regional system that achieved world-leading levels of technology, trade, and prosperity. By the nineteenth century, however, the ruling Qing dynasty was at low ebb, and European powers forced their way into China, demanding acceptance of free-trading privileges and imposing humiliating conditions on the Chinese government and people.[2]

By the late nineteenth century, all the signs of a declining empire were evident, as the Qing Dynasty entered a period of social, economic, and political crises. The oppression of peasant masses intensified, poverty widened, and discontent among broad segments of the population, including sections of the elite, mounted. With growing encroachments of Western imperialism in China and the worsening internal social-economic situation that affected millions of peasants, as well as resentment against the wealthy landed elite that became allied more and more with Western imperialist interests, feelings of nationalism and nationalist ideology spread and became a mobilizing force among the common population. Nationalist elements within government and elite circles became more and more critical of the prevailing situation and "resented the increasing role of Westerners and Western ideas and wanted reforms that would reestablish China's independence and prominence as a great world civilization."[3] This led to increasing nationalist activity among ruling circles at the close of the nineteenth century:

> In 1898 radicalism intensified. The Reform Movement of 1898, led by Kang Youwei, played an important role in consolidating elite discontent. In 1899 a famous revolt known as the Boxer Rebellion broke out. The Boxers were highly nationalistic; in 1900 they attacked missionaries, other foreigners, and Chinese converts to Christianity. In league with the government, they declared war on Japanese and Western powers and tried to expel them from the country.[4]

"However, their efforts were quickly put down," relates Sanderson. "Foreign troops occupied Beijing and killed thousands of people, and China was forced to accept a humiliating peace settlement that intensified its economic problems and actually increased foreign influence."[5]

Despite this defeat, however, the conditions that millions of Chinese peasants and workers endured during this period of persistent poverty and oppression were to reignite mass discontent into political action some years later. Engaging in radical political activities from the 1890s on, a major nationalist leader, Sun Yat-sen, emerged to take on the task of a national revolution to rid China of both foreign domination and the corrupt dynasty that sustained it—forces that had kept China in perpetual poverty, subjugation, and humiliation. Founding an organization to accomplish this task while in exile in Japan for some years, Sun Yat-sen and his United League became a prominent nationalist organ that launched a major offensive during the first decade of the twentieth century.

> The United League engaged in numerous revolts and attempted to assassinate government officials, including members of the imperial family. Revolutionaries increasingly infiltrated the army. Things had reached the crisis stage. The government responded to these actions and to earlier demands for reforms by undertaking a number of changes. . . . But the reforms were too little too late. Little was done to improve China's economic position vis-à-vis Japan and the West, and poverty and a strong feeling of social injustice were still widespread. China was ripe for revolution, and there was essentially no turning back after 1908.[6]

Intensified political activity by the rebel forces over the next three years, coupled with the deteriorating social-economic structure in China during this period, opened the way to direct political action resulting in a series of rebellions that culminated in the mass uprising that overthrew the Qing Dynasty in October 1911.

During the period following the 1911 uprising, China was ruled by various nationalist governments, from Sun Yat-sen in the nationalists' initial accession to power to Chiang Kai-shek and his right-wing authoritarian dictatorship. The nationalist period in China (1911–1949), much of it under Chiang Kai-shek's iron rule directed against the communists and the labor movement, became the most violent and bloody episode in modern Chinese history, as thousands of communists and their sympathizers were executed. Thus, while Chiang's Kuomintang government laid the groundwork for the reversals of the earlier reforms initiated under Sun Yat-sen in the immediate postrevolutionary period, it increasingly came to identify its mission along the lines of the dominant landowning and commercial interests and failed to address the problems faced by the Chinese masses, as most Chinese workers and peasants fell further into the depths of poverty and destitution. This deteriorating social-economic situation, together with the brutal repression of the regime's critics, especially the communists, set the stage for increased peasant support for the communists, with more and more intellectuals and students joining workers and peasants in their struggle against Chiang's authoritarian dictatorship.

During this prolonged period of nationalist repression, crisis, and turmoil lasting nearly four decades—a period that included the Japanese occupation of Manchuria in 1931 and the full-scale invasion of China proper in 1937, until Japan's final defeat and forced withdrawal in 1945—the Chinese communists were able to regroup and fight back. The communists built the Red Army, and under Mao's leadership took control of parts of southeast China, where a Chinese Soviet Republic was founded with Mao at its helm.[7] However, a series of major nationalist campaigns against the communists forced the latter to retreat: "The Red Army was routed and had to flee. Thus began one of the most famous events in modern Chinese history—the Long March [of 1934–1935]":

> Mao and about 100,000 men retreated from pursuing Kuomintang forces, traveling from the southeast to the southwest and then up to the northwest, a journey of some 6,000 miles. At most only a fifth of the men who started out were left when the Long March was finished. It was during this year of retreat that Mao became the unrivaled leader of the Communists.[8]

However, as Sanderson points out, "Mao and the Communists were able to reconstitute themselves militarily, and they continued to attract support from the peasantry, for whom they were strong advocates":

> Between 1937 and 1945 they expanded their influence enormously. In the former year the Red Army contained 80,000 men, but by the latter it had the better part of 1 million and a militia of more than 2 million. Moreover, in 1937 it ruled over only 1.5 million peasants in a single northern province, whereas by 1945 it governed 90 million peasants across much of northern China. The CCP (Chinese Communist Party) had grown to include over a million members by the end of World War II.[9]

With such strength in numbers and organizational skills, Mao and the communist forces were able to move on to the next stage in the struggle by creating the People's Liberation Army in mid-1946. With civil war under way, crucial battles began to take place in 1948:

> In April, Yenan was captured by the army, and shortly thereafter the two largest cities in the provinces of Honan, Loyang, and Kaifeng fell to Communist forces. By September the Communists had taken all of Manchuria. The most decisive battle was the Hwai-hai campaign, which was fought for two months from November of 1948 until January of 1949. This proved to be Chiang's Waterloo, for the Kuomintang forces were decimated and the Liberation Army had achieved a numerical superiority.[10]

"Recognizing defeat," writes Sanderson, "Chiang made known his desire to negotiate an end to the conflict. The Communists made it clear that Chiang himself had to go, and on January 21 he resigned as president. He and many of his allies fled to Taiwan, a former Japanese colony that had been reclaimed by China with the Japanese defeat in World War II."[11]

Thus, "by 1949, with their vast peasant base of supporters, the communists succeeded in driving U.S.-backed Kuomintang forces out of mainland China."[12] By taking state power, "the communists took control of China and proclaimed the foundation of the People's Republic of China in October 1949."[13] Thus began a new era in Chinese history—an era shaped by a state and a revolutionary leadership dedicated to the development of China along the socialist path.

POSTREVOLUTIONARY DEVELOPMENTS

The post-1949 revolutionary experience of China has in a number of ways been similar to that of socialist construction in Russia following the October revolution. After the 1949 revolution, China went through several important stages in its political economic development: the three years immediately following the revolution (1949–1952), the socialist transformation of the economy (1953–1957), the Great Leap Forward (1958), the crisis years (1959–1961), the New Economic Policy (1961–1964), the Cultural Revolution (1966–1969), the growth years of the early 1970s (1970–1976), the great reversals of the late 1970s and 1980s (1976–1989), and the expansion years (1990–Present).

The First Three Years (1949–1952)

Before the revolution in 1949, China was a poor and backward country. The predominant mode of production was feudal; less than 10 percent of the population (made up of landlords and rich peasants) owned 70 percent of the land; about 80 percent of the population was employed in agriculture; disease, hunger, and mass starvation were not uncommon. The industrial sector was small and largely owned by foreign capitalists.

After the revolution, the immediate strategic objective of the socialist state was to bring order to the chaotic economic situation of the country. During the initial period, economic control was secured over the major branches of the national economy, and a series of broad-based measures of land reform were put into effect, which redistributed the estates of landlords and rich peasants. The national bourgeoisie was viewed as a progressive force; hence, with the exception of the industrial assets belonging to those allied with foreign capital, no large-scale nationalization policy was initiated to confiscate private capital. Rather than a revolutionary transformation in the ownership of the means of production, the economic policy of the state during this period was one of gradualism.

The Socialist Transformation of the Economy (1953–1957)

In 1953, China launched its First Five-Year Development Plan, the aims of which were to lay the foundations for a comprehensive industrial base as rapidly as possible. In the initial stage of this industrialization process, emphasis was placed on the production of capital goods (over 50 percent of the state's investment funds was tied to heavy industry), and agriculture remained in the background. By placing strong emphasis on industrialization, China's objective was to replicate the Soviet experience into the framework of a development strategy based on the particular historical context in which the country found itself. This was clearly stated by Mao:

> In order to turn our country into an industrial power, we must learn conscientiously from the advanced experience of the Soviet Union. The Soviet Union has been building socialism for forty years, and its experience is very valuable to us. . . . It is perfectly true that we should learn from the good experience of all countries, socialist or capitalist, and there is no argument about this point. But the main thing is still to learn from the Soviet Union. Now, there are two different attitudes towards learning from others. One is the dogmatic attitude of transplanting everything, whether or not it is suited to our conditions. This is no good. The other attitude is to use our heads and learn those things which suit our conditions, that is, to absorb whatever experience is useful to us. That is the attitude we should adopt.
>
> To strengthen our solidarity with the Soviet Union, to strengthen our solidarity with all the socialist countries—that is our fundamental policy, this is where our basic interest lies.[14]

Following the post-1928 Soviet strategy, planning became highly centralized, and targets were fixed by the central government, which administered the various development programs through the ministries. Long-term loan agreements were set up with the Soviet Union to begin a large number of diversified modern industrial plants throughout the country.

> Most industrial targets of the First Five-Year Plan were achieved and some surpassed. Heavy industry constituted 48 percent of industrial output by 1957. Over the period of the plan, crude steel output increased from 1.35 million metric tons to 5.35 million; coal from 66.5 to 130.7 million; petroleum from 0.44 to 1.46 million; cement from 2.9 to 6.9 million; sulfuric acid from 190 thousand metric tons to 632 thousand; and electric power from 7.3 billion kilowatt hours to 19.3 billion.
>
> According to official figures, the gross output value of all industry, including handicrafts, increased by 128.4 percent during the plan, an annual average of 18 percent.[15]

In the agricultural sector, the strategy was to extend collectivization gradually. This was done in several stages: (1) mutual aid teams were developed, especially during 1949–1952; (2) the movement into cooperatives occurred in 1955–1956; and (3) communes were introduced in rural areas by the end of the decade.

Significant advances were made in both industry and agriculture. Although the major emphasis was on the expansion of heavy industry, the gross output value of agriculture increased by 24.7 percent at 1952 prices, and the output of food grains increased by 19.8 percent. And as the movement toward cooperative (and, in broader terms, the collectivization of agriculture) was speeded up in late 1955 through Mao's major policy intervention, by the end of the following year, over four-fifths of peasant households had become members of higher cooperatives.[16]

Despite the relatively sizeable advances made in agriculture, the state's emphasis on heavy industry placed agriculture in the background; a mere 6.2 percent investment in the latter was nowhere near the level needed to generate the rapid production of food and agricultural goods crucial for maintaining a high level of heavy industrial productivity. The slow progress in agriculture, coupled with the relative neglect of light industry, created problems for peasant incentives:

> Just as in the Soviet Union in the 1920s, the encouragement of a marketable surplus in agriculture depended largely in investment in agriculture, and on making available supplies of light industrial goods for peasants to buy in exchange for their product, so in China it was found that, under conditions of only gradual collectivization, peasant productivity lagged as a result of lack of incentives. Without steadily growing surpluses of agriculture, not only were there problems in supplying food to urban areas, but the financial backing (derived from taxation on agriculture and state profits from resale of agricultural deliveries) for industrialization was not there. Lack of expert surpluses did not permit the alternative method of industrialization, of exporting grain to obtain imported machinery.
>
> In 1956–57 the State procurements of grain and taxation in kind fell to 25.1 percent of the value of all grain produced, compared to 29.1 percent in 1953–54.[17]

One method of dealing with the emergent problems of industrialization generated during the course of the First Five-Year Plan was, as pointed out, the rapid growth of agricultural collectives in 1955–1956. Two other methods, initiated by Mao, also were designed to overcome these problems: (1) the commune system in agriculture in 1958 and (2) the encouragement of the Great Leap Forward in industry in 1958–1959.

Writing on the relationship between heavy industry, light industry, and agriculture, Mao, after pointing out that "heavy industry is the core of China's economic construction," stressed that "full attention must be paid to the development of agriculture and light industry." His message was clear:

> Industry must develop together with agriculture, for only thus can industry secure raw materials and market, and only thus is it possible to accumulate fairly large funds for building a powerful heavy industry. Everyone knows that light

industry is closely related to agriculture. Without agriculture there can be no light industry. But it is not yet so clearly understood that agriculture provides heavy industry with an important market. This fact, however, will be more readily appreciated as gradual progress in the technical improvement and modernization of agriculture calls for more and more machinery, fertilizer, water conservancy and electric power projects and transport facilities for the farms, as well as fuel and building materials of the rural consumers. . . . As agriculture and light industry develop, heavy industry, assured of its market and funds, will grow faster.[18]

Hence, during 1958, the movement toward the communalization of agriculture occurred concurrently with the decentralization of light industry. Earlier, in *Report on the First Five-Year Plan of Development*, Chief Planner Li Fu-Chun had announced a policy of "appropriately locating new industries in different parts of the country so that industrial production will be close to the sources of raw materials and fuels as well as consumer markets."[19] And this policy was in line with the measures advocated later during the Great Leap Forward.

The Great Leap Forward (1958)

The decentralization of industry and the communalization of agriculture were the central aims of what came to be known as "the Great Leap Forward." This period saw the creation of the communes and the industrial policy of "walking on two legs":

The aim of the commune system was the intensification of agricultural socialism to increase the marketable agricultural surplus and widen local agricultural and other investment opportunities. The industrial policy of "walking on two legs" aimed to tap the sources of industrial growth inherent in widely spread, easily mined coal and iron ore deposits, and small-scale indigenous technology, by the rapid development of small and medium industry in the interior of the country, both within and without the communes. In this respect it can be viewed as a kind of "crash industrialization" program, but within the context of developing agrarian socialism, without large-scale labor transfers to the cities.[20]

The Great Leap Forward was thus designed to achieve industrialization in a rural setting that was both complementary to the agrarian sector and decentralized enough to meet local demand for industrial goods. The coordination of the agrarian and industrial sectors within the context of a developing socialist society was the key to the success of the Great Leap Forward and of Chinese socialism in general—one that was to take place within the framework of communal social relations.

The Crisis Years (1959–1961)

While in 1958 the Great Leap Forward facilitated the development of industrial production within a rural communal setting, China in 1959 was on the eve of a major crisis that was to continue for the following two years. Two major developments were primarily responsible for the disastrous effects of the crisis years: (1) widespread natural disasters in agricultural regions, brought about by drought, typhoons, floods, and pests, destroyed more than half of the cultivated area, leading to a serious food shortage; and (2) the sudden withdrawal of Soviet economic aid in 1960 caused major disruptions in heavy industry, as some 150 enterprises (with more than a thousand Soviet technicians) were stopped. These two problems not only slowed down growth in both the agricultural and industrial sectors but also had adverse effects on operations throughout the economy. The Chinese industrialization process, based largely on Soviet aid, came to an end. And these events gave rise to sharp political and ideological debates over China's future economic policy toward agriculture and industry.

The New Economic Policy (1961–1964)

The economic crisis of 1959–1961 led the state to adopt a new strategy of economic development and a new set of policies that would put such strategy into motion. The new course of development came to be known as the New Economic Policy (NEP).

The basic similarity between this and the Soviet NEP of 1921–1928 was the granting of concessions for the expansion of free-market forces and the return of the profit motive in both agricultural and industrial production. As in the Soviet Union, of course, this was to take place within the framework of proletarian political leadership and the state's ownership of the major means of production and exchange.

In January 1961, an official declaration was made "to reinforce the agricultural front by making agriculture the foundation of the national economy and giving industry second priority":

> It was pointed out then, and later, that the Chinese countryside constituted eighty percent of the market of light industrial goods, as well as a large market for heavy industrial goods. It was proposed to adjust the rate of development of industry to the amount of raw materials and foodstuffs that agriculture could supply, and that industry should supply the flow of goods made necessary by agricultural development to help mechanize the rural sector.[21]

One of the first moves under the NEP was the gradual introduction of a free market in the countryside. Later, further concessions were made to the peasants through the adoption of the policy of *san zi yi bao*, which involved the restoration of private plots to peasants; the use of the household as the main accounting unit in communes; and the assumption by enterprises in communes of sole responsibility for profit and output quotas. Although the implementation of these policies made it possible to increase agricultural production, it also meant widespread diffusion of private cultivation practices throughout China's rural interior. And this, in turn, gave rise to the formation of a *kulak* peasant class.

It is clear that many of the steps taken during China's NEP resembled closely the situation that existed in the Soviet Union during the 1920s. Lenin's plans under NEP were clear; it was a transitional policy that was necessary for the full-scale development of industry and agriculture to prepare the road for the transition to socialism. Was this also true in China? Certainly the parallel is clear; and while agriculture in China got the upper hand, it nonetheless was to be coordinated with the development of industry. But the important question is, were the policies adopted under the NEP in China from the beginning regarded as temporary? Or was such a move a response to unexpected changes in material conditions at the time? The reason we raise these questions is that although things were clear in Lenin's mind with regard to the future transition to socialism when he introduced the New Economic Policy in 1921, the consistency of this policy was threatened after his death in 1924 by rightists within the Communist Party under the leadership of Bukharin, who essentially wanted to change the transitional NEP into a permanent one. This was almost exactly the situation in which the Chinese Communist Party found itself in the early 1960s; at the same time, capitalist forms of production and exchange (at least at the small-scale level) were in full swing throughout the rural areas. Moreover, this vigorous movement to the right (led by Bukharin's Chinese counterpart, Liu Shao-chi, who had once strongly supported revolutionary policies), was multiplied by the growing emphasis on profitability, expertise, and bureaucratization, in addition to the reappearance of traditional patterns of industrial organization and ownership. Again, the question to be asked is whether the NEP was a transitional stage in Chinese socialist development, or was it to become institutionalized into the mainstream of Chinese economy and society?

To clarify this point, and to place the post-1960 policy changes within the proper historical context, Wheelwright and McFarlane put it this way:

> Broadly speaking, Mao's technique in 1960–64 was to prepare and issue warnings about the implications of the "rightist" trend in economic policy and culture, and to counterpose "the revolutionary tradition of the masses," the need to train reliable successors to the revolution who would not follow the Soviet road,[22] the need for everyone to be a soldier, and the need to implement, wherever possible, the line of "from the masses to the masses," which had fallen into

disarray with the "seventy points" in industry and the "san zi yi bao" policy in agriculture. Mao also took certain organizational steps, notably in obtaining the adherence of the People's Liberation Army and General Lin Piao. . . .

By 1965 the tensions in Chinese Society were building up. The official ideology of the Chinese Revolution remained Maoist. But the State organizations and enterprises, and large sectors of cultural and ideological life, were governed by different rules. The years 1964 and 1965, in particular, saw the beginning of the struggle to resolve the question—"Which will transform which?" between State and Party practice, and Maoism? In this sense, 1965 marked the prelude to the Great Proletarian Cultural Revolution.[23]

The Cultural Revolution, which raised the crucial political issues confronting the Chinese state to the level of collective action, was intended to resolve this imbedded contradiction between theory and practice, ideology and practical politics—a contradiction that could be resolved, as it turned out, only through a mass action that the Cultural Revolution came to represent in the political uproar of the late 1960s.

The Cultural Revolution (1966–1969)

Closely observing the changes brought about by the NEP and disturbed by the direction in which it was moving, Mao, by launching the Great Proletarian Cultural Revolution, once again brought China under revolutionary leadership guided by proletarian principles and strategies.

The Cultural Revolution was launched, above all, to end entrenched bureaucratization of political life at the highest levels of the Chinese state, including the political officialdom and the intelligentsia, in an effort to halt the development of bourgeois values and privileges among a cadre of self-serving "revisionist" bureaucrats who were "communist" in name only. The attack on bourgeois ideas and privileges within the party and the promotion of class struggle at the ideological level (between the communists and the "capitalist roaders" within the party) was an effort to halt the danger of capitalist restoration while at the same time consolidating the gains of socialism.

We cannot go into a detailed analysis of the Cultural Revolution here, but its main features can be summarized as follows: (1) In political terms, the Cultural Revolution meant a clear victory for the Maoists in the fierce struggle against the "revisionists," led by Liu Shao-chi; (2) by taking power away from the rightists, the Maoists were able to resume the strategy of economic development launched by Mao during the Great Leap Forward in 1958; (3) culturally, it was a campaign against Confucianism and tradition—the tradition based on bourgeois and feudal ideologies—in the process of which the supremacy of the Maoist ideology over "revisionism" was assured; (4) at the mass level, it was a major effort to involve the masses deeply in the revolutionary fervor, an exercise in reminding them of the central importance of the class struggle; and (5) again at the mass level, it was an educational campaign directed at the younger generations—a learning process in the midst of the revolutionary experience of the masses. The Cultural Revolution thus opened up a new phase in China's development that was to continue to the end of the 1960s.

The Growth Years (1970–1976)

During the 1970s, China made great advances in economic development and social progress. Production increased, exports grew, and industrialization forged ahead, with impressive rates of growth in major branches of industry, especially in crude oil production, machinery, and manufactured goods. By the mid-1970s, China was producing 259 million metric tons of grain, 24 million metric tons of steel, 655 million metric tons of crude oil, 25 million metric tons of chemicals and fertilizers, 133 thousand tractors, and 5 million bicycles.[24]

This period also saw a marked growth in small industries that produce many of the inputs required by agriculture (cement, steel, fertilizers, etc.) and process the sector's output of food, cotton, sugar, tobacco, and other commercial crops. Moreover, with its strides in rapid industrialization, China reached a position by the mid-1970s of exporting one-quarter of its oil production and a large volume of manufactured goods (including bicycles, sewing machines, cameras, watches, and radios) to countries around the world. At the same time, the planning authorities promoted greater intensity of land use, further mechanization, and other measures to keep food supplies ahead of population, including a nationwide effort to limit birthrates. All these policies were implemented within the framework of a revolutionary program of social transformation leading to the consolidation of socialism that guaranteed a higher standard of living for the people.

The Great Reversals (1976–1989)

With the death of Mao in 1976, China entered another period of reversals and setbacks in socialist construction, as rightist forces within the Chinese Communist Party, headed by Deng Xiaoping, took advantage of the advances made in the economic sphere and made a comeback, repositioning China on the "capitalist road" and away from the socialist programs of the previous period. As a result, China began moving during the 1980s in the direction of a process that would restructure its socialist economic base through superstructural reforms of a market-oriented nature.

The changes that China underwent during this period were the result of a new approach adopted by the Chinese Communist Party toward private capital, including foreign capital, with which the state entered into joint ventures in various industries. While this approach facilitated the evolution of the Chinese economy along a development path that was export oriented, the state's strong controls to curb the negative impact of the opening to foreign and domestic capital helped mediate the process whereby the central authority (the state) would retain its reign over the major means of production, while at the same time accelerate the development of the productive forces and increase China's position in world trade. China's decade-long drive for modernization of its economy through a tactical alliance with foreign capital for further domestic growth and diversification in the direction of consumer goods production for export thus fed into its rising prospects for international trade—one that necessitated changes in the domestic economic structure, affecting the social-economic position of millions of Chinese who more and more engaged in small-scale entrepreneurial activities, hence facilitating the expansion of the private sector.

The changes China underwent in its domestic and global economic relations during this period inevitably necessitated a fundamental change in its foreign and domestic policy in the political sphere that was far more significant than the reversals of the early 1960s and comparable in magnitude to the Cultural Revolution, but in the opposite direction.[25]

China's opening to the West and increasing collaboration with foreign capital during the 1980s not only led to the further reversals of the policies promoted during the Cultural Revolution but extended the economic progress made during the growth years of the 1970s and set the stage for China's fuller participation in the world economy beyond the 1980s and well into the first decade of the twenty-first century.

The Expansion Years (1990–Present)

With the emergence of Li Pang and the opposition forces within the Chinese Communist Party in the late 1980s, the new party leadership began to tighten China's "pragmatic" economic policies that it had embarked on earlier, and led the country in a direction that placed the economy under greater state control. Thus, during the 1990s, the market reforms of the previous period evolved within the framework of an expanded role for the state—a role that complemented the enormous economic gains of the 1980s.

However, China's continued integration into the world economy during this period, through joint ventures with foreign capital, increased trade with the advanced capitalist countries, especially the United States, and membership in international financial and trade organizations—which regularly impose stringent economic conditions for compliance with regulations concerning international capital flows, global financial transactions, and social policy—have had a serious negative effect on the Chinese state, economy, and society. While such an outcome has come as a surprise to the pragmatic leadership of the Chinese Communist Party during this latest phase of China's economic development tied to the world economy, the process in place during this period has generated a new set of problems for the Chinese state.

The contradictions embedded in this process, subjecting the state to the dictates of the global political-economic structure and its institutions, has had a heavy toll on the evolution of Chinese socialism, forcing on the state setbacks and distortions that it has so far been unable to avoid. The effects of global political-economic relations on China and its role in the world economy in this and the coming period have thus become hot topics for discussion and debate—topics that are of critical importance for China's further development.

What the final outcome of this evolving situation will be in the next stage of the development process in China in the twenty-first century, only time will tell. But it is clear that the process of socialist construction in China, as in the former Soviet Union, has been a cyclical and contradictory one with many setbacks along the way—a process that is characteristic of the transition from capitalism to socialism throughout the world.

NOTES

1. Mark Selden, "The Chinese Communist Revolution," in *Revolutions: Theoretical, Comparative, and Historical Studies*, ed. Jack A. Goldstone, 3rd ed. (Belmont, Calif.: Wadsworth/Thomson Learning, 2003), 191.

2. Selden, "The Chinese Communist Revolution," 191.

3. Stephen K. Sanderson, *Revolutions: A Worldwide Introduction to Political and Social Change* (Boulder, Colo.: Paradigm, 2005), 36.

4. Sanderson, *Revolutions*, 36.

5. Sanderson, *Revolutions*, 36.

6. Sanderson, *Revolutions*, 37.

7. Sanderson, *Revolutions*, 39.

8. Sanderson, *Revolutions*, 39–40.

9. Sanderson, *Revolutions*, 40.

10. Sanderson, *Revolutions*, 41.

11. Sanderson, *Revolutions*, 41.

12. Selden, "The Chinese Communist Revolution," 191.

13. Selden, "The Chinese Communist Revolution," 191.

14. Mao Zedong, "China's Path to Industrialization," part 12 of "On the Correct Handling of Contradictions among the People," in *Selected Readings from the Works of Mao Tse-Tung* (Peking: Foreign Languages Press, 1971), 477–78.

15. E. L. Wheelwright and B. McFarlane, *The Chinese Road to Socialism* (New York: Monthly Review Press, 1970), 36.

16. Higher cooperatives were large units that embraced whole villages, containing from one hundred to three hundred households, whereas lower cooperatives consisted of from twenty to forty households. The former became the basic economic unit in the countryside during this period. For the nature, size, extent, and central importance of cooperatives in the early phase of China's collectivization of the agricultural sector, see Mao Zedong, "On the Question of Agricultural Cooperatives," *Selected Readings*, 389–420.

17. Wheelwright and McFarlane, *The Chinese Road to Socialism*, 40.

18. Mao Zedong, "Correct Handling of Contradictions," 476.

19. Li Fu-Chun, *Report on the First Five-Year Plan of Development* (Peking: Foreign Languages Press, 1950), 50.

20. Wheelwright and McFarlane, *The Chinese Road to Socialism*, 43.

21. Wheelwright and McFarlane, *The Chinese Road to Socialism*, 66.

22. The reference here is to the "revisionist" policies of the Soviet leadership following Stalin's death and the "restoration of the capitalist road" by the Khrushchev forces.

23. Wheelwright and McFarlane, *The Chinese Road to Socialism*, 93.

24. John Gurley, *Challengers to Capitalism* (San Francisco: San Francisco Book, 1976), 136–37.

25. Charles Bettelheim, "The Great Leap Backward," *Monthly Review* 30, no. 3 (July–August 1978).

6

The Vietnamese Revolution

People's War and the Protracted Struggle for Independence and Socialism

David L. Elliott

Modern Vietnam is first documented as having emerged as a separate society two millennia ago as an ethnic group at the southern reaches of China; as a distinct culture, the Nam (south of China) Viets (non-Chinese peoples) are probably twelve thousand years old. However, the Chinese and Vietnamese have traditionally shared many social structural and cultural attributes. With respect to religion, Buddhism was probably more deeply embedded in Vietnamese society than in Chinese. Philosophically, Daoism influenced the outlook of Vietnamese and Chinese alike. The Confucian social order that originated with the Chinese philosopher Kong Fuzi provided the rigid hierarchy and moral foundation for both peoples. Confucian society was characterized by peasant communes ruled nationally by a hereditary dynasty served by a meritocratic intelligentsia; so similar were these social orders that Vietnamese scholars were known as *mandarins*. The economic structure of both societies is probably best described as the Asiatic mode of production as opposed to feudalism: unlike feudalism, the peasants' relationship to the land was not mediated through lords to whom the peasantry owed rent and labor. To be sure, the peasantry was exploited by royal satraps and sycophants, such as the mandarins, traders, and tax collectors, through appropriation of the surplus product but not necessarily realized directly as labor.

China and Vietnam shared another common characteristic: at the height of their respective periods of power and influence both were expansionist. Indeed, China ruled Vietnam directly or indirectly for nine of the last twenty centuries. By the last quarter of the nineteenth century, Vietnam had absorbed other peoples including parts of the ancient Khmer Empire and had expanded to roughly its present borders, though not without internal strife and divisive wars. Weakened by conflict and unable to match imperialist France's military might, Vietnam fell to French colonial rule in 1887. In short order, France eviscerated the Confucian social order; imposed wage labor in mines, plantations, and factories; and offered favors to the Vietnamese compradors that had converted to Catholicism and served as the nascent bourgeoisie.

EARLY RESISTANCE

As the twentieth century opened, the Vietnamese intelligentsia that opposed French rule realized that the traditional Confucian-based political and social organization that had served Vietnam for many centuries was no longer viable, a lesson being learned at that time by the Chinese, as well, who faced the onslaught of European and Japanese imperialism. The traditional Confucian hierarchy of Emperor, intelligentsia, and peasantry could sometimes resist Chinese rule and even expand the nation. But it could not resist the military power of French colonialism. The intelligentsia, however, by virtue of its knowledge base and ability to communicate in writing, was the only segment of Vietnamese society capable of organizing resistance to French domination. The class struggles resulting from the imposition of French rule remained localized, at first.

The Vietnamese resistance movement saw increased literacy as a key strategy of the resistance. It encouraged adoption of the phonetic *quoc-ngu* system based on the Roman alphabet, which could be learned more easily and quickly than the traditional Vietnamese script. As literacy spread, and nationalist writings proliferated, two nationalist branches of the intelligentsia emerged, reformist and revolutionary.

The nationalist intelligentsia expanded and from it emerged a Vietnamese petite bourgeoisie employed by the French or running small commercial establishments. Many were reformists, not revolutionaries, in the sense that they viewed Japan as a model for Vietnam's modernization. Neither scholars in the classical Confucian tradition, nor nationalists in the long tradition of Vietnamese resistance to foreign rule, they felt estranged from both their families and the French. With their exposure to French culture, they began to adopt Western individualistic ideology.

> Many Vietnamese intellectuals found themselves in desperate need to create a dynamic and authentically Vietnamese form of individualism that could articulate more satisfactorily with the world in which they lived, a world shaped by family, by tradition, and by a stifling reality of colonial domination.[1]

Thus, Western individualism served as a new vehicle for Vietnamese expression of nationalism, especially by the petite bourgeoisie.

The most important organization based in the petite bourgeoisie was the Viet Nam Quoc Dan Dang (VNQDD, Vietnamese Nationalist Party). The VNQDD appeared in 1925 in Hanoi and quickly spread to other Vietnamese cities. It was created "with the dual aim of achieving commercial success and promoting revolution."[2] The VNQDD and associated revolutionary organizations were successful in fomenting revolt, and hundreds of VNQDD members were arrested with many sentenced to long prison terms.[3] The remaining leadership decided to initiate violent revolution. The VNQDD greatly overestimated its support among the people and the uprisings it initiated in 1930 failed. Remnants of the VNQDD retreated to China and linked up with the right-wing Kuomintang under the leadership of Chiang Kai-shek. The retreat into China effectively spelled the end of revolutionary activity by those associated with the petit bourgeois intelligentsia. It did, however, help to raise the consciousness of Vietnamese in the cities.

NATIONAL RESISTANCE:
PEASANTS, WORKERS, RADICAL INTELLIGENTSIA

The single largest social class in Vietnam was the peasantry, forced to grow both its own food and cash crops to pay the taxes levied by the French. Far less numerous, but no less oppressed than the peasantry, was the working class. Members of the working class toiled in mines, on plantations, or in factories for French companies that paid their wages and they were more surely subject to the vicissitudes of the capitalist economy.

In 1911, a twenty-one-year-old nationalist and future leader of North Vietnam departed his country, not to return for over thirty years. He traveled widely, including to the United States, working his way as a ship hand and at other menial jobs. As was the practice of some Vietnamese—and some Chinese, as his father was a Confucian scholar in the ancient tradition—he changed his name a number of times. By the time he arrived in Paris, he had adopted the name Nguyen Ai Quoc, "Nguyen the Patriot," the name he was best known by until 1945.

Nguyen Ai Quoc, like the traditional intelligentsia of his father's generation and the radical intelligentsia of his own, was a nationalist who sought an independent Vietnam. In his early adult years, living in France, he turned to France for support for the independence of Vietnam. He wrote and spoke and joined French organizations in an attempt to convince the French people and government to grant independence to Vietnam. In 1919, he even appealed for assistance to U.S. president Woodrow Wilson, who was in France attending the Versailles Peace Conference ending World War I.

Like Wilson, the French Socialist Party that Nguyen Ai Quoc was associated with endorsed the general principle of independence but provided no real support for *Vietnamese* independence. What first attracted Nguyen Ai Quoc to V. I. Lenin were Lenin's writings about the right of all nations to self-determination.[4] Nguyen Ai Quoc was aware of the plight and the small size of the Vietnamese working class, but he also knew that the working class in Russia was relatively small, as well. He saw the socialist revolution in Russia as a model for Vietnam's revolution for independence.

In the early 1920s, Nguyen Ai Quoc journeyed to Moscow and from there to Canton. He was sent to China by the Fifth Comintern Congress with the mission "(1) to establish a liaison between all communist organizations in Southeast Asia with the Comintern headquarters in Moscow, and with its bureau in the Far East, centered at Shanghai, and (2) to supervise the founding of the first communist organization in French Indochina."[5] In these early years of the Vietnamese communist movement, 1924–1930, much of the activity and organization took place outside Vietnam, in the Soviet Union, China, and the British colony of Hong Kong. This early period closed with the capitalist crisis that reverberated throughout the world; Vietnamese peasants and especially workers were the hardest hit, and this opened the door to anticapitalist ideologies.

In the face of intractable conditions that were presented to the Vietnamese workers and peasantry by the collapse of nationalist leadership by the VNQDD, the Vietnam Communist Party was founded in 1930 by Nguyen Ai Quoc. Its membership was recruited from among the remnants of revolutionary groups operating alongside the VNQDD. Within a year, with support from the Soviet Union, it had reconstituted itself as the Indochinese Communist Party (ICP). The ICP sought independence not just for Vietnam but for Laos and Cambodia as well, and it soon launched the first (unsuccessful) communist-inspired uprisings that took place in Vietnam, the so-called Nghe-Trinh soviets.

In the 1930s, Nguyen Ai Quoc remained outside Vietnam, organizing Vietnamese exile opposition to French colonial rule. He also continued to play a leading role in the communist movement as he had in the 1920s. Arrested by the British for these activities in the mid-1930s, he spent two years in a Hong Kong prison. After his release, he returned to Moscow and in 1938 went back to China to continue his work with Vietnamese exiles.

Nguyen Ai Quoc and other Vietnamese revolutionaries were able to find refuge in China because of a complicated struggle for power there. Two preeminent Chinese political party movements had emerged as opponents to Japanese aggression: the Kuomintang was backed by the United States and gave refuge to exiled members of the VNQDD, while the Chinese Communist Party was backed by the Soviet Union and provided shelter to members of the ICP. By the late 1930s, these parties had joined forces in opposition to Japanese aggression. With the fall of France to Germany in 1940 and Japan fighting in China, Japan was allowed to occupy Vietnam.

The Japanese military occupation of Vietnam relied on French administrators and collaborationist Vietnamese emperor Bao Dai. Nominal though his leadership was, Bao Dai was one important symbol of Vietnam as a nation. The ICP led uprisings against the French and the Japanese throughout Vietnam. While these uprisings were quickly put down, the surviving fighters were to form the basis of the army that would eventually defeat France in the 1950s, and then defeat the United States a generation later.

In the south of China in 1941, Nguyen Ai Quoc and the ICP formed the League for the Independence of Vietnam, better known as the Vietminh. During the period of Japanese occupation while World War II was waged, the Vietminh organization spread across Vietnam. The Vietminh obtained widespread peasant support for independence and the ejection of both the French and the Japanese from Vietnam.

Following the formation of the Vietminh, Nguyen Ai Quoc was arrested and spent another year in a Chinese prison. On his release, he linked up with the surviving remnants of the VNQDD in China, but toward the close of World War II, the Vietminh organization formed an army under the leadership of General Vo Nguyen Giap, the brilliant strategist who would eventually lead Vietnam's military forces to independence.

The year 1945 was a turning point in Vietnam. Under the leadership of Nguyen Ai Quoc and General Giap acting on behalf of the ICP, the Vietminh continued to strengthen its support throughout the country. Meanwhile, World War II had turned against the Germans and the Japanese. In a desperate move to remain in Vietnam after France was liberated from German rule, the Japanese installed the puppet emperor Bao Dai as the leader of a Japanese "protected" independent Vietnam. The nationalist fires for independence burned still stronger, and the communist-led Vietminh had come to be the only credible organization that could claim widespread popular support in Vietnam.

To end World War II, the United States deployed nuclear weapons on Japanese cities, and the Japanese surrendered to the United States on August 15, 1945. Technically, Vietnam was now independent and under the rule of Bao Dai. But this did not last. The day after the Japanese surrender, the Vietminh called for revolution throughout the country to rid Vietnam of both French and Japanese control.

No longer the young man he was when he left Vietnam over thirty years before, his body weakened by illness contracted during his years of imprisonment in China but his mind sharpened by struggle, Nguyen Ai Quoc returned to Vietnam and changed his name for the last time. Nguyen Ai Quoc renamed himself Ho Chi Minh, "he who enlightens."

THE VIETNAM DECLARATION OF
INDEPENDENCE AND PROVISIONAL GOVERNMENT

In the next two weeks, Ho Chi Minh assembled a provisional government, and Bao Dai abdicated in favor of Ho's provisional government, which appointed Bao Dai as supreme counselor. On September 2, 1945, Ho Chi Minh issued the Vietnam Declaration of Independence that included the following passage:

> "All men are created equal. They are endowed by their Creator with certain inalienable rights; among these are Life, Liberty, and the pursuit of Happiness."
>
> This immortal statement was made in the Declaration of Independence of the United States of America in 1776. In a broader sense, this means: All the peoples on the earth are equal from birth, all the peoples have a right to live, to be happy and free.[6]

Vietnamese nationalists (including communists) were informally allied with the United States in opposition to Japanese occupation of southern China and Vietnam, and the Vietnamese knew that the United States had freed the Philippines from a brutal Japanese occupation, setting into motion plans for Philippine independence. Consequently, Vietnamese nationalist leadership expected the United States to be instrumental in helping Vietnam achieve independence. However, the Potsdam Conference ending World War II directed the Nationalist Chinese to occupy the north of Vietnam until the French could return, and the British were to occupy the south. The British rearmed the defeated Japanese and ordered them to maintain control until they could be relieved by French troops. With the United States in agreement, any hope for peaceful transfer to independence in Vietnam was demolished.

The French, however, still recovering from German occupation, were in no position to prevent the formation of a provisional independent Vietnamese government, and the Democratic Republic of Vietnam (DRV) took office on the first day of 1946. The ICP was dissolved, since "Indochina" was a French colonial designation for Vietnam, Laos, and Cambodia. Following the end of German occupation, French leaders and their British and American allies looked to the reinstitution of colonial rule over Indochina as one means of restoring France's prestige and rebuilding her economy. The only credible Vietnamese opposition to the reimposition of colonial rule came from the Soviet-backed DRV.

Meanwhile, when the Nationalist Chinese withdrew from the north, France declared Vietnam a "free state" within the French Union. In May, Ho Chi Minh traveled to France to negotiate the details, but while he was there, a French admiral with the support of pro-France Vietnamese declared a separate government in the south. Vietnam was divided, once again. France continued to reassert its power in Vietnam by bombing Haiphong harbor near Hanoi in November 1946, forcing the DRV government out of the city and into the countryside. The following month, the Vietminh attacked the French in the north, and the war for independence had resumed.

In 1948, U.S. State Department official George Keenan published an anonymous article in the U.S. journal *Foreign Affairs* that defined the U.S. "containment" policy that was a foundation of U.S. anticommunist policy in Southeast Asia. Shortly thereafter, in the attempt to contain communism in Asia, France once again called on its puppet leader, Bao Dai, to assume rule over the Associated State of Vietnam from Saigon. In 1949, the Chinese communists forced Chiang Kai-shek's army off the China mainland to the island of Taiwan. This event, along with the ongoing Vietnamese Revolution, was yet one more justification of a policy of containment of communism that was to shape the politics of East Asia for decades to come.

In Vietnam, the fighting between the Vietminh and the French continued. U.S. dollars continued to flow into France to support its war effort, while the Vietnamese Revolution for independence from France spilled over into neighboring Laos, with France granting Laos and Cambodia their independence in 1953. By the end of that year, the Vietnamese city of Dienbienphu was poised to become the site of the last and most decisive battle of the independence phase of the Vietnamese Revolution. Tensions had then reached a point where a peace agreement in Vietnam was supported by leaders throughout the world—from the United States to France and Britain, the Soviet Union to China—and the Geneva Conference on the Vietnam question began on May 8, 1954. In the closing weeks before the peace talks began, the Vietminh launched an attack on French-held Dienbienphu. A fierce battle raged as the DRV army recaptured the city resulting in a major French defeat on May 7.

THE GENEVA ACCORDS:
DIVISION AND PROBLEMS OF INDEPENDENCE

Cochaired by Britain and the Soviet Union, the Geneva Conference also included France, the United States, the People's Republic of China, the "State of Vietnam," the "Democratic Republic of Vietnam," Laos, and Cambodia. These nations worked until July of that year to come up with a cease-fire and other documents aimed at bringing independence to Vietnam. The conference also intended to bring a lasting peace to the region, an ill-fated intention.

The 1954 peace accords called for the *temporary* division of Vietnam at the seventeenth parallel. This provisional division was only intended to stand until nationwide elections could be held two years later. It is important to note that in the conference *two state apparatuses claimed to represent one country: Vietnam.* The State of Vietnam was headed by Emperor Bao Dai and was a creation of the French. The Democratic Republic of Vietnam (DRV) was headed by Ho Chi Minh and was created by the Vietminh forces with Soviet sponsorship at the close of World War II. The Geneva Accords did not create two countries; rather, they recognized rival claims to one independent country, Vietnam.[7] The Geneva Accords did not anticipate a permanent or even indefinite division of Vietnam into two countries; it envisioned electoral resolution of the rival claims.

Both of the rival governments questioned the settlement. The DRV, which was given temporary authority over the north of Vietnam, was concerned about the settlement because it had loyal Vietminh troops in the south that would come under the rule of the State of Vietnam. However, under pressure from conference participants China and the Soviet Union, Ho Chi Minh's government agreed to the accords.

The French-formed State of Vietnam that was given control over the south of Vietnam opposed the settlement and refused to sign. The situation in the south was more complex and involved the United States. During the three months the conference was in session, from April to July 1954, a major change took place in the government of the State of Vietnam. At the urging of the United States, the Bao Dai government appointed Ngo Dinh Diem as prime minister. Diem's nationalist sentiment and opposition to colonialism were well known and respected, even among the Vietminh. In fact, Ho Chi Minh's provisional government in 1945 had approached Diem to cooperate in the establishment of an independent Vietnam. But Diem's staunch Catholicism and vigorous opposition to communism were apparently stronger than his views for independence from the west. Diem quickly gained power within the government. When the Geneva Conference came to a close, Diem was influential enough to prevent the State of Vietnam from signing the accords, a refusal that the United States also adopted. Neither the State of Vietnam in the south nor the United States agreed to the temporary division to be followed in two years with democratic elections. In his memoirs, President Dwight Eisenhower said that "had elections been held at the time of the fighting [that the Peace Accords was intended to end], possibly 80 per cent of the population would have voted for the communist Ho Chi Minh as their leader."[8]

Astute political maneuvers with support from the United States led Ngo Dinh Diem to assume the presidency of what was renamed the "Republic of Vietnam" the year after the Geneva Conference. Diem refused to participate in the nationwide elections scheduled for 1956, and he set about the task of further consolidating his rule in the south.

Even though nationwide elections were not held as scheduled, and even though France withdrew from Vietnam, the cease-fire held. For the first time since France imposed colonial rule, Vietnam (albeit divided) was independent and thus set the stage for a resolution of its internal social and class contradictions that would lead to its impending social transformation. Following French disengagement, the Vietminh began a series of assassinations of low-level South Vietnamese officials who were agents of the oppressive Diem regime. By 1958, Vietminh in the south had been organized and were operating in collaboration with the DRV in the north. The following year, to unify the country and to further the drive toward socialism throughout Vietnam, the north began to infiltrate the south with fighters and arms traveling secretly down the "Ho Chi Minh Trail," a network of paths through the jungles of Laos and Cambodia used by Diem's opponents to reach South Vietnam.

The leading counterrevolutionary in the south, Ngo Dinh Diem, with his retinue, favored Catholics and oppressed the Buddhist and peasant majority of the population with the backing of the United States. The hated Diem regime also supported large landowners over the poor peasants, while the communists promised land reform and redistribution of land to the poor and landless peasants.

SOCIALIST CONSTRUCTION AND COUNTERREVOLUTION

In North Vietnam, Ho Chi Minh and General Giap, who led the assault against Dienbienphu, remained the most powerful figures. They had been joined in 1960 by Le Duan, a longtime follower of Ho who had replaced the aging Ho as head of the Vietnam Workers' Party, the ruling party in North Vietnam. The authorities in the North were faced with a number of challenges. As leaders of a nationalist revolution as well as a socialist revolution, they saw a need both to win over the entire country, North and South, and build a socialist society. The socialist society envisioned would be one in which there would be no sharp distinctions between rich and poor. There would be no advantage taken of workers and peasants by the rich and powerful, as had taken place under French rule and continued under Diem in the South. North Vietnam's goal of winning over the South was understood only too well by the United States and the Diem regime, but North Vietnam's goal of building a socialist society was profoundly misunderstood by U.S. leaders.

Contrary to U.S beliefs in the existence of a monolithic form of communism controlled from Moscow, Ho, Giap, and Le Duan were determined that Vietnam would define its own socialist future without any external control. Whereas both the Soviet Union and the United States advocated for national self-determination in word, only the Soviets supported Vietnam in deed. No small part of that support was the organizational capabilities learned from the communists. According to Le Duan:

> Before the seizure of power and in the pursuit of that aim, the only weapon available to the revolution, to the masses, is organization. The hallmark of the revolutionary movement led by the proletariat is its high organizational standard. All activities aimed at bringing the masses to the point where they will rise up and topple the ruling classes may boil down to this: to organize, organize, organize.[9]

One of the key ways that the communists in the North attempted to organize society so as to provide for its welfare was by redistributing land from the large landowners to the landless peasantry. This is what the Chinese communists had begun to do in the 1950s and what the Cubans were to do in their revolution, too. But there were many problems in implementing the land reform. First, land and the labor that worked it was not the only source of wealth. The industrial infrastructure that emerged under French rule was systematically dismantled by its departing owners leaving behind a landless and unemployed working class. The large landowners who remained, like virtually the entire Vietnamese population, were patriots and nationalists who heard Ho's declaration of independence in 1945, only half completed by the mid 1950s, but not his call for socialist revolution.[10]

One problem facing Ho and Giap was maintaining sufficient support in the North for the continued revolution in the South and the struggle for its reunification with the North—in addition to the building of socialism in the North. Ho and Giap attempted a balancing act that would sow the seeds of socialism while maintaining the support of the landowners, large and small, for the struggle for liberation in the South. But there was a split in the Workers' Party, with the ultraleft supporting the immediate class struggle pitting the poorest of the workers and landless laborers against landowners and peasants, large and small. Perhaps the greatest problem, therefore, was oversimplification of the class struggle and the idealization of the landless peasant as the moral superior of the large landowners. Despite the fact that many landowners had resisted French rule alongside the communists, the building of socialism in a united Vietnam was hindered by divisive repression of some landowners in the North who were not themselves directly responsible for exploitation of the masses.[11]

By 1956–1957, a crisis brewing within the Workers' Party was resolved by the purging of the ultraleft by Ho, Giap, and their followers who were able to rebuild their organization and resume the strategy of pursuing both liberation in the south with reunification and the building of socialism. Both the nationalist ideology that was deeply embedded in Vietnam and the socialist ideology that was less well understood and supported were essential for the ultimate victory of the socialist revolution a quarter of a century later.

After the refusal of Diem in the South to participate in national elections and reunification in 1955, Ho and Giap increased their support for guerilla warfare against that regime by way of organizing the masses into a people's army. With their backing, in 1960 a revolutionary mass organization was formed in the south, the National Liberation Front (NLF), and its military wing, descendent from the Vietminh, was formed the following year.

North Vietnam's military strategy of "people's war," as conducted by Giap,[12] used guerrilla warfare to strike revolutionary violence against the enemy (the South Vietnamese Army and the U.S. military) when and where the guerrilla leaders chose. The mobility of Giap's guerrilla army and its ability to blend in with the Vietnamese people made larger and more sustained battles possible because the place and timing of the battle was determined by the commanders of NLF fighters. Giap was emphatic about the importance of a small power selecting the time and place of engagement. Essential to support Giap's tactics was the widespread acceptance of the struggle among the people; thus its name, "people's war." This strategy was borrowed from Mao Zedong's successful approach in the Chinese communist revolution of the 1940s. In addition to guerrilla infiltration and mobile warfare, Mao successfully practiced a more conventional strategy of fighting from territory gained in previous battles. This strategy Giap was to find most difficult to accomplish in the face of superior conventional U.S. military capabilities, a strategy at which the United States excelled.

By 1962, therefore, Ho and Giap had adopted a people's war strategy of infiltrating villages in the South with NLF agents, accompanied by armed fighters.[13] To combat dissident influence, the Diem regime in South Vietnam removed peasants from their ancestral lands, relocating them in "agrovilles," later strategic hamlets,[14] surrounded by barbed wire to keep Vietminh and the NLF out. The relocated villagers, "protected" from the communists, were formed into quasi-feudal organizations providing free labor ostensibly for community projects. This impaired the ability of the villagers to earn enough to sustain their families, and they were not sufficiently compensated for the lands they were forced to give up. Consequently, relocated villagers were often unable to purchase sufficient farm land, and were reduced to landless laborers.

The tragedy of the agrovilles, which "suffered from Diem's myopic vision of Vietnamese rural life,"[15] was lost on the Diem regime. He simply did not understand the peasantry, especially regional differences within Vietnam. Diem and his clique were urban intellectuals, not farmers rooted to the land. In Diem's view, everyone—city and country folk alike—would have a small plot of land. A garden plot, however, simply would not keep a rural village family alive. Realization of Diem's ideal in the country would have forced the peasants into working for wages on plantations and in mines, a direct return to the oppressive French colonial practices. Ironically, onetime nationalist Ngo Dinh Diem, who strongly opposed French rule, advocated a lifestyle for villagers that would have meant little difference to them in daily life. While French rule had been replaced by U.S.-backed Vietnamese rule, opponents to the Diem regime saw no improvement in village conditions.

Diem's vision differed markedly from Ho Chi Minh's in the North. Ho advocated that after land was redistributed, it would be collectivized. Neither of these visions met with success. In the North, land redistribution remained the primary objective. By contrast, in the South, Diem's agroville strategy proved to do little more than strengthen the hand of the NLF.

DIRECT U.S. INTERVENTION

The U.S. strategy of propping up the Diem regime continued, and in 1962, U.S. military advisers, originally sent to aid the South Vietnam government under the Eisenhower administration, began flying helicopters, dropping South Vietnamese troops to fight the NLF troops. U.S. advisers took the South Vietnamese counterrevolutionaries on bombing and strafing missions.[16] Moreover, President John "Kennedy authorized use of defoliants to deny guerrillas cover and secure major roads and, on a limited basis, the use of herbicides to destroy enemy food supplies."[17] By the end of 1962, the number of U.S. military advisers in South Vietnam had increased from fewer than one thousand when Kennedy took office to about twelve thousand as U.S. opposition to the Vietnamese revolution increased.

On the second day of 1963, NLF guerilla fighters won a remarkable battle at Ap Bac over South Vietnamese forces that were backed by U.S. military advisors. Outnumbered ten to one and using captured U.S. arms, the NLF fighters shot down five helicopters with South Vietnamese and U.S. Army adviser crews. Journalists Stanley Karnow and Neil Sheehan reported that the counterrevolutionary South Vietnamese command was characterized by incompetence, cowardice, and failure to follow counsel of the U.S. advisers accompanying the operation. Sheehan added that the North Vietnamese–aligned NLF forces fought such a battle as to gain the grudging respect of key U.S. advisor, Colonel John Paul Vann. This was in sharp contrast to most U.S. opinions of South Vietnamese officers.[18]

Four months later, South Vietnamese troops turned on their own people. Soldiers of the Catholic-dominated South Vietnamese army fired on demonstrating Buddhist monks. South Vietnamese government attacks against Buddhist monks continued well into August, despite U.S. and world protest. In the midst of the series of attacks, in June 1963, a monk killed himself by self-immolation. This horrifying event was pictured in newspapers around the world, raising cries of criticism against the South Vietnamese forces.

The monk's suicide was perceived by Buddhists differently from the way it was seen by the rest of the world. According to one expert, in the quest for nirvana, devout Buddhists "seek to escape all sense of attachment to a bodily self and a personal life, and the complete destruction of his body by a monk is applauded by several sacred texts."[19] Similar to a later suicide in prison by a Vietnamese poet, the monk's suicide was an ultimate personal and clearly public statement in opposition to the Diem forces that were oppressing the Vietnamese people. Accordingly, "these acts of self-destruction demonstrate more clearly than anything else the fact that culturally Viet-Nam is quite beyond the normal range of occidental comprehension. This fact is of immense political significance."[20] Ironically, U.S. Defense Secretary at that time, Robert McNamara, only recognized its significance some thirty years after the monk's death with the 1995 publication of his book, *In Retrospect*: "I had never visited Indochina, nor did I understand or appreciate its history, language, culture, or values. The same must be said, to varying degrees, about President Kennedy . . . and many others."[21]

Given Diem's autocratic and oppressive behavior, incompetence, and the intense opposition it generated, the United States came to accept the need for regime change in South Vietnam. Diem's assassination in November 1963 could not have come as a surprise to the United States, but Kennedy's assassination that same month did. These assassinations resulted in profound leadership changes in both countries. In South Vietnam, a succession of coups was set into motion, and direction of counterrevolution effectively defaulted to the United States. U.S. fighting forces remained in the background, however. It was not until the middle of 1965 that strong leadership once again came to the South in the person of Nguyen Van Thieu. Thieu remained in power until the fall of South Vietnam in 1975.

BEYOND THE TONKIN GULF:
U.S. ESCALATION OF THE COUNTERREVOLUTION

On August 2, 1964, the U.S. destroyer *Maddox* sailing in the Gulf of Tonkin was attacked by North Vietnamese patrol boats and a few days later reported erroneously a second attack. This incident served as the rationale for the Tonkin Gulf Resolution in the United States that legalized continuing support on the part of the United States for the counterrevolutionary regime in South Vietnam, and for the entrance and then the massive buildup of U.S. fighting troops. In February 1964, months before the Tonkin Gulf Resolution, the United States had begun the secret bombing of NLF supply lines from North Vietnam, along the Ho Chi Minh Trail in Laos.[22]

By the end of 1964, the United States had massively escalated its hostilities against the Democratic Republic of Vietnam in its effort to suppress the socialist revolution, though war was never formally declared. Rolling Thunder was the code name for a shift from air strikes in retaliation for specific NLF attacks to sustained bombing, including attacks against North Vietnam. The air war had begun.

A year later, U.S. suppression of the Vietnamese Socialist Revolution had erupted into full-scale war: 636 U.S. troops had been killed by then, and 184,300 U.S. troops were stationed in Vietnam.[23] From 1965 to 1968, the war continued to expand. President Lyndon Johnson's politically driven policy ordered punishing and prolonged bombing attacks, halting periodically to see whether the North Vietnamese would agree to peace. Johnson did not believe North Vietnam's position that the only peace they would agree to was one that featured the prior withdrawal of U.S. forces from Vietnam. Bombing halts only gave the North and the NLF a chance to recover, regroup, and resupply.

Johnson's commander in Vietnam, General William Westmoreland, had a somewhat different strategy. Westmoreland believed that the revolution could be crushed through "attrition," the eventual wearing away of revolutionary forces. The belief was that if enough Vietnamese were killed and enough land and property damaged, they would give up. Westmoreland also failed to understand the revolutionary strategy. While Westmoreland claims to have studied the writings of Giap, he apparently did not take the people's war approach seriously.[24]

Tet is the Vietnamese Lunar New Year and usually takes place near the end of January or the first of February. It is the biggest holiday of the year, and even in war-torn Vietnam in January 1968, a cease-fire had been arranged. Secret negotiations between the DRV and the United States were going nowhere. NLF fighters struck the U.S. embassy in Saigon on the first day of Tet, January 30, 1968. With substantial popular support and no effective opposition from counterrevolutionary forces, NLF fighters had thoroughly infiltrated Saigon. Not only did the NLF fighters break into the embassy compound, but they even blasted their way into the embassy building itself. The chaos, bloodshed, and destruction from that incident drove home to the world the fact that the United States was not invulnerable to the revolutionary forces. A few months before, Giap had announced that the DRV and the NLF would redirect their efforts from the countryside to the cities of the South, and the U.S. embassy in Saigon suffered attack, as did more than 150 other cities and hamlets in the South.[25]

The outcome of the Tet offensive, however, was unsatisfactory to all sides. The DRV expected a mass uprising against the United States and the Saigon regime. While the North Vietnamese and the NLF fighters were able to infiltrate the cities with ease, because villagers and city folk did not report their presence to the authorities, no general uprising occurred. Because it had wildly optimistic expectations of support among the people of the South, North Vietnam failed in its objective to start an uprising. Moreover, the major losses to the NLF and DRV were its revolutionary fighters. Never again would the NLF fighters based in South Vietnam launch an offensive like the 1968 Tet offensive. Such large-scale operations in the future would rely much more on DRV regular army troops. The counterrevolutionary U.S. and South Vietnamese forces succeeded in driving the NLF fighters out of the cities, and they suffered far fewer personnel losses than the NLF.

Johnson's conduct of the war after Tet differed in two significant ways from the pre-Tet strategy. Escalation diminished; bombing halts replaced stepped up bombing operations as a primary strategy. Additionally, insistence on greater South Vietnamese army participation in the hostilities and more serious negotiations with North Vietnam became U.S. policy.

Le Duan had been a follower of Ho Chi Minh since 1928 and a cofounder of the Indochinese Communist Party, the predecessor of the Vietnam Workers' Party. Le Duan had extensive experience working with the NLF, and since 1960, he had been head of the Vietnam Workers' party in the one-party government of North Vietnam. As head, day-to-day leadership had long since passed from Ho Chi Minh to Le Duan. When Ho Chi Minh died in 1969, General Vo Nguyen Giap and Le Duan were the most powerful figures in the DRV. No change in strategy was in sight. According to Le Duan,

> The revolutionary struggle unfolds without cease in all spheres of life: political, social, cultural. Hence, to win step by step means in each arena of combat to mobilize and organize the masses with a view to frustrating the enemy's successive policies and foiling every one of his schemes and maneuvers; to point out and attain at all costs all objectives.[26]

TOWARD CLOSURE

Peace negotiation as a strategy had begun tentatively and without success during the Johnson administration. One of the reasons for the lack of success by Johnson, and then by Richard Nixon during his first term of office, was a grave misunderstanding of the nature of the war: this was Vietnam's revolution. Nonnegotiable conditions were established by all sides. North Vietnam's conditions included the withdrawal of all U.S. troops and the formation of a coalition government including the NLF to replace the Thieu regime.[27] Thieu demanded that North Vietnam withdraw all troops and that the NLF lay down its arms and agree to abide by his Constitution that forbade "communist" and "neutralist" activity.[28]

The conditions of the NLF were recognition of the 1954 Geneva Accords and the withdrawal of all U.S. troops. Reunification of the North and South would take place peacefully and over time.[29] The United States' conditions included the gradual withdrawal of all non–South Vietnamese troops (including U.S.) under supervision of an international body "acceptable to both sides" with internationally supervised elections and observation of the 1954 Geneva Accords.[30] Moreover, Nixon's underlying strategy was development of positive U.S. relationships with the Soviet Union and China to isolate Vietnam diplomatically from the Soviets and the Chinese.

While there was room for some agreement in these conditions, far more obstacles to an agreement existed. The greatest were the United States' and South Vietnam's steadfast refusal to accept a coalition government that might give equal footing to the NLF, and the NLF's and DRV's insistence on prior withdrawal of the U.S. military and U.S. support for Thieu.

After the major losses that resulted from the 1968 Tet offensive and the failure to stir a general uprising against the South Vietnamese regime, the DRV leadership resolved itself to "protracted warfare." The leadership believed that eventually the United States would tire of the war and would withdraw, as Nixon had pledged to his country, leaving a relatively unprotected counterrevolutionary South Vietnamese regime. Essentially, this was the Westmoreland "attrition" strategy turned on its head.

As Giap told journalist Stanley Karnow many years after the war was over, "We were not strong enough to drive a half million American troops out of Vietnam, but that wasn't our aim. . . . We sought to break the will of the American government to continue the conflict." When Karnow asked him how long they would have continued to fight the United States, Giap immediately replied, "Another twenty years, maybe a hundred years, as long as it took to win, regardless of cost."[31]

With the official peace talks with North and South Vietnam and the NLF going nowhere, in February 1970, Secretary of State Henry Kissinger had begun secret talks with the North Vietnamese in Paris. These talks, through many twists and turns, and much more fighting, would eventually lead to the success of the Vietnamese revolution. By the end of 1971, the number of U.S. troops in Vietnam was down to less than half what it had been in Nixon's first year in office.

The last year of negotiations between the United States and North Vietnam and the NLF did not go smoothly. That year began with Nixon's celebrated 1972 visit to China. While China had offered support for North Vietnam in its war with the United States, the Vietnamese leadership did not fully trust China. Not only had China ruled and bullied Vietnam for nine centuries, but the problematic relationship between China and the Soviet Union was troubling; these onetime allies came to experience very strained relations, including armed border clashes with one another. Under Le Duan, North Vietnam tended to lean more toward the Soviet Union, questioning the reason for the newfound friendship between China and the United States. What would be the impact of this on Vietnam? This was also an election year in the United States. Leaders in North Vietnam understood that the people of the United States were tired of the war and wanted out. In March, the North Vietnamese launched an offensive against the South that rivaled the Tet offensive of four years earlier. This one came to be known as the "Easter" offensive. DRV committed one hundred thousand of its troops to the battle and the counterrevolutionary South Vietnamese forces that took the impact of the attack were ineffective. Despite an impending election and growing U.S. opposition to the war, Nixon called for renewed bombing of the North and mining of the harbor at Haiphong.

The Easter offensive and Nixon's counteroffensive brought the two sides (DRV and the United States) back to the bargaining table—now with the United States having a psychological upper hand. The DRV leadership misjudged Nixon's resolve. For the first time in four years of negotiations, just two months before the scheduled election in the United States, both sides gave ground. The DRV dropped its demand for a coalition government in the South. Thieu could stay in South Vietnam. The United States agreed to a cease-fire "in place" and to withdraw its forces. With the proposed in-place cease-fire, DRV troops could stay in South Vietnam. With great excitement, Henry Kissinger declared that "peace is at hand." His announcement came too soon.

The counterrevolutionaries refused to join in the agreement, aggravating the United States and extending the U.S. direct involvement three months longer. The United States took Thieu's demands back to Paris to meet again with representatives of the DRV. When, by the end of 1972, little progress had been made on Thieu's demands, Nixon applied pressure. The last major offensive of the United States in the war in Vietnam is called the "Christmas bombing." Once again, the United States bombed North Vietnam and this time the North agreed to some of Thieu's terms. Could this bombing have been more intended to convince Thieu of U.S. willingness to continue bombing, rather than to convince Hanoi to sign the agreement?[32] Under intense pressure, Thieu finally agreed; and on January 27, 1973, the United States, South Vietnam, DRV, and the NLF signed the agreement. Among the terms of this agreement, U.S. prisoners of war held by the North were to be returned, the United States was to withdraw from Vietnam, but the North Vietnamese troops could stay where they were in the South.

The United States was the only party to the agreement that fulfilled its military obligations—by withdrawing. Both the counterrevolutionary Thieu government and the DRV/NLF forces attempted to gain advantage at the expense of the other. At first, it was the counterrevolutionary South Vietnamese forces, well equipped by the United States, that violated the agreement by attacking positions held by the war-weary NLF. But soon the DRV began resupplying and reinforcing NLF troops in the South, and by January 1974, Thieu announced that the war had resumed. While the United States retained a substantial presence in Thailand, it was not directly involved in the renewed war in Vietnam.

On August 9, 1974, Richard Nixon resigned the presidency. Nixon's final disgrace came sixteen months after the last U.S. troops were pulled out of Vietnam. With Nixon gone, the United States dramatically cut its aid to the counterrevolutionaries. In South Vietnam, the situation quickly deteriorated. In January 1975, six years after Tet and two years after the Easter offensive, DRV soldiers once again swept through the South. This would be the last time. With inept military leadership and no support from the Vietnamese people, the counterrevolutionary forces were unable to stop the attack. If President Eisenhower was right that Ho would have won a free election in 1954, apparently little change in political preference had taken place.

Since the fall of Saigon and the triumph of the DRV forces, the Vietnamese, like a number of other socialist countries, have adapted their economy to articulate to global capital with the final outcome still to be revealed. Moreover, in the immediate years following Vietnamese reunification, isolated but troubling border conflicts with China erupted into violence. More troubling, three years after gaining its own independence, Vietnam unilaterally invaded Cambodia deposing the infamous Pol Pot regime and installing its own puppet rule. The irony of this action is made all the more vivid in the Cambodian national memory of past Vietnamese aggression coupled with a shared colonial history under French rule. But perhaps most salient, Cambodia's decades of turmoil with U.S. military assault and occupation that led up to the Pol Pot debacle was almost solely because of Cambodia's proximity to Vietnam and the spillover from the Vietnamese revolution.

CONCLUSION

What can we learn from the Vietnamese revolution? First, injustices suffered by one people at the hands of another are not easily forgotten. National domination and foreign rule, class exploitation and conflict, imperialist domination, foreign interference in the internal political affairs of a country, and military assault and occupation were all suffered by the Vietnamese people.

Vietnam suffered all of these injustices and overcame them, but at what cost? Because the United States elected to support France's imperialist claim to Vietnam after World War II and because the United States elected to cast Vietnam as the leading domino in the Cold War, the cost was great. Clearly, the Vietnamese revolution succeeded in bringing about independence and national reunification with progress toward socialism. Will Vietnam succeed as a socialist country in an era of capitalist globalization? The answer remains to be seen.

NOTES

1. Neil L. Jamieson, *Understanding Vietnam* (Berkeley: University of California Press, 1995), 112–13.

2. William Duiker, *The Rise of Nationalism in Vietnam, 1900–1941* (Ithaca, N.Y.: Cornell University Press, 1976).

3. Duiker, *The Rise of Nationalism in Vietnam*, 161.

4. See "The Path Which Led Me to Lenin," in *Vietnam and America: The Most Comprehensive History of the Vietnam War*, ed. Marvin Gettleman et al., rev. and enlarged 2nd ed. (New York: Grove, 1995), 20–22.

5. "The Political and Military Line of Our Party," in Gettleman et al., *Vietnam and America*, 199–200.

6. Gettleman et al., *Vietnam and America*.

7. See the text of the accords with additional explanation in Gettleman et al., *Vietnam and America*.

8. Gettleman et al., *Vietnam and America*, 65.

9. Le Duan, *The Vietnamese Revolution: Fundamental Problems, Essential Tasks* (Hanoi: Foreign Languages Publishing House, 1970), 51.

10. Ken Post, *Revolution, Socialism and Nationalism in Viet Nam*, vol. 1: *An Interrupted Revolution* (Aldershot, U.K.: Dartmouth, 1989), 268–92.

11. Post, *Revolution*.

12. See General Vo Nguyen Giap, "The Political and Military Line of Our Party," in Gettleman et al., *Vietnam and America*, 193–201.

13. Incredibly, the NLF even placed its agents at high levels of the South Vietnamese government.

14. William Duiker, *Sacred War: Nationalism and Revolution in a Divided Vietnam* (New York: McGraw-Hill, 1995), 152.

15. Jamieson, *Understanding Vietnam*, 237.

16. George C. Herring, *America's Longest War: The United States and Vietnam, 1950–1975*, 3rd ed. (New York: McGraw-Hill, 1996), 96.

17. Herring, *America's Longest War*, 95.

18. Neil Sheehan, *A Bright Shining Lie: John Paul Vann and America in Vietnam* (New York: Random House, 1988), 201–6; and Stanley Karnow, *Vietnam: A History* (New York: Penguin Books, 1991), 76–79.

19. Ralph Smith, *Viet-Nam and the West* (Ithaca, N.Y.: Cornell University Press, 1971), 3.

20. Smith, *Viet-Nam and the West*, 4.

21. Robert McNamara, *In Retrospect: The Tragedy and Lessons of Vietnam* (New York: Random House, 1995).

22. Francis Fitzgerald, *Fire in the Lake: The Vietnamese and the Americans in Vietnam* (New York: Vintage Books, 1972), 352.

23. James S. Olson and Randy Roberts, *Where the Domino Fell: America and Vietnam, 1945 to 1990* (New York: St. Martin's, 1991), 301.

24. See editors' preface to Giap, "The Political and Military Line of Our Party," in Gettleman et al., *Vietnam and America*, 193–94.

25. Fitzgerald, *Fire in the Lake*, 523. See also Herring, *America's Longest War*, 206.

26. Le Duan, *The Vietnamese Revolution*, 49.

27. Duiker, *Sacred War*, 223.

28. Gettleman et al., *Vietnam and America*, 430.

29. Gettleman et al., *Vietnam and America*, 431–33.

30. Gettleman et al., *Vietnam and America*, 433–34.

31. Quoted in Karnow, *Vietnam*, 20.

32. In a personal communication to the author on March 8, 1998, Tom Grunfeld raised this possibility.

7

The Cuban and Nicaraguan Revolutions

Imperialism, Dictatorship, and Popular Resistance

James F. Petras

Two monumental developments in twentieth-century attempts at socialist transformation in Latin America have been the Cuban and Nicaraguan revolutions. These two mass, popular uprisings in the Western Hemisphere in the mid to late twentieth century mark a major turning point in Latin American history since the infamous Mexican revolution that set the stage a half century earlier by providing the historic context of the struggle against dictatorship and oppression, as well as foreign domination imposed on Latin America by U.S. imperialism. This chapter takes a close look at the Cuban and Nicaraguan revolutions as two parallel socialist experiments that have their origins in popular struggles over the course of the twentieth century and that culminated in the taking of state power through revolutionary mass action, which marked the beginning of a new era in Latin American politics.

THE CUBAN REVOLUTION

The Cuban revolution must be studied and understood as a *process*, not as an event, although particular configurations of activities and personalities at given moments certainly define important benchmarks or turning points in history. In particular, to establish the boundaries of the Cuban revolution, we must identify the essential features of the revolutionary process. It is clear that the Cuban revolution was a *socialist* revolution in the sense that its overall thrust was to expropriate the major privately owned productive forces and collectivize them. This is not to deny the importance of other

elements of the revolutionary process—the nationalist, antidictatorial, an-
ticorruption aspects, which were certainly present. However, all these components were ultimately subsumed within the social process that transformed all of Cuba's property relations.

Thus, to periodize the Cuban revolution, the point must be identified in
Cuban history when socialism ceased being an idea discussed in limited circles and became the driving force of a social movement and immediately
threatened the capitalist relations of production. The starting point is the
popular upheaval of 1933.

The 1933 revolution contained within it the first massive socialist movement of the Cuban working class. Under socialist leadership (and sometimes without), major sections of the Cuban working class directly attacked
the owners of property, took control over a number of the productive units
in several regions of the country, and established class hegemony over important sectors of the non-working-class regions of the country and sectors
of the state apparatus (municipal government, police, and army).

While this uprising was eventually defeated, this movement had long-
term influence on the consciousness of the working class and on all subsequent governments, parties, and trade union activities. The uprising and the
threat it represented was always present in the minds of most decision mak-
ers. Policies formulated henceforth, even by non-working-class (and even
anti-working-class) governments had to take account of the presence of the
working class. Moreover, all revolutionary and pseudorevolutionary parties
and groups, each in its own way, attempted to derive their legitimacy, in-
spiration, and lessons from the experience of 1933. The legacy of the popular uprising was not directly expressed in new revolutionary upheavals, but
it permeated society at all levels and found multiple expressions institu-
tionally and legally, as well as in the memories of the participants.

If 1933 defines the beginning period in the struggle for a socialist revolution, it must be kept in mind that its trajectory did not follow a straight
line but was refracted through a variety of nonrevolutionary working-class
experiences that nonetheless generated a crisis of regime. Capitalism was secured at the level of the state, but labor's presence was codified and institutionalized to the point of seriously impairing capitalism's capacity to re-
produce itself with any dynamism. The development of the anticapitalist
struggle was a contradictory one, combining socialist and reformist elements. The result was a deadlock in which *both* capitalist development and
working-class struggle was contained. This contradictory development
found reflection in myriad economistic strikes, flights of capital abroad, investment in nonproductive areas, pillage of the state treasury, and, in general, an emphasis on short-term gains. Class consciousness among all social
strata created a perspective based on uncertainty, in which systemic crisis
was always present although mostly latent.

The armed struggle initiated in the 1950s by the July 26th Movement broke with and continued this contradictory development in a new form: state power was challenged, but seemingly for narrow ends. The previous pattern espoused by the Cuban Communist Party of advocating socialist ideology and practicing state subordination was reversed. The pattern followed by the July 26th Movement in the 1950s involved a conventional national-popular program and sustained efforts at breaking the state apparatus. The July 26th Movement accumulated social forces, many politicized and radicalized in previous decades. It gained massive support in provincial productive regions, and it drew support from a variety of fractions of classes and races open to its appeal. Traditional, regionalist, and anti-imperialist forces were recruited and combined with new social revolutionary forces seeking state power. The social revolutionary process was accelerated with the overthrow of Batista in 1959 and culminated four years later with the expropriation of the major productive forces, the destruction of the old repressive apparatus, and the creation of the revolutionary state.

In summary, this argument can be stated in propositional form. (1) The socialist revolution in Cuba was the product of an accumulation of social and political forces and experiences resulting from the social upheaval of the early 1930s. (2) The content and legacy of that defeated revolution and the threat that it represented for all propertied groups shaped the content and style of Cuban politics in the direction of labor-influenced policies and institutions. (3) The central contradiction of Cuban society was rooted in the fact that while capitalist forces controlled the state, the labor movement's presence blocked the accumulation of capital; thus, both capitalist development and the working-class struggle for socialism were contained. (4) The consequences of this stalemate were an emphasis by both labor and capital on short-term gains, reflecting the general perception by all social strata that a systemic crisis was always imminent. (5) The coup by Batista in 1952 was aimed at breaking this deadlock at the expense of labor and unleashing a new phase of capitalist development from above, promoting large-scale foreign investment. (6) The revolutionary struggle led by the July 26th Movement represented an effort to break the deadlock by mobilizing forces from below, extending the social gains and in the postrevolutionary period moving toward an effort to reorganize the pattern of collective ownership and control to create a new base for economic expansion.

Four distinct periods can be identified within the overall time frame of the social revolutionary process encompassed in the 1932–1963 period, which reflect changes in the scope, size, and orientation of the mass movement and working class. Within each period, activities and organizations emerged that conditioned the context and struggles in the ensuing period and the overall character of the political-economic system. Thus, the revolution in Cuba must be seen as a complex mosaic involving overlapping events and activities whose cumulative effects created the context and movement for a socialist transformation.

In this interpretation the Cuban revolution is not seen as a willful act of a handful of dedicated idealistic guerrillas. In contrast to this voluntaristic approach, historical processes—structure and action—that created the "will" should be emphasized, as well as the political and social conditions for its realization.

Mass Socialist Revolutionary Mobilization, 1932–1935

The struggle against the Machado dictatorship took place in the context of a society that had been profoundly transformed by advanced capitalist expansion and the subsequent world capitalist depression. The former created a large class of wage workers linked to the productive process through the cash nexus; the latter led to the massive displacement of labor and depression of wages.

As James O'Connor notes, "By 1907 the island's social economy already featured a typically capitalist class structure. The rural proletariat was (statistically) well developed; according to the census of that year, of roughly 770,000 Cuban wage workers about 40% or 310,000 laborers were farm workers. Also included in the agricultural labor force were 40,000 tenant farmers and 17,000 farm owners."[1] The process of proletarianization was evidenced in the declining number of small farmers. Before 1894, there were 90,960 small and lease farms; in 1899, this figure was reduced to 60,711; and by 1935, it further declined to 38,105.[2]

Real per capita income in Cuba fell from 239 pesos per year in 1924 to 109 in 1933. The combined process of massive proletarianization and precipitous socioeconomic dislocation created propitious conditions for class organization. The revolutionary political and social forms within which class organization developed reflected the absence of any substantial reformist-mediating structures capable of channeling the discontent. Machado's repression of the anarchist and socialist trade unions, newspapers, and offices undermined their organizational position in the labor movement and laid the groundwork for the emergence of the Communist Party.[3]

The rapid and massive incorporation of employed/unemployed wage workers into social revolutionary activity was largely the result of the autocratic/centralized structure of the Cuban political system, which undermined independent forms of representation and articulation. Autocratic centralism, however, was one of the basic ingredients, conditioning the massive and sustained flow of capital, guaranteeing its reproduction and accumulation. Massive proletarianization of labor, the product of large-scale and precipitous expansion of capital, emerged in the context of an autocratic-centralized state. The cohesion of the whole ensemble was sustained by the expanding global economy during the 1920s. Cuba's thorough transformation into a capitalist society was rooted in its incorporation into the productive and exchange relations of the global capitalist system. The crises of that system, beginning with the crash of 1929, directly and massively affected the Cuban class structure in much the same way that it affected the economies and societies of the United States and Europe. There were few precapitalist subsistence units to cushion this collapse of capitalist relations of production. Moreover, unlike Europe, Cuba's capitalist transformation was telescoped into a few decades, under the aegis of autocratic regimes, and thus it lacked the accumulation of bureaucratic working-class reformist organizations capable of deflecting the working-class struggle into purely economistic channels or into demands for change of regime.[4]

The objective transformations wrought in the organization of productive units (concentrating masses of propertyless workers in large-scale integrated production and processing networks) and social relations (cash payments tied to the creation of surplus value and privately accumulated capital) found social expression in the massive organization of class-oriented unions. The generalized depression served to homogenize wage-labor demands, because all workers, independent of wage difference, suffered sharp declines in salary and were threatened by unemployment. The autocratic-centralized regime of Machado, which penetrated relations down to the local enterprise level—intervening to repress struggles at the point of production—politicized the working class. One participant observer early on noted Machado's tendency to either subordinate and emasculate representative organization or to repress it: "In 1926 Machado crushed the railroad strike and the strike of the Camaguey sugar workers, thereby fulfilling his promise that under his government 'no strike in Cuba would last more than 24 hours.' The dictatorship launched an uncontrolled terror. It dissolved unions, arrested or deported hundreds of militant workers, and assassinated such outstanding leaders as Enrique Varona and Alfredo López."[5]

The extensive control exercised by absentee U.S. corporate owners and the impersonal relations within production eroded the exercise of "cultural hegemony"—highlighting the specific socioeconomic forms of exploitation, the unequal relations within the enterprise, and the polarized nature of the productive process (between owners and producers). Thus, to the objective effects of capital accumulation at the global level were added the class *homogenizing* effects of economic crisis, the *politicization* effects of a centralized state, and the *polarizing* effects resultant from the absence of a culturally hegemonic ruling class. These ingredients set the stage for the political confrontation between capital and labor, culminating in the insurrectionary efforts embodied in the short-lived "soviets" encountered in many parts of Cuba. "Direct-action" syndicalist activity had been prominent within the working-class movement preceding the insurrectionary phase. This tradition was embodied in the anarcho-syndicalist leadership that led the Cuban trade unions in the 1920s. The impact of anarcho-syndicalist tradition and rank and file on the increasingly communist-led labor struggle was clear in the strike wave of 1932. As one writer notes, "The strike movement of these years (1930–1932) was strongly influenced by the traditions and tendencies of anarcho-syndicalism . . . the application of the united front, the implacable struggle against reformist leaders and the systematic and daily propaganda on the necessity of applying revolutionary union methods involving mass participation, strike committees elected by the workers, pickets."[6]

The destruction and demise of this leadership during the Machado dictatorship led to the disarticulation of the organization, but not the methods of struggle, which remained ingrained in the consciousness of working-class militants. In the preinsurrectionary period, the Communist Party laid claim to the tradition of direct action, class struggle, and class solidarity that preceded, although not always acknowledging it. The communist innovation was the diffusion of these ideas and their translation into mass organizational forms among the sugar workers, located in the new, modern industrial areas. The creation of mass industrial unions in the sugar fields and factories linked to a revolutionary Communist Party conditioned the further development of the class struggle in Cuba. The centrality of this sector of the working class to Cuban capitalism and its organization laid the basis for the challenge to state power. Having moved to the center of capitalist development, the Communist Party confronted the main task of organizing its overthrow.

During this insurrectionary period, political and economic demands were combined: Wage demands were linked to general strikes to overthrow the regime; struggles for trade union rights were joined with the organization of organs of dual-power workers' councils. The revolution against the Machado dictatorship and its supporters was quickly transformed into a struggle against the major corporate property holdings on the island—many of the same owners who were nourished and sustained by the Machado regime.

The observations by the researchers of the Foreign Policy Association present us with a detailed and vivid account of the worker-led social revolution.

> The discontent was generalized throughout the interior. Students, communists and some members of the ABC were reported active in the task of labor organization. Strikes were spreading on the sugar plantations, the workers demanding higher wages, recognition of their unions and better living conditions. On August 21, the workers seized the first sugar mill—at Punta Alegre in Camaguey Province. Within less than a month the number of mills under labor control was estimated at thirty-six. Soviets were reported to have been organized at Mabay, Jaronu, Senado, Santa Lucia, and other *centrales*. At various

points mill managers were held prisoners by the workers. Labor guards were formed, armed with clubs, sticks and a few revolvers, a red armband serving as uniform. Workers fraternized with soldiers and police. . . . This wave of agitation and discontent extended to almost all the sugar mills and zones, reaching even the most remote areas. In the far west of the island, in the province of Pinar del Rio the tobacco workers declared themselves on strike; the coffee workers of Oriente did likewise. In the same region the Bethlehem Steel mines in Daiqiuri were closed and in the hands of the working class. . . . In Antilla the red flag waved from the city hall and in Santiago a communist demonstration obliged the mayor to abandon the province.[7]

The transparent linkages between the Machado state and U.S. capitalist expansion and exploitation facilitated mass mobilization against both: The antidictatorial and the anti-imperialist struggle were fused, and, among workers, anticapitalist consciousness flourished. As the movement grew in size, this animus to corporate capitalism was extended to new strata of the population.

At the height of the insurrectionary movement, observers noted that

the strikers included young and old, whites and blacks, natives and foreign [workers]. In many places the whole working class was drawn into the movement; joining the sugar-mill workers were field workers, office and shop employees, and even inspectors and guards. The tenant farmers formulated their own demands. In some sugar mills the cooks, laundry workers, and domestic servants went on strike asking for higher pay. The small farmers and businessmen of the neighboring towns lent their solidarity.[8]

This opposition movement was instrumental in engraving a profound antagonism to labor's relation to capital. The expression of hostility to capital provided one impetus to the social revolution. More important, however, was the organization of class-anchored revolutionary organs—workers' councils that threatened to disintegrate capital's state and property relations.

The original nationalist and antidictatorial movement based on petit bourgeois and working-class forces found expression in the populist Grau San Martin regime (1933–1934). The latter, while purging the old bourgeois officers, retained the lower echelon of the capitalist state as its own guardian against the *social* threat embodied in a working-class movement, which was not to be contained within the bourgeois-nationalist program espoused by the Grau regime. The military sectors of the reconstructed capitalist state retained by Grau and led by Batista were not content with repressing workers. Sergeant Batista turned against his petit bourgeois political mentors, including Grau, in the course of reconstructing an alliance with U.S. imperialism.

Above everything else, the 1933 revolution demonstrated the capability of the Cuban working class to organize and actively support a revolutionary socialist insurrection. This fact was deeply etched in the minds of U.S. investors and officials, as well as among Cuban politicians and bourgeois leaders. Henceforth, the Cuban working class was seen as an important factor to be taken into account in any political calculation—whether the regime pursued policies of repression, concession, or a combination of both. The threat of another "1933" was an ever-present reality that hung over Cuban politics for the next twenty-five years and was evident in much of the debate and discussion that surrounded government policy to labor organizations and legislation, as well as its attitude toward strikes and labor/management conflicts.

In terms of its long-term diffuse impact on the political system, the insurrectionary period of 1933 had a profound effect in shaping the boundaries and content of all subsequent developments in Cuba. U.S. investments, the development of a Cuban bourgeoisie, the position of the *colonos*, the overall process of capital accumulation (and lack of it—the problem of stagnation), and the orientation of investors toward short-term speculative gain and politicians to immediate pay-off (graft) must be seen in the context of the constraints imposed by the organizational strength of labor against capital, one of the long-term results of the 1933–1935 period.

The Working-Class Presence, 1936–1952

In the period following the insurrection (1933–1934) and its repression (1935–1936), the Cuban working-class movement reemerged as a major actor in the Cuban political and social system. Throughout this period, a whole series of legislation and policy decisions was instituted that reflected the real power and potential threat of a reenactment of 1933. This period was marked by the growth and institutionalization of workers' power, providing incremental gains to the working class and confining it within the framework of the capitalist state. The Communist and later Auténtico parties and their representatives in the labor movement followed a similar policy of actively engaging with the state as a means of enlarging the institutional influence and economic share of the labor movement. The net result was a vast labor presence focused on a narrow set of interests. The consequences of this set of circumstances were adversely to affect the capacity and willingness of capital, especially U.S. capital, to expand where labor was organized.

From the 1930s, U.S. capital began to divest itself of holdings in Cuban sugar, and, even after the crisis, Cuban sugar production remained at levels commensurate with the 1920s. U.S. mills produced 62 percent of sugar prior to 1933; this dropped to 55 percent in 1939, 43 percent in 1951, and by 1958 only 37 percent. Likewise the number of U.S. mills declined from sixty-six in 1939 to thirty-six in 1958. Foreign-owned land declined from

1.7 million hectares in 1946 to 1.2 million hectares in 1958.⁹ The crucial problem cited repeatedly by foreign and domestic capitalists for Cuba's accumulation crisis was "the labor problem."

One of the most thorough and searching reports of Cuban economic development, prepared by the International Bank for Reconstruction and Development, concludes that "Conflicts in labor management relations in Cuba today [1951] are undoubtedly among the chief obstacles to economic progress."¹⁰ The report went on to provide the historical and sociopolitical reasons underlying capitalist stagnation.

> In view of the important role by the government in these matters [collective bargaining] the political strength of organized labor, which has become very great since the political and social revolution of 1933, is in many respects a more important factor than its economic bargaining power. Before the 1933 revolution, the government was usually on the side of the employers in disputes with workers. Since then the pendulum has swung so far towards the other extreme that it is now employers and investors who complain that every issue seems to be settled against them.¹¹

The crisis expressed in Cuba's economic stagnation was thus a result of the class struggle and the institutional strength of labor. The electoral regimes that sought to promote capitalist development by necessity of survival gave way to labor pressure. Batista's second regime, following the coup of 1952, sought to resolve this crisis by weakening the institutional constraints that labor imposed on efforts at capitalist rationality. Even in this case, however, Batista's efforts were constantly stymied by his efforts to secure the support of the labor bureaucracy to enable him to sustain political power. Thus, his regime vacillated between overtures to capitalist investors and promises of labor discipline, on the one hand, and the need to recognize and concede concessions to trade unions, on the other. The crisis of accumulation was exacerbated in both directions; insufficient capital responded, labor discontent multiplied, repression increased, the labor bureaucracy became more isolated, the political legitimacy of the regime declined, and the July 26th and other revolutionary movements consolidated their support.

The convergence of guerrilla and insurrectionary forces in the general strike that toppled Batista at the end of 1958 symbolized the merger of the forces of revolution of the 1930s with those of the 1950s. The stalemate between capital and labor, which paralyzed Cuban society, was once again challenged, only this time from the Left: The pattern of the 1930s, the reemergence of workers' militias, the intervention of *centrales*, and the takeover of land was repeated, only this time with the backing of the national government and the rebel army. Cuba had come full circle: The aborted social revolution of 1933 was consummated in 1963. The role of the mass labor movement was decisive in initiating the process, sustaining the anticapitalist animus, constraining the development of capital, and providing the organized mass forces to sustain the reorganization of the state and the collectivization of property. The period between 1936 and 1952 can be subdivided into several phases, each corresponding to different moments in the working-class struggle.

The Repression of Insurrection, 1935–1936

The defeat of the revolutionary wave of 1932–1934 was organized and directed by Batista in consort with U.S. imperialism. Essentially, the defeat was the result of the "regional" nature of the revolutionary movement, the sectarian policies of the Communist Party, the fragmentation of the Left forces (revolutionary petit bourgeois nationalists and the communist working class), and, most important, the fact that the workers were not armed or able to politicize the army sufficiently and win decisive sectors over to its side. The result was a confrontation between the reconstructed capitalist state apparatus, armed and disciplined, versus a mobilized but unarmed working-class movement. The outcome was predetermined: the general strikes were broken, land and factory occupiers were dislodged, and local councils and elected officials responsible to the working class were purged and replaced by functionaries loyal to the regime.

The immediate and direct targets of the repression were the revolutionary organs of the working class: the areas of greatest concentration of working-class militancy; and the leaders and political parties most directly linked to the anti-imperialist, anticapitalist movement. Although the counterrevolutionary repression soon spread to encompass nationalists, middle-class political leaders, and the less radical trade unionists, its prime goal was to destroy the basis of revolutionary working-class action. The soviets (workers' councils) were the earliest targets, followed by the Communist Party, the left-wing nationalists around Antonio Guiteres (a member of the cabinet of Grau San Martin), the trade unionists affiliated with them, and the industrial workers who were militants in one or another of the direct action groups.

A confidential memorandum written by the U.S. consul in Havana sums up the repressive policies of Batista-backed president Mendieta's regime and its political isolation:

> The Mendieta Government has unquestionably met the issue of labor, red as it has seemed, squarely if not fairly. Its defense of the Republic Decree virtually suspending constitutional guarantees—the word "constitutional" seems out of place in these days of government by executive decree—and resorting again to military law to forestall the general strike was undoubtedly most opportune and necessary for the preservation of civil peace. It had reached its limits in ne-

gotiating with the strike organization. Only the use of troops with threats of violence and actual jailing of the communistic agitators could have saved it from downfall. . . . Its hold on power in the final analysis still rests upon the backing it receives from the military branch of the Government. Without this support last week the general strike would have been consummated. . . .

However, if his government does not proceed with the dissolution of the syndicates declared by decree illegal, and continues to take drastic measures against the communistic labor agitators, arresting the natives and deporting aliens, danger of another revolution threatens.[12]

The dismantling of revolutionary organizations was accompanied by physical assaults on trade union and party facilities and assassination of revolutionary leaders and militants. The purges in the trade unions and working-class centers were destined to prevent any counterattack by the revolutionary Left. More fundamentally, the repression was not only designed to *prevent* revolutionary action, but to put the workers back in their place within the organization of capitalist production—to re-create capitalist work discipline among the labor force and restore managerial prerogatives at the plant level and government authority at the state level. The rupture in the system evidenced during the 1932–1934 period raised grave problems for the functioning of the capitalist state and enterprise: The incapacity to rule and enforce capitalist laws and the threat of massive flight of capital and/or U.S. military intervention were uppermost concerns in the minds of the leaders of the counterrevolution. The growth of a "dual-power" situation, in which two sets of competing authorities governed within the same national boundaries, was incompatible with the development of capital. The counterrevolution was designed to resolve this anomaly.

The targeting of the revolutionary vanguard and its immediate periphery was designed to try to divide the working class—to separate the socialist revolutionaries from the less politicized workers. The purges were extensive and affected almost all areas of public life, reaching beyond working-class organs and affecting the press, the rights of free speech, assembly, and so on. The relentless pursuit of all protesters and the breakup of all opposition activity was designed to fragment the working class and its organization and dissolve the material basis for class consciousness rooted in collective mobility through collective activity. By destroying the *political* basis of class organization, the regime sought to restructure the working class in corporate bodies that were dependent on the state and cooperated with capital. To this end, the regime sought to retain most of the social legislation approved during the insurrectionary period, while destroying the organizations that had brought it about.

Clearly, repression was a short-term measure that could be applied to limited sectors of the working class. Its continual application to broad sectors of the class would destabilize and dislocate production, in addition to homogenizing the class experience of all sectors of labor and creating a common basis and bond for future action. The policy of the counterrevolution—to combine repression against the revolutionary sectors of the working class and attempt to gain the loyalty of the rest through nationalist rhetoric and the retention of the progressive social legislation—did not succeed because the working class was denied the instruments by which to enforce the legislation and to raise its most elementary demands. The employers and their supporters within the regime took advantage of the counterrevolution to attack all the gains of the labor movement, thus undermining the regime's attempt to impose a new order in which deradicalized labor participated in the system through its ties to social welfare programs.

The immediate outcome of the counterrevolutionary offensive was quite successful. There was a sharp decrease in strikes, political or economic, and other forms of mass activity. The working-class movement suffered a historical defeat that set the movement back in terms of organizational capabilities. The democratic gains that had created the space for further mobilization were destroyed. The terror unleashed by the regime, compounded by disintegration of mass organization, led to widespread political intimidation: Political demobilization and disarticulation of organizations isolated the revolutionary forces, who fell back on their organizational nuclei and seasoned cadres.

However, these political victories of the counterrevolutionary regime over the working-class movement at the same time destroyed any capacity to secure substantial support. Cuba's labor force, composed of wage workers, and petty-commodity producers and employees, who suffered the brunt of the repressive measures, were in no mood to concede any legitimacy to the regime. Cuba's capitalist class was weak and ineffective (where they were not on the verge of bankruptcy). Only the U.S. corporations and state stood as staunch allies of the regime, and, in a sense, this support undermined the only nonclass appeal, "nationalism," that the regime could float in an effort to capture some semblance of popular support. Hence the very terms (its social base and political program) of the counterrevolutionary success created the conditions for its *political isolation*, a condition that, by its pervasiveness, threatened the middle-range stability of the regime and the operation of the social system.

Equally important, the regime recognized that the repression was not destroying the social commitments of the working class but driving it underground. Whatever the lack of public expression, there existed widespread and substantial loyalty to the revolutionary Left and more fundamentally to the working-class organizations that had gained the social benefits and had provided a certain degree of job freedom and protection from the employers. The experience of 1932–1934 could not be obliterated from the consciousness of the working class, which could directly contrast its present adversities and its recent liberties. Beneath the satisfaction that the holders of power expressed was fear that a generalized decline in workers' standard of living could once again coalesce with the residual revolutionary forces in a new insurrectionary wave. The continued economic crisis, the pervasive presence of U.S. corporate power, and the lack of any popular loyalties to the state dictated that Batista adopt a new approach to securing the stability of the capitalist system that went beyond repression.

The Reemergence of Working-Class Institutions, 1937–1944

Beginning in early 1936, the Communist Party in Cuba, as elsewhere, shifted its political orientation toward what is described as "popular fronts," essentially political alliances in which the Communist Party allied itself with capitalist parties and subordinated the struggle for socialism to a variety of reform goals, including welfare legislation, democratic rights, modified colonial rule (in the colonies), and, above all, antifascist declarations. In Cuba, the shift from a revolutionary to a reformist perspective was aided by the defeat of the revolutionary upsurge and the demise of revolutionary democratic institutions. Hence, the counterrevolutionary ascendancy, the disarticulation of popular organizations, argued for a *reconstruction* of the movement, which in turn depended on reattaining democratic rights. However, while the conditions in Cuba facilitated the shift in political orientation, as the circumstances changed and the Left regained its organizational position, it became clear that the reformist orientation was not contingent on the adversities resulting from the repressive phase of the counterrevolution (nor on the "mistakes" during the insurrectionary period). Rather, it reflected a fundamentally different conception of Cuban sociopolitical reality and thus a different strategy, one in which socialist transformation was put on the back burner.

Between 1937 and 1944, the Communist Party developed a close and cooperative relationship with the Batista regime, exchanging political support of the capitalist state for legality, organizational freedom to organize the working class, and access to cabinet ministers, especially the labor ministry. In affirming communist support for Batista in 1942, Bias Roca, the Communist Party's general secretary, cited his "democratic positions . . . his categorical declaration in favor of popular demands, opposition to fascism and finance capital, his support of democracy and the complete independence of our country."[13] Batista reciprocated by stating that "the Communist Party has my respect and my greatest consideration."[14]

Thus, the move toward "popular front" politics translated itself into a policy of state collaboration, organizational expansion, and incrementalist social gains, especially prior to World War II. With the coming of the war, the social gains diminished, and what remained was essentially the consolidation of state/party ties and organizational expansion, as the Communist Party, in line with its "antifascist" program, opposed even the limited economic struggles for incremental gains that it promoted until 1941.

The shift in communist orientation during the late 1930s and the emerging political crises facing the regime (isolation, illegitimacy) converged and allowed Batista to forge a new political orientation. The Batista of the counterrevolutionary terror was set aside and the image of Batista the social democrat was fashioned. For Batista, there were two basic concerns within which his "popular turn" operated: (1) to prevent any overturn of capitalist property relations, including U.S. corporate holdings and (2) to secure governmental power for his particular political entourage to facilitate personal enrichment and the expansion of economic holdings. Within those boundaries, Batista was willing to pursue a very flexible program of reforms and concessions to a variety of groups and classes, including the working class. The Communist Party accepted those boundaries and fashioned its party and trade union activities to maximize its gains and those of its followers within that framework. The problem was no longer one of state power but of elaborating a reform program that was sufficiently "advanced" or "progressive" to secure immediate gains for the working class and institutional stability for the party and the unions. The new nonclass vocabulary introduced was symptomatic of the larger shift from socialist revolution to capitalist reform.

The relationship between Batista and the Cuban Communist Party, however, was reciprocal. The communists did not surrender the social revolution gratis but realized a series of substantial gains that had far-reaching, if indirect, effects on the operations of the capitalist system. While Batista received mass support, mobilized by the Communist Party, he had to recompense those supporters with more than symbolic payoffs. Batista granted the sugar workers 15 to 25 percent wage raises prior to the 1942 harvest, 50 percent prior to the 1943 harvest, and 10 percent prior to the 1944 harvest.

Per capita income increased from 109 pesos in 1933 to 240 pesos in 1944. Laws dealing with minimum wages, maternity insurance (women workers received full pay six weeks before and after giving birth), and labor immobility (guaranteeing workers against dismissal) were instituted. Laws passed during the Grau period creating a Ministry of Labor, providing an eight-hour day and guaranteeing 50 percent of all employees in a given category were Cuban were maintained.[15]

As early as 1936 and continuing throughout the 1930s, capitalists complained about the prolabor policies of the regime, and the U.S. embassy frequently intervened with the Cuban government on their behalf. One among many memos from the U.S. embassy to the State Department reported that the president of the American Chamber of Commerce complained that "the present administration of Cuba's labor laws is causing great hardship to American companies established in Cuba." The memo accused the secretary of labor of "seeking to secure the support of labor" and thus going "much further in instituting measures favoring labor than previous administrations."[16]

The cost of popular legitimacy and communist support, at least up to 1941, was not at all cheap. New legislation was passed, and previous legislation approved during the insurrectionary period was enforced. Trade unions were recognized and union organizing drives, collective bargaining, and strikes were legalized. Moreover, the regime frequently intervened to support the economic demands of labor or, more likely, refrained from the use of force. The Communist Party was legalized, and while it promoted Batista's candidacy and gave support to his regime, it also, until 1941, disseminated socialist and anti-imperialist ideas, recruited and organized working-class militants and developed a "subculture" of working-class solidarity. Although the Communist Party and its trade union leaders eschewed the general strike as a political weapon against Batista, they were not averse to organizing strikes at the industrial level on the basis of economic and social issues. Moreover, the Communist Party used its political influence to secure a series of laws that virtually made it impossible to fire workers, thus overcoming one of the great fears that had always plagued the Cuban working class in a high-unemployment economy. The combined impact of organizational legality, political access, limited class struggle, social legislation, and prolabor state intervention in wage disputes contributed to incremental gains in income for the working class and substantial expansion in labor organization.

Using dues collected as an indicator of the growth of the organizational strength of the Cuban Labor Confederation (CTC) demonstrates the extraordinary growth of the labor movement. In 1939, 4.7 million pesos were collected, while in 1944, 41.5 million pesos filled the treasury. In 1939, 282 unions were dues-paying members; in 1944, there were 913.[17] By 1945 approximately one-third or 406,776 workers were organized out of a labor force of 1.2 million.[18]

The spread of reforms and the resurgence of communist influence in the labor movement were, however, premised on the institutionalization of that power. The cooperation between labor and the regime was translated into the election of Batista and the demise of mass revolutionary political action. Nevertheless, an unforeseen consequence that resulted from the institutionalization of the labor movement was that its increasing capacity to impose wage solutions, and its ability to curtail some of the prerogatives of capital regarding control over labor in production, limited the process of capital accumulation. The continual needs of capital to modernize and rationalize production, to hire and fire labor, were in constant conflict with the institutional power of labor. Hence, while Batista sought and effectively did co-opt labor to preserve capital, he did so in such a fashion as to hinder the mechanism that facilitated its dynamic development.

This was not altogether evident during the war years (1941–1945), for both the communists and *Auténticos* (the populists organized into the Partido Revolucionario Cubana [Auténtico], or PRC[A]) outdid each other in collaborating with the "allies," their corporate subsidiaries, and the local capitalist class. Incrementalism, wage gains, and social legislation were put on the shelf in the interests of supporting the antifascist effort, democracy, and the Soviet Union. A resolution passed at the 1942 CTC Congress succinctly summed up the position of the communist leadership:

> While war conditions last, the Cuban workers wish to avoid all strikes and conflicts capable of paralyzing production but at the same time they insist that their suggestions for the creation of machinery for conciliation and arbitration shall be given due consideration as well as the suggestion for direct negotiations between the unions and management.[19]

One U.S. embassy intelligence study provides data on Communist Party growth between its founding and the immediate post–World War II period.[20] The first big gain (sixfold) occurred during the 1933 insurrection. The subsequent expansion occurred during the alliance with Batista, beginning in 1937. The war period thus witnessed the deepening ties with the state apparatus: organizational growth and the further weakening of the class struggle ideology. The trade unions were more concerned with maintaining production than with defending workers' interests. The extension of working-class membership was more the result of cooperation with the employers than the result of organization from below.

Institutionalization, and Class Collaboration, 1945–1952

The degree to which the Communist Party contributed to the growth and conservatism of the labor movement cannot be overemphasized, especially during the war years. The basic relations of state collaboration in exchange for labor legislation between regime and labor confederation were established, extended, and sustained during the 1945–1952 period. The process, however, was contradictory: For as the communists extended organizational networks, they limited class conflict; as they cooperated with capitalist regimes, they diffused socialist ideas; as they promoted the Marxist doctrine of class struggle, they practiced the politics of class collaboration; as they purported to represent the historic interest of the working class, they became integrated into the capitalist state apparatus.

The contradictory class position of the Communist Party and its working-class organizations reflected the dual realities of Cuban political economy:

its flexibility and capacity for absorption of labor demands filtered through a bureaucratized labor movement and the perennial struggles generated by stagnant capitalist development with chronic high rates of unemployment. The change of government in 1944—the victory of the Auténtico Grau San Martín—did not lead to any qualitative changes in working-class politics. Grau was amenable to the same relationship with the Cuban Communist Party that Batista had cultivated: exchange of incremental reforms and salary increases for political support of his essentially capitalist regime. Shortly after taking office, Grau raised the wages of the sugar workers 32 percent prior to the 1945 harvest.[21]

With the end of World War II, limited class conflict again reemerged, fanned in part by the competition between the Auténticos and communists for leadership of the CTC. While the labor unions were firmly entrenched, communist leadership within them was less so. Years of dependence on regime support, years without any serious effort at revolutionary mobilization, and constant emphasis on immediate gains over and against the historic goals of socialism obscured the differences between the socialist and nonsocialist working-class struggle. The blurring of political differences, the decline in socialist consciousness among the trade unionists, and the dependence on agreements at the top contributed to the displacement of the communist leadership from the labor movement once the regime changed hands. Despite its apparent massive growth, the *quality* of membership and leadership had changed. As Charles Page notes, "During the Batista-Communist Party pact many young would be proletarians without legal education saw the way open to political power through the Communist organized labor movement. . . . The aspirants to these positions . . . with scant Communist ideology, easily recanted."[22]

The organizational challenge mounted by the Auténticos could not be answered in the streets, but in the offices of the government. Offers to share power, to divide leadership posts, and to prefer support to the regime were of no avail. When the Grau regime finally endorsed the Auténtico seizure of the CTC offices and buildings in 1948, the Communist Party was no longer politically or psychologically in a position to offer any resistance. The years of practice involving the extension and enforcement of legislation, the limited struggles for economic demands, and the bureaucratic nature of the organization vitiated the capacity for political warfare. The communist labor movement was a giant with clay feet. Many members transferred their loyalties to the new bureaucracy, which sustained the old policies of the Communist Party, engaging in struggles and demands for wage increases, new legislation, and so forth, without the accompanying socialist educational campaigns.

As Page observes, "The Popular Front in union affairs proved to be a weakness for the Communists. One after another, formerly subservient syndicate officials joined the Auténtico rebellion. Only those syndicates with large rank and file Communist membership remained loyal."[23] Union membership grew along with the economic demands, continuing the pressures on the accumulation process. The labor movement, and its organization and demands, was so institutionalized that it easily withstood the shift in leadership and continued on its bureaucratic way. The purge of the Communist Party during 1948–1952 did not have any noticeable effects at the level of labor-state relations. The Auténtico–President Prio relationship was not very different from the Communist Party–Batista–Grau relationship; wages and salaries were increased, protective legislation was pursued, and so on. The only difference was an increase in class conflict at the plant level, as both factions competed for worker loyalty, thus fanning greater labor strife.

The conspicuous loser in this situation was the Cuban economy. Economic stagnation, speculative investments, overseas bank accounts, and political corruption highlighted a society in which local and foreign capital refused to invest in an economy that had powerful labor influence. With communist leadership and without, the labor movement was a major force *within* capitalist society, but it was impotent to change it. Likewise, capitalism controlled the means of production but was unable to develop them. This stalemate defined the prolonged crisis in Cuban society, which the Batista coup of 1952 sought to resolve.

Military Dictatorship and Revolution, 1952–1958

Many episodes and idiosyncratic factors can be analyzed to account for the coup of 1952. But the long-term structural factors that underlay the coup must be taken into account. Cuba's economy was stagnating: Sugar production, the mainstay of the economy, remained at levels comparable to earlier decades. Cuba was still overwhelmingly dependent on sugar, productivity was low, the local bourgeoisie was not investing on a significant scale or in areas to promote structural changes.

As James O'Connor notes:

> Productivity of investments in Cuba was unusually low, reaching barely one-third of the level of capital productivity in most advanced capitalist countries. One of the reasons was that commercial and public construction took a relatively large share of total capital outlays; also an inordinate amount of investment funds were expended in trade and commerce and in consumer goods industry.[24]

Moreover, foreign capital regarded Cuba as unattractive because of its strong labor movement and the constraints that it imposed on the development of capitalism. In 1950, a thorough survey of the Cuban economy by the International Bank for Reconstruction and Development (IBRD) documented the constraints that existed and were felt by the capitalist class: The power of labor and social legislation were cited as fundamental concerns for the lack of capitalist involvement. The IBRD report complained that "few of them [Cuban workers] have had good educational opportunities, and any economic education has probably been at the hands of class struggle doctrinaires."[25]

Batista's "historic mission" was to break this paralysis, to restructure Cuban society to facilitate capital accumulation. In the 1930s, his mission had been to prevent a socialist revolution and to stabilize a capitalist regime, which he did, first through repression and then through co-optation. The very terms of his success in stabilizing and legitimizing his regime, however, created the conditions for the paralysis of capitalist expansion. In 1952, capitalism appeared to be secure from any insurrectionary threat, and Batista's efforts were turned toward creating conditions for rapid and substantial capital expansion—at the cost of the very labor programs that he had initiated earlier. In launching his offensive against labor, Batista not only failed to restructure society to facilitate capitalist advance but also succeeded in re-creating the conditions that undermined the security of the system of labor–regime collaboration, which he had so laboriously contributed to creating in an earlier period.

During the period immediately preceding Batista's coup, the labor movement, largely purged of Communist Party leaders and militants, extended and deepened its collaboration and subordination to the state. As Page observes:

> The rank and file of the left-wing labor were intimidated by the arrests of its leadership—assemblies removed their former officers and elected pro Cofiño [Auténtico, anticommunists]. Where assemblies did not act the Ministry of Labor intervened . . . Management proceeded to fire thousands of Communist supporters for participating in the strike.[26]

Militancy at the local level was attacked, and national union leaders kept a heavy hand on radicalized locals and an open hand toward the employers and state. Corruption within the labor movement eroded the loyalty of many members and went far beyond any previously experienced during Communist Party leadership. Bureaucratization and purges forced the labor movement to depend more and more on top-level agreements with the regime to secure minimal gains—which were necessary to maintain organizational control. Differentiation between national union leaders and their apparatus supporters and the rank and file became very marked. Page notes that "in the federation we find scant contact between the leadership and the rank and file."[27]

The virtual integration of the labor bureaucracy into the state allowed for specific union protection, legislation, and trade union cooperation with the state, but it led to the neglect of the broader social problems of unemployment (20 percent), underemployment (seasonal work in the sugar fields), vast regional and class disparities, and racism. Page summarizes the situation:

> The present CTC(A) leaders drew their strength from the government. They are the government's lobby with the labor movement. Since 1947 . . . the workers pressure has been directed against their leaders and the government, rather than with their leaders against the government. . . . The most advanced social legislation . . . are circumvented by all parties concerned. Economic and political strength still dictates the solution of an issue outside of an artificial legal framework.[28]

Nevertheless, the class struggle existed within industries and especially because of rank-and-file pressure. The Communist Party, now in opposition and lacking ties to the regime, was more responsive to local rank-and-file demands for direct action. The Auténtico militants at the local level, fearful of losing their following, competed with the Communist Party in militancy. Thus, clear and profound breaches began to appear within the labor movement: between a militant rank and file organized in local unions and an increasingly privileged and corrupt bureaucracy tied more to the state than to the membership; between the regional unions located in the provinces and the Havana headquarters; and between certain national federations and the central federation. There were several crosscurrents operating to realign working-class forces within the national pattern of class collaboration, immobilization, and corruption.

The ease with which Batista took power—the lack of any sustained opposition—appeared to vindicate his assessment of the weakness of his political opponents and his shrewd understanding of the dependence and immobility of the so-called mass organizations. As the leader of the CTC, Eusebio Mujal, described it, "Only one out of seventy CTC leaders voted for a general strike to protest the coup—the remaining sixty nine said that 'Batista was useful.'"[29] The bureaucratized nature of Cuban political and social life and the lack of any consequential mobilization and sustained participation from below prevented any effective response. President Prio ran for an embassy: Mujal and the trade union bureaucracy almost immediately and unanimously sought to come to terms with Batista. According to Mujal, Batista offered the CTC bureaucracy "legality and social legislation"[30] in exchange for support of the dictatorship. The ease of the transfer of political loyalties captures well the fundamental concern with maintaining organizational control and political sinecures over and against membership concerns and political programs.

Batista's inheritance included a strong labor presence and a crisis in capital accumulation. The needs of capital dictated a break with the constraints that labor represented. However, Batista, an experienced politician, recognized that he needed some form of labor cooperation. He resolved the apparent dilemma by relying on the labor bureaucracy, signing a pact with its leaders, and attacking regional, sectional, and rank-and-file members who created obstacles to the expansion of capital. The Batista–CTC bureaucracy pact was successful; each respected the other. According to Mujal, "Batista offered a pact that he honorably and loyally fulfilled."[31] Batista allowed the CTC bureaucrats to draw their salaries, secure favors, and even to make selective gains, while the bureaucracy attempted to block each and every effort by rank-and-file groups to oppose Batista's economic policies and political regime.

As the policies of the Batista regime began to affect the labor movement adversely, and as the bureaucracy continued to support Batista against the rank and file, a crisis within the labor movement and outside among non-affiliated wage workers began to develop: Divisions reflecting class, regional, and generational differences began to appear. Among bank, telephone, and transport workers, dissidents gained strength. An editorial in *El Rodante* of the Transport Workers Union captures the emerging opposition to Batista regime. "What attitude should we adopt before these measures. . . ? Should we allow our miserable salaries to be lowered and that they throw us out in the streets, so many family heads. . . ? If these functionaries do not resolve our problems we will go directly to General Batista . . . and explain our rights."[32] The failure to secure a response through petitions to the Labor Ministry in the traditional fashion "radicalized" workers around "standard of living" arguments.

Within the CTC, Mujal attempted to disguise his subordination of the trade unions to the Batista regime by defining his program as "Third Force." Nonetheless, his Third Force rhetoric was fundamentally directed toward destroying any dissident reformist or revolutionary trade unionist group. Mujal editorialized:

> We close ranks in the great struggle for the liberation against all totalitarianisms and repressive regimes, but we know who we have to defeat first, in order to pursue the struggle. The CTC supports free thought among its members but we have a statute and program to defend and that is anti-communist and absolutely democratic. . . . The Communists are not workers, they do not have a race, nor sex, they are simply communists.[33]

Within the official publications of the union bureaucracy and the hierarchically controlled conventions, there were few signs of the increasing discontent evidenced among rank-and-file workers, who were increasingly turning to other forms of pressure and protest and closer to the direct action tactics proposed by new groups outside of the official labor movement.

Batista's main preoccupation after the coup, in addition to self-enrichment, was to seek ways and means of implementing the IBRD recommendations. The strongly entrenched position of labor, however, dictated a cautious piecemeal approach in close cooperation with the labor bureaucracy, lest a broadside unite labor and provoke a massive response. Thus, while Batista appeared to follow the same co-optive strategy of the earlier period, in reality his position rested, of necessity, on a much narrower base. Rather than attack the bureaucratic institutions per se, his policies were designed to weaken labor's positions in the factories and at the point of production. Although cordial relations were maintained with the labor bureaucracy at the top, there was no concomitant payoff at the bottom. Thus, in place of the sustained and effective trickle-down approach promoted between 1936 and 1944 through the trade unions, there developed a policy of horizontal payoffs to the leaders and tightening of political and social controls at the bottom.

In pursuing this different policy, Batista no longer faced the immediate threat of 1933, and he discounted the new challenge embodied in the armed movements of the 1950s. Operating within the framework of the old parties of the 1930s and 1940s, he was unimpressed by a weak and isolated Communist Party and ineffectual, corrupt Auténticos, a divided bureaucratized trade union movement, and a less politicized working class. The fading out of the past threat of 1933 blinded Batista to the reemergence of a new opposition: the July 26th Movement based on a new tactical and strategic approach, although rooted, in some cases, in social forces similar to those that exploded earlier. While Batista guarded against and looked for ways to crush an urban insurrection, he overlooked the possible success emanating from combined urban mass struggle and rural guerrilla activity.

Batista set the stage for the outbreak in the new revolutionary struggles by his increasing attacks on the cumulative economic, social, and political gains achieved by the working class over the previous twenty years. His forceful intervention against labor strikes, unions, and the steady increase in pressure on behalf of the employers reactivated working-class opposition and alienated an increasing number of local trade union leaders. State repression penetrating to the local level politicized union and nonunion members, independently of the trade union bureaucracy. Herbert Mathews's reports in Santiago de Cuba best capture the emerging working-class revolt:

> A group of nine trade union leaders representing a cross section of the workers of the province came to see me at the hotel. . . . "None of us is political or partisan. We speak to you as Cubans. We represent and we are the people of Cuba and we are against Batista and his clique. You may be sure that all workers are

good Cubans and feel the way we do, all except our top national leaders who are chosen by Batista and are in his pay." . . . Anti-U.S. feeling runs high in this city because of what is considered United States support for General Batista. There is a constant exodus from the city of youths who try to join Fidel Castro . . . the center and symbol of Santiago de Cuba's resistance. . . . The tension is almost palpable and is certainly very dangerous to the regime. Santiago de Cuba is a city living in a state of fear and exaltation and it is the exaltation that dominates.[34]

The unwillingness of the bureaucrats to channel this discontent or to provide any leadership opened the field to the direct action groups organized against Batista. The principal conflict within Cuban society was between the capitalist state embodied in the Batista dictatorship, which sought to restructure Cuban society for the capitalist class as a whole, and the Cuban working class, increasingly disposed to act outside the official party and trade union organizations. Thus, because the capital labor struggle did not take place primarily between private owners and labor unions, the fact that a highly politicized class struggle was taking place—and not merely an amorphous political struggle against a dictatorial regime—should not be obscured.

Moreover, while Batista was pushing to reverse previous gains, the working class in Cuba was looking beyond its previous achievements toward a new set of demands that went beyond the capacity of Cuba's dependent capitalist society: The demands for full employment and improved and increasing social services came into conflict with the imperatives of capitalist rationality, which demanded an end to work definitions that multiplied employment. The reinsertion of U.S. capital to promote a diversified economy necessitated a lowering of social overhead costs and a reallocation of state expenditures from social services to capital expenditures and infrastructure investments. The pursuit of this new development strategy forced Batista to cut off labor's access to the state and to increase his ties with U.S. and domestic capital. The result was to re-create the basis for mass confrontation politics—similar to the early 1930s. Following a similar development model—"from above and outside"—Batista ended up creating the same revolutionary situation in which a military-centralist autocratic state linked to U.S. business provoked a massive popular movement that fused democratic, anti-imperialist, and anticapitalist forces into one broad movement outside the official parties and trade unions.

From General Strike to Collectivization, 1959–1963

A number of striking aspects of the social revolutionary process that occurred between 1959 and 1963 have been inadequately dealt with by both friends and foes of the Cuban revolutionary process. The first is the massive activity and active support of the working class in the collectivization of capitalist property and the construction of revolutionary organs of state power. The second is the *speed* and *scope* of the action directed toward realizing these revolutionary ends. Third is the unquestioned and unambiguous *success* of these efforts. The explanation usually set forth is that Castro and his inner circle were able, because of their personal influence and because of the deficiencies in political organization of the local bourgeoisie, to engineer this revolution with the support of the masses who were brought into this process. The conflict with the United States facilitated this change, for the leadership was able to mobilize on a nationalist basis forces that otherwise might not have responded to a purely anticapitalist or socialist appeal. The long and short of these "explanations" is that they do not go far enough—whatever their simplicity and appeal to "obvious" facts. Why was there such a massive response in such a short period for such monumental changes if there was not a whole history of struggles and activities that preceded it? What elements in Cuban society weakened the bourgeoisie's social and political position, vis-à-vis labor, even as the former's position with relationship to U.S. capital was improving?

It is clear that Cuban national capital was growing in importance in sugar, relative to the United States, yet its capacity to exercise hegemony was severely constrained. Hence, the thesis of U.S. corporate capital "undermining" the basis of social domination by the bourgeoisie was less tenable in the late 1950s than it was earlier. Castro's actions and revolutionary measures—intervening enterprises, nationalizing large-scale foreign enterprises—followed a pattern that had been initiated by the workers' movement in the early 1930s and followed the labor/capital strife that was endemic to Cuban labor relations throughout the preceding period. The post-1959 struggles in Cuba, culminating in nationalization and collectivization, deepened and extended the class struggle, frequently a direct response to the labor/capital conflicts emerging in the post-1959 period. The leadership drew sustenance and, in turn, was influenced by the generalized anticapitalist animus that pervaded rank-and-file labor and animated its activities for a quarter of a century. The revolutionary regime was able initially to build on the juridical structure and social legislation, which reflected past working-class struggles, in implementing and extending laws to secure and provide employment, increase the standard of living, and lower costs of essentials. The "continuities" with the past, however, were in some ways superficial: The depth, scope, consistency, and coherence of application were *qualitatively* different after 1959 because the state was not trying to deflect working-class action from a revolutionary overturn, but to provide space for its consummation.

But it is a mistake to speak of the "state" at least in the immediate period following Batista's overturn, for the situation was much more fluid. The dismantling of the military/police apparatus was in full force (the civil bureaucracy was still in place, although quite passive), cautiously waiting to see whether they could be individually or collectively assimilated to the new order. The expansion and growth of the rebel guerrilla army and the proliferation of local armed committees served as transitional forms of state power in the immediate circumstances. The armed struggle launched by the counterrevolutionaries against the regime precipitated a massive movement demanding the arming of the people—a movement that paralleled the insurrectionary experiences of the 1930s *and* grew out of the armed struggle of the 1950s.

The extension and deepening of the revolutionary process was as much through mass pressure as it was through leadership initiative. In the sugar fields mass action occurred: "The revolutionary militia have converted the 161 sugar centrales of the island into 161 bulwarks of the revolution. These militias guard their own work centers against criminal sabotage."[35] In the petroleum refineries, similar mass action occurred: "It was the militias of these work centers, those who were alert and vigilant before the interventions and who proceeded to make them function, with the decided support of the Cuban technicians and engineers."[36]

In all the major unions—railroad, metallurgical, and sugar workers—new revolutionary slates were elected. In addition, the Castro government was pressured from below for a militia form of army. "But in the same measure that these [U.S.] aggressions were consummated the Cuban people with a profound revolutionary spirit . . . clamored for military instruction and necessary preparation in order to defend the country. . . . Thus emerged the National Revolutionary Militia."[37] This popular working-class army was instrumental in defeating the U.S.-backed invading force at the Bay of Pigs in April 1961. The movement from below for a working-class militia as an alternative form of state power culminated in the transfer of state power from the capitalist to the working class, deepening U.S. and Cuban bourgeois opposition. If this mass movement for militias *originated* in a struggle to defend the limited gains attained in early 1959, it resulted in further polarizing class forces, internally and internationally, and ultimately extending the collectivization process throughout the productive units within which the armed workers were employed.

The genius of the Castro leadership was not to "create" consciousness among Cuban workers but rather to respond to the historic legacy of Cuban class politics, to facilitate its organizational expression, and to synthesize and articulate the sometimes inchoate strivings and tumultuous activities. In many ways, Castro's success was based on the fact that his revolutionary trajectory was similar to the "average" class-conscious militant: a historic sense of capitalist and imperialist exploitation that had built upon an organizational movement defending Cuban national and working-class interests, a commitment to new forms of struggle, including arms, and a profound rejection of the compromised parties of the past. In other words, it was a clear understanding of the adversaries and a commitment to defeat them, a willingness to use all necessary political and military means, and a vague general idea of what postcapitalist society and state should emerge. The strong point of both Castro and the militants in the Cuban working class was a concrete sense of the past and present and a consequential commitment to rectify or abolish exploitative relations. Where they both were weak was in their sense of the social system that should emerge. The movement of militants and leadership were more anti-imperialist and anticapitalist than socialist—the product of twenty-five years in which immediate militant struggles were not illuminated by a socialist perspective.

The resurgence of revolutionary class struggle began in the mid-1950s. Among the myriad forces that began to percolate in the campaign against the Batista dictatorship were sectors of the working class. Beginning in mid-1955, strikes and demonstrations by employees in diverse industries, including the sugar industry, began to be manifested. The original impetuses in many cases were "economic"—wages, bonus payments, job security. The limitations that Batista tried to impose on labor's power in relation to capital and the collaboration of the CTC leadership with his "development" scheme *alienated* rank-and-file labor and politicized the struggle. As worker discontent was not deflected by regime policy and as the CTC leadership was incapable of mediating the disputes, new local leadership emerged to articulate grievances.

The expression of labor discontent outside official channels was repressed by the regime, transforming the economic discontent into political opposition to the regime. The first major indication of mass working-class opposition was the successful general strike organized by Frank Pais and others in Santiago de Cuba in Oriente Province in 1956. This mass working-class action was not an isolated event but reflected the constant tension and hostility that existed there between the regime and the laboring masses and included a substantial number of local and provincial working-class leaders. The revolutionary mobilization reflected the dialectical interplay between the mass struggle of the cities and the armed guerrilla movement in the countryside. Beyond the tactical differences, the success of the struggle depended upon the interdependence and articulation of both struggles.

Castro's rupture with the conventional collaborationist politics of the 1940s, and his mass appeal to join the revolutionary movement, was based on an accurate perception of two basic facts: that the insurrectionary tradition of the 1930s was still alive; and that a significant mass of Cubans, in and out of the official labor organizations, who were not represented in the class struggle, were capable of engaging in a confrontation with the regime. The guerrilla movement was seen by its organizers as an instrument to weaken the regime and organize the general strike leading to the mass in-surrection. The "foco" concept, of guerrilla action being a substitute for mass action, was foreign to Cuban history and thus to the thinking of the revolutionary vanguard of the July 26th Movement. The movement was a national political formation, anchored in the mass struggle of provincial towns, drawing support from wage and salaried workers of the cities and peasants in the countryside, and finding active collaboration among the younger generation of local trade union leaders. As the struggles developed, the movement expanded and drew to itself and reactivated many of the militants from the earlier insurrectionary period. These physical links between the revolutionary past and the younger militants of the 1950s laid the groundwork for the radicalization of the post-Batista period.

The working-class presence in the anti-Batista struggle and its specific class interests were subsumed within the general democratic, antidictatorial framework. It shared, along with other petit bourgeois and bourgeois forces, an opposition to the political repression of the regime—but from a differ-ent class perspective. This temporary convergence would immediately dis-solve after the overthrow of Batista in the competing and conflictive efforts to restructure and define the nature of the state apparatus. The working-class struggle against Batista was directed toward maximizing its weight and in-terests within the state and society and ensuring that its gains would not be endangered. Hence, there is historic importance of the working-class demand for "arming the people"—thus blocking the attempt by the bourgeois coali-tion to demobilize the populace and to restructure an armed apparatus sym-pathetic to its class interests. The precipitous reaction of the more extreme sectors of the bourgeoisie in launching armed actions against the initial structural changes of the coalition regime served as a catalytic force, alerting the working class to the inherent dangers in the politically fluid post-Batista period. The armed mobilization of the masses, accompanied by sociopolit-ical pressures within each productive sector and firm in which they were em-ployed, accelerated the radicalization process. Nationalization and state in-terventions multiplied, breaking up the coalition regime and forcing the bourgeois cabinet minister to abandon responsibility for the expropriation of their closest capitalist associates.

The emerging power bloc of guerrilla leaders and armed mass working-class organizations overwhelmed both the political and economic organi-zations of the bourgeoisie. The latter lacked comparable instruments to "confront" the revolutionary forces with the disintegration of the old (Batista) state apparatus; they lacked any comparable organization within the trade union apparatus and any "special formations" derived from the anti-Batista struggle. Their only recourse was the U.S. imperial state appara-tus, to which they had recourse. The surprisingly rapid and drastic shift from "reformist" ministers of a "democratic," "nationalist" regime to open collaborators with imperialist and dictatorial forces (as one encounters during the Bay of Pigs invasion) is explained by the absence of any alternatives between the organized armed power of the Cuban working class and the organizational apparatus of U.S. imperialism. Having broken with the first, the second remained the only choice; having to choose to live under working-class power or dependent dictatorial capitalism, the bourgeoisie belatedly chose the latter—symptomatic of the behavior of the bourgeoisie throughout the continent for the next two decades.

For the working class, the anti-Batista mobilization was a form of class struggle, directly political and with an immediate set of grievances directed at the capitalist system. The original limitations of that struggle—that it was confined at the political level and was informed by a series of social reforms—did not prevent it from deepening and extending in the post-dictatorial period. The multiple conflicts between labor and capital after the overthrow and the enormous number of demands that the populace placed on the new leadership can be seen as attempts by the working class to put its social class content into the emerging democratic forms. The class struggle in the post-Batista period became clearer, and the social dimension of the revolution became predominant—essentially through the penetration by the working class of the critical new institutions, the embryonic revolutionary state, the Rebel Army, and the popular militias. The transition from the democratic to the socialist phase of the revolution, punctured as it was by conflicts and some violence, was relatively peaceful, because the working-class role in the armed struggle for democracy had secured it a strategic position, allowing it to undermine all bourgeois opposition.

THE NICARAGUAN REVOLUTION
IN HISTORICAL PERSPECTIVE

The Nicaraguan revolution has great substantive importance for the country and even greater symbolic significance for the continent. For the first time in more than twenty years after the Cuban revolution, it was demonstrated that a U.S.-armed and -trained military dictatorship could be defeated in a popular armed upheaval.[38] The defeats in Chile, Uruguay, Argentina, and other countries during the 1960s and 1970s weighed heavily on all popular movements. Beginning in the 1980s, however, there emerged a resurgence of mass popular democratic movements throughout Latin America, of which the Sandinista-led forces were the earliest and most developed that succeeded in taking state power.

Just as the Nicaraguan revolution has a profound symbolic impact on Latin America, so did many Latin Americans contribute with lives and arms to the victory of it. From all over Latin America, volunteers from fifteen to forty years of age joined the Frente Sandinista Liberación Nacional (FSLN, the Sandinista National Liberation Front), among them veterans and novices, militants and idealists, to oust Somoza, symbol of tyranny, corruption, and wealth, of U.S. training, support, and subservience. The internationalists included Costa Ricans who, coming to politics, saw the gap between the professions of democracy and the practice of privilege; Chileans, who had suffered the defeat of a revolution without a struggle at the hands of the military and the United States and who sought to redeem themselves; and Mexicans, who came out of the peasant struggles and who saw in Nicaragua a chance to relive the struggles of the past, equalizing the odds. Also included were those from Guatemala, El Salvador, and Honduras, who suffered similar terror and destruction and saw a chance to even the score, ending the reign of the regional gendarme and perhaps opening a new chapter—the first truly sovereign state in Central America governed by the people, not by the oligarchies of a few dozen families, or less. They came from Colombia's occupied universities, the offices and factories of Caracas, from the Chilean and Argentine diaspora, from Zapata country—the Latin American revolutionaries building barricades with the embattled street fighters from Managua, Masaya, Esteli, León, cities made famous throughout the world by the thousands of anonymous militants who took the streets and defended their barrios with rifles against Sherman tanks and moved from city to city until they captured the last bunker in Managua.[39]

Nothing ran in Managua except by permission of the FSLN: factories were closed or in ruins; ports and transport were paralyzed. The workers traded their tools for guns; everywhere, everyone, made a decision to struggle to victory or die. The expression "the final struggle, cost what it may" passed from being a rhetorical exhortation of a guerrilla band to being the living expression of a determined and committed people. The marketplaces were empty; the stalls were burned, and the vendors had nothing to sell. Weeks earlier, they had hid scores of clandestine guerrillas entering the city; even the prostitutes, wielding knives, advised the guard patrols to keep going.

Several features of the Nicaraguan revolution bear discussion for their import to the rest of the third world, especially Latin America. The writings that focus exclusively on the uniqueness of the Somoza dynasty and wealth overlook several historical processes that are operating on a world scale and that found expression in Nicaragua. Here we will focus on (1) the historical developments that generated the revolutionary upheaval; (2) the nature of the revolutionary process, the changing patterns, and the configuration of forces, strategies, and alliances; and (3) the contradictory development in the transition period—that is, the relationship between the organs of popular power, which were instrumental in the insurrectionary phase, and the governing organs.

Capitalist Development: Autocracy and Revolution

It is important, first, to deal with several misconceptions about the socioeconomic context of the revolutionary struggle. Nicaragua was not a simple "underdeveloped" country wallowing in stagnation and backwardness. From the 1950s to the mid-1970s, the Nicaraguan economy went through a period of rapid growth—large-scale commercialization of agriculture and high-powered expansion of industry, services, and finance. While most observers have noted the private wealth and corruption of Somoza, the fact is that a portion of that wealth took the form of capital investments. The growth of capitalism was accompanied in part by the proletarianization of the peasants in the countryside and the artisans in the city, along with the displacements of others and their incorporation into a large, surplus labor pool, which crowded the central cities in each region.

The state—the Somoza clan—and foreign capital played a decisive role in implanting capitalism and capitalist social relations. The whole process of rapid growth from above was made possible by the autocratic dictatorship and its "free market" and repressive labor policies, a pattern not unknown to other Latin American countries. This configuration of forces displaced many factions and sectors of traditional mercantile society, while they failed to integrate or provide mechanisms of representation for the new classes generated by the new pattern of capitalist development. The very terms for success of the autocratic development ("from above and outside") model prevented the dominant forces from any sustained and consequential *democratization*. Rather, the pattern was one of selective and time-bound *liberalization*—modification of dictatorial policies—followed by widespread, systematic repression.[40]

While the competitors for power were lodged largely within the two capitalist parties (Liberals and Conservatives), and while the adversaries were mostly capitalist competitors, conflict, including armed and mass activity, was a bargaining weapon to secure a better share of government revenues (subsidies, credit) and led to pacts between Somoza and his bourgeois critics. This pattern began to change only with the massive entry of the FSLN. In fact, parallel to the intransigent opposition of the FSLN, the bourgeois opposition continued to attempt to "deal" with Somoza and the United States in much the traditional pattern; the only difference was that the unsatisfactory results, from the point of view of the masses, gave further sustenance to the FSLN and ultimately undermined bourgeois hegemony over the mass movement. Hence, the growth of capitalism and intrabourgeois conflicts provided a gloss of "competitive" politics, limited by the overwhelming concentration of power in the hands of the autocratic dictatorship and the total subordination of the National Guard to his rulership.[41]

Rapid capitalist growth premised on large labor surpluses, labor discipline (no strikes, protests), and extensive as well as intensive exploitation provided a fertile basis for social mobilization in the cities and larger agro-industrial complexes. Unlike the early Sandino-led movement, largely based on peasant recruits, the Nicaraguan revolution was generally rooted in the *most urbanized, industrialized areas—the most "advanced" sectors of production and social reproduction.* The revolutionary movement contained the most retrograde forces displaced by dynamic state and foreign capitalist development: the small and medium-size producers, as well as the new industrial working class, middle-class professionals, employees (employed in the modern industrial and service sectors), and the large reserves of underemployed, unemployed, semiproletarianized youth of the cities and countryside, all products of the same process of uprooting that accompanies capitalist development. Generally, the most passive, least rebellious sectors, with some notable exceptions, were the agricultural areas least affected by commercial-capitalist activity, the isolated villages and communities of the south.

The concentration of employed and unemployed workers in the cities, the growth of impersonal wage relations instead of payments in kind, and the decline of personal forms of domination and control in the sprawling urban slums facilitated antagonistic relations. The autocratic state, prime mover of capitalist growth, emasculated legitimate organs of representation and prevented effective articulation of demands for urban services. The social-overhead costs for the reproduction of labor were borne directly and totally by the direct producers. Hence, barrio organizations, initially activated around local and immediate needs, became the vehicles for FSLN mobilization. Only the most radical and determined organizations capable of withstanding the dictatorship could sustain a consequential struggle for incremental gains. The point of habitation became the principal point of organization, the common meeting ground, for employed and unemployed workers, proletarians, and semiproletarians. And the target was the state: the dispenser of social services, controller of social expenditures, and the critical agent for urban real estate speculation and slum eradication.

While the economic boom increased the social weight of the working class and employees in the cities, the economic downturns marginalized the bourgeoisie, especially those medium and small owners without access to state credits and subsidies, pushing them closer to bankruptcy and threatening their property-owning status. The crisis and the lack of access to the Somoza-dominated state pushed the marginalized bourgeoisie into opposition.[42] The convergence of workers, middle class and bourgeoisie, into a common anti-Somoza struggle and for democracy obscured the fundamentally different interests being pursued and the different concepts of the state. For the bourgeoisie and its petit bourgeois political representatives, the issue is one of securing access to the state to promote its class interests, financing, credit, protection, subsidies, contracts—and the rapid demobilization and disarming of the masses in order to create a new state apparatus in the most proximate image of itself. For the masses, democracy is the generalization and sustenance of the local organs of popular power—their extension to control of the productive forces to serve barrio needs. Thus, *the most crucial issue in the post-Somoza period has been political, not economic: reconstruction by whom and for whom?*

The concentration of the insurrectionary struggles in the cities and among the most radicalized working-class forces raises the issue of the *socialist* potentialities inherent in the struggle. With the uneven nature of capitalist development, its concentration in certain urban/rural areas finds expression in the uneven development of the revolutionary struggle. The insurrectionary struggle in the cities developed far in advance of the struggle in general. More important, the tempo and tasks of the revolution are not dictated by the *general* level of the productive forces in the *country as a whole*, but by the level of *class struggle* in the most *advanced* areas.

The Nature of the Revolutionary Process

The revolutionary process in Nicaragua covers a wide array of complementary and combined forms of struggle over a long period. Moreover, the revolutionary movement went through several phases: correcting itself, altering its course, and dividing and converging for the final assault on the Somoza dictatorship. The unquestionable central organization responsible for the overthrow of the autocratic regime is the FSLN, whose origins and development are derived from the Nicaraguan revolutionary experience of the 1920s and 1930s, and from more recent Latin American history.

From Sandino, the guerrilla leader and revolutionary opposed to U.S. occupation in the 1920s and 1930s, the FSLN derived several aspects of its program and orientation: (1) *nationalism* and *anti-imperialism* as the basic tenets of its program, in opposition to other pro-U.S. oppositionists who presented themselves to the embassy as "democratic alternatives"; (2) *reliance on mass support*, as opposed to efforts mainly by the bourgeoisie to organize elite conspiracies and military coups behind the backs of the masses, thus substituting one elite for another; and (3) *development of armed struggle* as the only effective means of overthrowing the Somoza dictatorship (hence, rejection of all "negotiations," "pacts," and U.S.-sponsored mediations, as ploys to prolong the life of the regime and/or modify it in nonessential ways).

Founded in 1961, FSLN heavily influenced by the "foco" theory of guerrilla warfare and by the success of the Cuban revolution, launched a series of military actions designed to detonate popular uprisings. These isolated military actions, led largely by students and professionals, were easily put down by the military, inflicting substantial losses but failing to destroy the organization. With the failure of the foco strategy, a complete change in tactics and orientation was introduced and applied beginning in the late 1960s and early 1970s. The decisive shift was toward the organization of mass support in the countryside and cities. The new perspectives envisioned a prolonged, popular war that would combine rural guerrilla activities (to harass the National Guard) and mass struggle in the cities, immediate struggle on local issues and political demands, legal and illegal organization, culminating in the organization of a general strike, the arming of the masses, and a national insurrection.[43] The revolutionary insurrection was seen as a process, not as an event. The process leading to the insurrection can be divided into three phases.

Phase I: Accumulation of Forces in Silence, 1970–1974

The FSLN, which generally did not act in its own name, engaged in organizing, mobilizing, and agitating in the barrios, trade unions, and schools through intermediate organizations that projected the basis for the organization of popular power. Through these intermediate organizations, the FSLN began to forge links with the mass movement and establish its legitimacy as a representative of the people. In everyday struggles for light, water, and sewers, combined with its organizational demands for political rights, it began to project itself as a national alternative to Somoza. The FSLN's insertion in the strikes and protests following the 1972 earthquake—when the workday for workers was arbitrarily extended, aid funds were pocketed, and businessmen displaced—augmented its importance, especially among the urban working and middle class.

Phase II: Accumulation of Forces with Offensive Tactics, September 1974–August 1978

On September 22, 1974, the FSLN captured a number of high officials in the regime and was able to liberate a substantial number of political prisoners. This action signaled the beginning of a new turn in the struggle, which saw local demands increasingly combined with national political issues: neighborhood issues, with attacks on the dictatorial nature of the state; and trade union rights, with demands for the freeing of political prisoners. A rising wave of mass protests and demonstrations forced the liberal bourgeoisie to augment its pressure on Somoza. With the assassination of *La Prensa* editor Pedro Joaquín Chamorro in January 1978, the bourgeoisie attempted to channel the discontent through a general strike (during which the workers were paid). But the strikes begun by the bourgeoisie passed beyond their control; the incapacity of the bourgeois-led general strike to topple Somoza and their unwillingness to sustain the struggle to the end severely eroded their mass support and hastened the mass exodus toward the FSLN. Throughout this period, mass organization in the cities and guerrilla harassment in the countryside increased.[44]

Phase III: Accumulation of Forces in
Strategic Offensive, September 1978–July 1979

The constant mobilization, conflict, and regime repression created the objective conditions for insurrection. Whole neighborhoods and sectors of the city were openly defiant of the regime; the intermediate organizations welded together in the United People's Movement (MPU) openly recognized the FSLN as its representative leader. The FSLN was converted from a guerrilla organization to a mass one. The Somoza regime was increasingly isolated: the bourgeoisie organized in the Broad Opposition Front (FAO): the liberal democrats, calling themselves The Twelve (Los Doce), were openly calling for the overthrow of Somoza, the disbanding of the National Guard, and a coalition including the FSLN; and the MPU increased its organizational network to virtually every area of the country. While politically vulnerable, Somoza was still militarily strong.

The insurrection of September 1978 was partly spontaneous and partly the result of the initiative of a faction of the Sandinistas (the Tercerista, or Insurrectional, wing). A general strike was called by the MPU following the seizure of the Government Palace by the Terceristas and the uprisings in Matagalpa, uprisings in Monimbó, Masaya, León, Chinandega, and the rest of the major cities and towns.[45] The National Guard and air force destroyed cities, houses, hospitals, and schools in their attempt to drown the insurrection in blood. They failed. The genocidal repression polarized the whole country *against* Somoza and *for* the FSLN. Several strategic tasks faced the FSLN: (1) to unify the three forces, (2) to organize and coordinate the insurrections at the national level, (3) to attack strategic areas affecting the regime, (4) to disperse its forces into several fronts, and (5) to arm the organized local committees in each city.

The strengths and limitations of the September uprising were analyzed. First, within the FSLN there were substantially different conceptions in relation to the political-military strategy—divisions over how to confront the dictatorship—that impeded a unified action. Second, the absence of sufficient arms forced the populace to rely on hunting weapons and handguns, revolvers against tanks. Both issues were resolved first by the unification of the Sandinista tendencies, formally signed in March 1979, and second through a concerted effort to organize and arm popular militias, Comites de Defensa Civil (CDCs), and Comites de Defensa de Trabajadores (CDTs) throughout the major cities. The positive results of the September insurrection were evidenced in the general recognition of the importance of the masses in the military tasks and the centrality of political organization.

The organizational experience prepared the masses for the political administrative tasks in the subsequent uprising in May–July 1979. Finally, tactically, the FSLN leadership recognized that the armed forces of the regime had to be engaged out of the population centers prior to the mass insurrection, to take some of the pressure off and allow breathing space for the local committees and militia to establish themselves. By the beginning of 1979, a new wave of unrest began to grow. In February, there was another uprising in Monimbó (Masaya); continual guerrilla and militia harassment of the National Guard; daily barricades; street demonstrations; and takeovers of churches, buildings, and schools. By May, the barrios were ready to explode once again, only this time the insurrection was organized, the militants were armed, and the FSLN command was unified. Within a month, twenty cities were in the hands of the people.[46]

From the beginning of the insurrection, the local committees took charge in León, Estelí, Masaya, and Matagalpa, areas of large concentrations of workers and with long traditions of militancy and political struggle, both of which weighed heavily in the level of organization. In León and Masaya, the CDTs were transformed into military organizations that organized the seizure of the town and took over the factories, continuing production. In the rest of the country, the CDCs functioned as political-administrative and defense units, sustaining defense, distributing food, and maintaining sanitary conditions.[47]

The FSLN leadership, especially where the GPP (Prolonged Popular War) and Proletarian Tendency predominated, envisioned the CDC and CDT playing a major role in all aspects of the insurrectionary effort. One document described the functions of the CDC: train the masses in all forms of civil defense; create groups of guards to protect and supply the neighborhoods, preventing the activity of anarchistic groups; create food and provision outlets; collect all types of material that serve to defend the barricades; concentrate all material that could serve for defense against punitive actions by the enemy forces; develop clandestine hospitals and clinics; establish operational barracks; collect medicine; orient the masses to recover food from the regime's supply centers; locate the strategic points through which the enemy might advance; create linkage and supply groups with the Sandinista military groups fighting in the barrios; and provide information to the militia and the military forces about the Somoza forces and their supporters.

The CDTs were oriented toward obtaining control of the principal factories, especially strategic ones in order to make them function in the manner of small war industries; taking hold of any and all objects that could be converted into a weapon, making it available to the combatants; maintaining the workers concentrated as a class, linking their revolutionary activity with that of the neighborhood masses; creating obstacles in the strategic transport lines, impeding the enemies' movement; gaining control of the means of communication; paralyzing the public sector and calling on the technicians to provide aid to the combatants; seizing of the haciendas of the Somozas and their supporters and transforming them into refugee centers for non-combatants; and incorporating fighters to the militias or Sandinista army.

The successful insurrection in all the major cities and in eastern Managua reflected the long-term political-organizational work of the FSLN covering the previous decade. Both the formal organizations and the informal networks functioned to bring about complete solidarity between barrio residents and combatants, evidenced in the flood of volunteers, militia units, and the saying that every house was a Sandinista fortress.

Although these mass organizations do not have an explicit class character, the bulk of their membership is drawn from the working class—employees and unemployed. The CDCs and the CDTs could serve as the basis for a new form of popular representation and government. During the insurrection, the interbarrio committees coordinated defense throughout the municipality and could serve as the instrument for popular control over reconstruction.

CONCLUSION

Several features of the revolutionary struggle should be underlined because of their importance not only in the Nicaraguan context, but in terms of future revolutionary struggles in the rest of Latin America.

- The combined guerrilla movement with mass urban insurrectionary organizations were both necessary ingredients to sustain each other's struggle. The previous debates that counterposed one approach to the other were surpassed.
- The urban mass movements, through their organized local power, were able to destroy the standing army located in their cities. The notion of the outdatedness of urban insurrections itself has been demonstrated to be outdated. What was clearly in evidence was the high level of political organization, availability of arms, and the broadest organizational unity.
- The prolonged nature of the struggle was evidenced in the several stages through which it passed and the concomitant shifts in tactics and strategy. The Nicaraguan experience illustrates the fact that revolution is a process requiring the gradual accumulation of forces, punctured by decisive actions that focus on the essential weaknesses of the

regime and mobilize previously uncommitted forces. The flexibility of the revolutionary leadership, reflected in its recognition of the specificities of the issues and problems facing urban/industrial organizations, was necessary in laying the groundwork for mass organization. The fusion of barrio and factory struggles and the dialectical interplay of both clearly demonstrated the critical importance of combining political action at the points of habitation and production. The necessity of combining extralegal and legal struggles provided the military and mass organization necessary to sustain insurrectionary activity. Tactical unity and organizational independence facilitated the maximum application of pressure at critical moments and, at the same time, allowed the revolutionary movement to raise the level of struggle beyond immediate issues to broader systemic problems.

- The insurrectionist activities of the Tercerista faction served to detonate action, while the GPP and Proletarian Tendency organizers laid out the mass organization that sustained the struggle. The *audacity* of the former and the organization of the latter were complementary, each requiring the other to make the revolution succeed.
- The development of the mass movement passed through a stage of bourgeois hegemony, which was undermined by its incapacity to sustain the struggle once the masses were mobilized. The FSLN displaced the FAO between February and September 1978, a period in which the struggle increasingly took the form of mass armed struggle. Having been displaced, however, the bourgeoisie was not eliminated from the scene.
- The self-directed and organized mass organizations evidenced in the uprisings of September 1978 and even more so in May–July 1979 demonstrate that the masses were not looking toward a bourgeois-democratic state dominated by notable personalities, but rather were determined to struggle for a regime that allowed them direct mass participation in the process of transformation.
- The mass organizations that were instruments of struggle against the dictatorship became also the instruments for "reconstruction." As before the revolution, the mass organizations took a leading role in the organization of production and distribution and in the administration of neighborhoods. The Factory Defense Committees, the Civil Defense Committees, and the militia, which were the parallel power to Somoza, came to play an important role to assure that the revolution succeeds.

During the period since the 1979 revolution, the Sandinista government faced numerous obstacles in implementing its revolutionary program directed toward the improvement in the social position of peasants and workers. Above all, the decisive threat to the stability of the revolution came from the U.S.-backed Contra war waged by remnants of the Somoza dictatorship, especially his notorious national guard, financed by U.S. imperialism.[48] The Contra war against the Nicaraguan revolution throughout the 1980s and other machinations of the United States against the Sandinista regime cost thirty thousand lives and upward of $4 billion.[49] The U.S.-backed Contra war devastated the country and subverted the political process through CIA support and funding of opposition political parties to oust the Sandinistas from power in upcoming elections.[50] The continuing U.S. economic embargo imposed on Nicaragua and the growing threat of outright imperialist invasion in the late 1980s forced the Sandinista leadership to give up power to opposition right-wing forces in the elections of 1990 and two subsequent elections in 1996 and 2001, all of which were heavily financed by the United States. Thus, during much of the 1990s and into the early years of the following decade, the United States was able to prolong its hold on Nicaragua through a series of pro-U.S. neoliberal regimes. Although the Sandinistas lost control of the executive branch, they still garnered a substantial percentage of the national vote (nearly half), while maintaining considerable presence and influence on other branches of the government, especially the judiciary and the national assembly. By 2006, they were hard at work to remobilize the masses to regain their lost power; and in the elections of November 2006 the Sandinistas scored a resounding victory and Daniel Ortega was elected president—an event that ushered in a period to transform Nicaragua once again in a socialist direction.[51]

NOTES

1. James O'Connor, *The Origins of Socialism in Cuba* (Ithaca, N.Y.: Cornell University Press, 1970), 22.

2. *Problems of the New Cuba* (New York: Foreign Policy Association, 1935), 54.

3. Charles Page, "The Development of Organized Labor in Cuba," Ph.D. diss., University of California, Berkeley, 1952, 62; Evelio Telleria Toca, *Los Congresos obreros en Cuba* (Havana: Editorial de Arte y Literatura, Instituto Cubano del Libro, 1973), 230 passim. Telleria cites Machado's destruction of the anarchist-controlled Sindicato Fabril as a crucial element in its decline.

4. Paradoxically, one of the outcomes of the defeat of the social revolutionary movement was the deliberate effort by Batista after 1935 to cultivate working-class organizations that would mediate the struggles in a fashion to contain them within capitalist state structures.

5. Fabio Grobart, "The Cuban Working Class Movement from 1925 to 1933," *Science and Society* 34, no. 1 (Spring 1975): 86. See also Mirtz Resell, *Luchas obreras contra Machado* (Havana: n.p., 1973); José Tabares del Real, *La Revolución del 30: Sus dos últimos años* (Havana: n.p., 1971); Lionel Soto, *La Revolución del 33*, 3 vols. (Havana: Editorial Ciencias Sociales, 1977).

6. Toca, *Los Congresos*, 235.

7. Toca, *Los Congresos*, 201–2.

8. Toca, *Los Congresos*, 202.

9. O'Connor, *Origins of Socialism in Cuba*, 27.

10. International Bank for Reconstruction and Development (IBRD), *Economic and Technical Mission, Report on Cuba* (Washington, D.C., 1951), 357. See also International Co-operation Administration, Office of Labor Affairs, U.S. Department of Labor, *Summary of the Labor Situation in Cuba* (Washington, D.C.: Government Printing Office, 1956), 1–3.

11. IBRD, *Report on Cuba*, 361.

12. U.S. Consul Lee R. Blohm to Department of State, March 15, 1934, in *Cuba Labor Notes*, U.S. Archives.

13. *El recibimiento al Corononel Batista* (Havana: Partido Comunista, 1938).

14. Carta del Coronel Batista a Pepin Rivero (Havana, May 25, 1940).

15. Page, "Development of Organized Labor in Cuba," 89 passim.

16. Memo from Laurence Duggan, U.S. embassy in Havana, to Department of State, Division of Latin American Affairs, August 19, 1936.

17. C.T.C. Secretaria Financias, *Balance General 1943* (Havana: Editorial CENIT, 1944).

18. Informe rendido al día 2 de diciembre 1944, IV Congreso Nacional de la CTC.

19. Lazaro Pena, *El Proletariado, las huelgas y la lucha contra el nazismo* (Havana, 1943). The clearest expression of the collaborationists' perspective is found in "La Colaboración nacional entre obreros y patronas," *CTC* 61 (March 1945): 14–15.

20. U.S. Embassy Report, *The Communist Party in Cuba*, March 1947.

21. Page, "Development of Organized Labor in Cuba," 96.

22. Page, "Development of Organized Labor in Cuba," 217.

23. Page, "Development of Organized Labor in Cuba," 121.

24. O'Connor, *Origins of Socialism in Cuba*, 18–19.

25. IBRD, *Report on Cuba*, 358.

26. Page, "Development of Organized Labor in Cuba," 128.

27. Page, "Development of Organized Labor in Cuba," 218.

28. Page, "Development of Organized Labor in Cuba," 223.

29. Interview with Eusebio Mujal, April 11, 1979.

30. Interview with Eusebio Mujal.

31. Interview with Eusebio Mujal.

32. *El Rodante*, September 1952, 1–2.

33. *El Rodante*, August 1954, 7–8.

34. *New York Times*, June 10, 1957, 10.

35. *Verde Olivo*, no. 17, July 10, 1960, 28–29.

36. *Verde Olivo*, July 17, 1960, 15.

37. *Verde Olivo*, November 12, 1960, 8.

38. George Black, *Triumph of the People: The Sandinista Revolution in Nicaragua* (London: Zed Books, 1982).

39. Black, *Triumph of the People*.

40. Thomas Walker, *Nicaragua in Revolution* (New York: Praeger, 1982).

41. Walker, *Nicaragua in Revolution*.

42. Morris H. Morley, *Washington, Somoza and the Sandinistas: State and Regime in U.S. Policy toward Nicaragua 1969–1981* (London: Cambridge University Press, 2002).

43. Black, *Triumph of the People*.

44. Walker, *Nicaragua in Revolution*. See also John Booth, *The End and the Beginning: The Nicaraguan Revolution*, 2nd ed. (Boulder, Colo.: Westview, 1985).

45. Black, *Triumph of the People*.

46. Booth, *The End and the Beginning*.

47. Booth, *The End and the Beginning*.

48. Holly Sklar, *Washington's War on Nicaragua* (Boston: South End, 1988). See also Thomas Walker, *Reagan versus the Sandinistas: The Undeclared War on Nicaragua* (Boulder, Colo.: Westview, 1987).

49. John Foran and Jeff Goodwin, "Dictatorship or Democracy: Outcomes of Revolution in Iran and Nicaragua," in *Revolutions: Theoretical, Comparative, and Historical Studies*, ed. Jack A. Goldstone (Belmont, Calif.: Wadsworth/Thomson Learning, 2003), 116.

50. See Dévora Grynspan, "Nicaragua: A New Model for Popular Revolution in Latin America," in *Revolutions of the Late Twentieth Century*, ed. Jack A. Goldstone, Ted Robert Gurr, and Farrokh Moshiri (Boulder, Colo.: Westview, 1991). See also Eric Selbin, *Modern Latin American Revolutions*, 2nd ed. (Boulder, Colo.: Westview, 1999).

51. The final paragraph of this chapter was written by Berch Berberoglu to update developments in Nicaragua from the early 1980s (when this chapter was originally published) to the present (late 2006).

Conclusion

The twentieth century was a century of revolution. The major socialist revolutions of our time all occurred in the twentieth century. The Russian, Chinese, Vietnamese, Cuban, and Nicaraguan revolutions—the most prominent socialist revolutions of the twentieth century—were examined in this book to show the complexities of the revolutionary process: the class nature of the revolutionary movement (its class base, leadership, and political objectives), the mass mobilization of the people for revolutionary action, the protracted class struggles laying the basis for political power, and the strategy and tactics that define the balance of class forces in revolutionary situations, as well as the role and response of the state, the reaction of the dominant classes, and the measures taken by the repressive institutions of society to maintain the prevailing social-political order. Taken together, these and related factors determine the nature and prospects of revolution and whether a revolutionary situation will actually develop into a full-fledged revolution that brings about a complete social transformation.

In this context, it is important to differentiate a political revolution from a social revolution, for while the former may bring about change in government and political structure of society, only the latter brings about a complete transformation of society and its social (class) structure. The transformation of the class structure of society thus requires a social revolution that involves the overthrow of one class by another and the transfer of power to the new victorious class that has succeeded in taking state power. Thus, while the 1905 and February 1917 revolutions in Russia were political revolutions, the Great Proletarian Socialist Revolution of October

1917 was a social revolution that completely transformed the social relations of production in Russia, replacing the tsarist semifeudal/semicapital-
ist system with a proletarian socialist one. The same can be said of the two
Chinese revolutions of the twentieth century: the revolution of 1911 was a
political revolution with a bourgeois orientation that was unable to transform the old despotic semifeudal state into a capitalist one; whereas the October 1949 revolution, led by Mao and the Communists, was a social revolution that transformed a semifeudal/semicapitalist society into a socialist
one. Among the other cases taken up for study, the Vietnamese and Cuban
revolutions were eventually able to achieve similar ends, while the
Nicaraguan revolution remained incomplete and was forced to retreat due
to the U.S.-backed Contra war that paralyzed its transformative features.

In examining the experience of these major socialist revolutions and the
subsequent evolution of the new postrevolutionary states over the course of
their development along the socialist path, one observes a number of features that are of decisive importance for future socialist revolutions that are
yet to come. The first is the centrality of proletarian leadership. The working-
class movement (and its leading organ, the Communist Party) has always
maintained that the struggle against capitalism and the capitalist state must
be based on the broad participation of the laboring masses led by a workers'
party that will guide the process of transition from capitalism to socialism.
On this score, most major socialist revolutions of the twentieth century were
quite successful, especially the Russian, Chinese, and Vietnamese revolutions, but to a great extent the Cuban and Nicaraguan revolutions as well.

The second, and equally important, is the level of commitment and support for the revolutionary organization and its leadership that is at the helm
of the revolutionary movement. This implies the existence of a high level of
class consciousness and ideological discourse, accompanied by democratic
practices among members of the movement at its social base, and between
the base and the leadership of the organization. This is of crucial importance because the structure and practices of a revolutionary organization in
the prerevolutionary period determine to a great extent the nature of leadership and forms of governance after the revolutionary organization has assumed power and governs in the name of the people. The experience of Russia and China, as well as Vietnam, and especially Cuba and Nicaragua,
show how important this is for the future prospects of a revolution. Without the commitment and support of the masses, there would be no revolution or a revolutionary movement to lay claim to a successful revolution.

The third and perhaps the most decisive thing for the success of a revolution is the nature of the postrevolutionary state and society and its relationship to the people. In the case of a socialist revolution, this involves the
application of proletarian principles to the cultivation of socialist (people's)
democracy—a process that requires the ongoing ideological vigilance of

both the state and the people. The viability of a socialist revolution in the postrevolutionary period thus depends on the extent to which a genuine socialist democracy is cultivated and maintained. The failure of a socialist state to actively engage the masses in this process of socialist construction may well lead to the demise of the socialist order. Whereas the revolutions in China and Cuba, and to a great extent in Vietnam and Nicaragua, succeeded quite well in this regard through continued ideological struggle and renewal, this was not the case in the Soviet Union and Eastern Europe, where the socialist state failed to provide the necessary stimulus for mass participation in ideological education—to understand, to protect, and to preserve the socialist order and to build the basis of a future communist society. It is this grand failure of the Soviet state to energize the masses and enlist their will in defense of socialism and communism that finally led to its collapse in the face of internal and external reaction to crush the socialist state in the final decade of the twentieth century.

The modest contribution made by this book toward the study of the major socialist revolutions of the past century is hoped to provide a broader understanding of the twists and turns of the revolutionary process and a heightened understanding of the dynamics of socialist revolutions that are yet to come in the twenty-first century.

Bibliography

Aguilar, Luis. 1972. *Cuba 1933: Prologue to Revolution*. Ithaca, N.Y.: Cornell University Press.

Alavi, Hamza. 1965. "Peasants and Revolution." In *The Socialist Register 1965*. London: Merlin.

Althusser, Louis. 1978. "What Must Change in the Party." *New Left Review* 109 (May–June).

Anderson, Perry. 1974. *Lineages of the Absolutist State*. London: New Left Books.

———. 1974. *Passages from Antiquity to Feudalism*. London: New Left Books.

Anonymous. 1976. *Brief History of the Vietnam Workers' Party 1930–1975*. Hanoi: n.p.

Aptheker, Herbert. 1960. *The American Revolution, 1763–1783*. New York: International Publishers.

———. 1976. *Early Years of the Republic*. New York: International Publishers.

Arendt, Hanna. 1965. *On Revolution*. New York: Viking.

Ash, Timothy Garton. 1990. *We the People: The Revolutions of '89 Witnessed in Warsaw, Budapest, Berlin, and Prague*. Hammondsworth, U.K.: Penguin.

Avineri, Shlomo. 1972. *Hegel's Theory of the Modern State*. Cambridge: Cambridge University Press.

Aya, Rod. 1979. "Theories of Revolution Reconsidered: Contrasting Models of Collective Violence." *Theory and Society* 8.

Balibar, Etienne. 1977. *On the Dictatorship of the Proletariat*. London: New Left Books.

Bambirra, Vania. 1978. *La Revolución cubana*. Mexico City: Nuestro Tiempo.

Banac, Ivo. 1992. *Eastern Europe in Revolution*. Ithaca, N.Y.: Cornell University Press.

Baran, Paul. 1957. *The Political Economy of Growth*. New York: Monthly Review Press.

Bell, David V. J. 1973. *Resistance and Revolution*. Boston: Houghton Mifflin.

Belov, Gennady. 1986. *What Is the State?* Moscow: Progress.

Belden, Jack. 1949. *China Shakes the World*. New York: Harper.

Berberoglu, Berch. 1994. *Class Structure and Social Transformation*. Westport, Conn.: Praeger.

———. 2001. *Political Sociology: A Comparative/Historical Approach*. 2nd ed. Boulder, Colo.: Rowman & Littlefield.

———. 2003. *Globalization of Capital and the Nation-State*. Boulder, Colo.: Rowman & Littlefield.

———. 2004. *Nationalism and Ethnic Conflict: Class, State, and Nation in the Age of Globalization*. Boulder, Colo.: Rowman & Littlefield.

Bettelheim, Charles. 1976. *Class Struggles in the USSR: First Period, 1917–1923*. New York: Monthly Review Press.

———. 1978. *Class Struggles in the USSR: Second Period, 1923–1930*. New York: Monthly Review Press.

———. 1978. "The Great Leap Backward." Monthly Review 30, no. 3 (July–August).

Bianco, Lucien. 1971. *The Origins of the Chinese Revolution, 1915–1949*. Stanford, Calif.: Stanford University Press.

Black, George. 1982. *Triumph of the People: The Sandinista Revolution in Nicaragua*. London: Zed Books.

Blackburn, Robin, ed. 1977. *Revolution and Class Struggle*. Atlantic Highlands, N.J.: Humanities Press.

Block, Fred. 1977. "The Ruling Class Does Not Rule: Notes on the Marxist Theory of the State." *Socialist Review* 33 (May–June).

Booth, John. 1985. *The End and the Beginning: The Nicaraguan Revolution*. 2nd ed. Boulder, Colo.: Westview.

Borkenau, Franz. 1937. "State and Revolution in the Paris Commune, the Russian Revolution, and the Spanish Civil War." *Sociological Review* 29, no. 41: 41–75.

Borón, Atilio. 1995. *State, Capitalism, and Democracy in Latin America*. Boulder, Colo.: Rienner.

Bottomore, T. B. 1966. *Elites and Society*. Baltimore: Penguin.

Bunyan, James, and H. H. Fisher. 1974. *The Bolshevik Revolution 1917–1918*. Stanford, Calif.: Stanford University Press.

Buttinger, Joseph. 1972. *A Dragon Defiant*. New York: Praeger.

Calvert, Peter. 1970. *A Study of Revolution*. New York: Oxford University Press.

Carnoy, Martin. 1984. *The State and Political Theory*. Princeton, N.J.: Princeton University Press.

Carr, Edward Hallett. 1950. *The Bolshevik Revolution, 1917–1923*. 3 vols. New York: Norton.

———. 1952–1958. *History of Soviet Russia*. Vols. 2, 4, and 5. New York: Macmillan.

———. 1958–1959. *Socialism in One Country*. Vols. 1 and 2. London: Macmillan.

Chaliand, Gerard. 1977. *Revolution in the Third World: Myths and Prospects*. Trans. Diana Johnstone. New York: Viking.

Chamberlin, William Henry. 1965. *The Russian Revolution 1917–1921*. 2 vols. New York: Grosset & Dunlap.

Chesneaux, Jean. 1968. *The Chinese Labor Movement 1919–1927*. Stanford, Calif.: Stanford University Press.

———. 1973. *Peasant Revolts in China, 1840–1947*. New York: Norton.

Chirot, Daniel. 1977. *Social Change in the Twentieth Century*. New York: Harcourt Brace Jovanovich.

———. 1995. "After Socialism, What? The Global Implications of the Revolutions of 1989 in Eastern Europe." In *Debating Revolutions*, ed. Nikki R. Keddie. New York: New York University Press.

Clarke, S. 1977. "Marxism, Sociology and Poulantzas's Theory of the State." *Capital and Class 2.*

Claudin, Fernando. 1975. *The Communist Movement: From Comintern to Cominform.* New York: Monthly Review Press.

Cohan, A. S. 1975. *Theories of Revolution.* London: Nelson.

Colletti, Lucio. 1977. "The Question of Stalin." In *Revolution and Class Struggle*, ed. Robin Blackburn. Atlantic Highlands, N.J.: Humanities Press.

Copleston, Frederick. 1994. *A History of Philosophy.* Vol. 7. New York: Doubleday Image.

Davies, J. C. 1962. "Toward a Theory of Revolution." *American Sociological Review* 27: 5–19.

DeFronzo, James. 1996. *Revolutions and Revolutionary Movements.* 2nd ed. Boulder, Colo.: Westview.

Deutscher, Isaac. 1949, *Stalin: A Political Biography.* New York: Oxford University Press.

———. 1977. "Maoism: Its Origins and Outlook." In *Revolution and Class Struggle*, ed. Robin Blackburn. Atlantic Highlands, N.J.: Humanities Press.

———. 1959. *The Prophet Unarmed.* London: Oxford University Press.

Diamond, M. D. 1998. *Women and Revolution: Global Expressions.* Dordrecht, Netherlands: Kluwer.

Dobb, Maurice. 1948. *Soviet Economic Development since 1917.* London: Routledge & Kegan Paul.

———. 1954. "The Soviet Economy: Fact and Fiction," *Science and Society* (Spring).

Dominguez, Jorge. 1978. *Cuba: Order and Revolution.* Cambridge, Mass.: Harvard University Press.

Draper, Hal. 1977. *Karl Marx's Theory of Revolution: State and Bureaucracy.* Parts 1 and 2. New York: Monthly Review Press.

Duiker, William. 1976. *The Rise of Nationalism in Vietnam, 1900–1941.* Ithaca, N.Y.: Cornell University Press.

———. 1995. *Sacred War: Nationalism and Revolution in a Divided Vietnam.* New York: McGraw-Hill.

Dung, Van Tien. 1977. *Our Great Spring Victory.* New York: Monthly Review Press.

Dunn, John. 1989. *Modern Revolutions: An Introduction to the Analysis of a Political Phenomenon.* 2nd ed. Cambridge: Cambridge University Press.

Eckstein, Susan E. 1980. "Capitalist Constraints on Cuban Socialist Development." *Comparative Politics* 12, no. 3: 253–74.

———. 1986. "The Impact of the Cuban Revolution: A Comparative Perspective." *Comparative Studies in Society and History* 28: 502–34.

Eisenstadt, S. N. 1978. *Revolution and the Transformation of Societies: A Comparative Study of Civilizations.* New York: Free Press.

Engels, Frederick. 1972. "Ludwig Feuerbach and the End of Classical German Philosophy." In Karl Marx and Frederick Engels, *Selected Works.* New York: International Publishers.

———. 1972. *The Origin of the Family, Private Property and the State.* New York: International Publishers.

——. 1976. *Anti-Duhring*. New York: International Publishers.

Erlich, Alexander. 1960. *The Soviet Industrialization Debate*. Cambridge, Mass.: Harvard University Press.

Eyal, Gil. 2003. *The Origins of Postcommunist Elites: From Prague Spring to the Breakup of Czechoslovakia*. Minneapolis: University of Minnesota Press.

Fanon, Frantz. 1963. *The Wretched of the Earth*. New York: Grove.

Fitzgerald, Francis. 1972. *Fire in the Lake: The Vietnamese and the Americans in Vietnam*. New York: Vintage Books.

Fitzpatrick, Sheila. 1994. *The Russian Revolution*. Oxford: Oxford University Press.

Foran, John, ed. 1997. *Theorizing Revolutions*. London: Routledge.

——. 2003. *The Future of Revolutions: Rethinking Radical Change in the Age of Globalization*. London: Zed Books.

Foran, John, and Jeff Goodwin. 2003. "Dictatorship or Democracy: Outcomes of Revolution in Iran and Nicaragua." In *Revolutions: Theoretical, Comparative, and Historical Studies*, ed. Jack A. Goldstone. Belmont, Calif.: Wadsworth/Thomson Learning.

Frank, Andre Gunder. 1969. *Capitalism and Underdevelopment in Latin America*. New York: Monthly Review Press.

Friedrich, C. J., ed. 1953. *The Philosophy of Hegel*. New York: Modern Library.

——. 1966. *Revolution*. New York: Atherton.

Gerschenkron, Alexander. 1951. *A Dollar Index of Soviet Machinery Output, 1927–28 to 1937*. Los Angeles: Rand Corporation.

——. 1962. *Economic Backwardness in Historical Perspective*. Cambridge, Mass.: Belknap Press of Harvard University Press.

Geschwender, James A. 1968. "Explorations in the Theory of Social Movements and Revolutions." *Social Forces* 42, no. 2: 127–35.

Gettleman, Marvin, et al., eds. 1995. *Vietnam and America: The Most Comprehensive History of the Vietnam War*. Rev. and enlarged 2nd ed. New York: Grove.

Giap, Vo Nguyen. 1995. "The Political and Military Line of Our Party." In *Vietnam and America: The Most Comprehensive History of the Vietnam War*, ed. Marvin Gettleman et al., rev. and enlarged 2nd ed. New York: Grove.

Goldstone, Jack A. 1980. "Theories of Revolution: The Third Generation." *World Politics* 32: 425–53.

——. 1982. "The Comparative and Historical Study of Revolutions." *Annual Review of Sociology* 8: 187–207.

——. 1998. *The Encyclopedia of Political Revolutions*. Washington, D.C.: Congressional Quarterly Press.

——. 2003. *Revolutions: Theoretical, Comparative, and Historical Studies*. Belmont, Calif.: Wadsworth/Thomson Learning.

——. 2003. *States, Parties, and Social Movements*. New York: Cambridge University Press.

Goldstone, Jack A., Ted Robert Gurr, and Farrokh Moshiri, eds. 1991. *Revolutions of the Late Twentieth Century*. Boulder, Colo.: Westview.

Goodwin, Jeff. 2003. "The Renewal of Socialism and the Decline of Revolution." In *The Future of Revolutions: Rethinking Radical Change in the Age of Globalization*, ed. John Foran. London: Zed Books.

Gottschalk, Louis. 1944. "Causes of Revolution." *American Journal of Sociology* 50, no. 1 (July): 1–8.

Gramsci, Antonio. 1971. *Prison Notebooks*. New York: International Publishers.

———. 1978. *Selections from Political Writings 1921–26*. London: Lawrence & Wishart.

Greene, Thomas H. 1974. *Comparative Revolutionary Movements*. Englewood Cliffs, N.J.: Prentice Hall.

Grobart, Fabio. 1975. "The Cuban Working Class Movement from 1925 to 1933." *Science and Society* 34, no. 1 (Spring).

Gross, Feliks. 1974. *The Revolutionary Party: Essays in the Sociology of Politics*. Westport, Conn.: Greenwood.

Grynspan, Dévora. 1991. "Nicaragua: A New Model for Popular Revolution in Latin America." In *Revolutions of the Late Twentieth Century*, ed. Jack A. Goldstone, Ted Robert Gurr, and Farrokh Moshiri. Boulder, Colo.: Westview.

Guevara, Che. 1966. *Episodes of the Revolutionary War*. Havana: Book Institute.

Gurley, John G. 1976. *Challengers to Capitalism*. San Francisco: San Francisco Book.

Gurr, T. R. 1970. *Why Men Rebel*. Princeton, N.J.: Princeton University Press.

Hagopian, Mark N. 1974. *The Phenomenon of Revolution*. New York: Dodd, Mead.

Halliday, Fred. 1999. *Revolution and World Politics: The Rise and Fall of the Sixth Great Power*. Durham, N.C.: Duke University Press.

Hatto, Arthur. 1949. "'Revolution': An Inquiry into the Usefulness of an Historical Term." *Mind* 58, no. 229 (January): 495–517.

Hegel, G. W. F. 1929. *Selections*, ed. J. Loewenberg. New York: n.p.

Hegel, G. W. F. 1942. *Philosophy of Right*. Oxford: Knox.

Hémery, Daniel. 1975. *Revolutionnaires vietnamiens et pouvoir colonial en Indochine*. Paris: Maspero.

Herring, George C. 1996. *America's Longest War: The United States and Vietnam, 1950–1975*. 3rd ed. New York: McGraw-Hill.

Hilton, Rodney, ed. 1976. *The Transition from Feudalism to Capitalism*. London: New Left Books.

Hinton, William. 1966. *Fanshen: A Documentary of Revolution in a Chinese Village*. New York: Vintage Books.

Hirsh, Joachim. 1979. "The State Apparatus and Social Reproduction: Elements of a Theory of the Bourgeois State." In *State and Capital: A Marxist Debate*, ed. John Holloway and Sol Picciotto. Austin: University of Texas Press.

Hobsbawm, Eric J. 1965. *Primitive Rebels: Studies in the Archaic Forms of Social Movement in the Nineteenth and Twentieth Centuries*. New York: Norton.

———. 1995. *The Age of Extremes, 1914–1991*. New York: Pantheon.

Ho Chi Minh. 1977. *Selected Writings*. Hanoi: Foreign Languages Publishing House.

———. 1995. "The Path Which Led Me to Lenin." In *Vietnam and America: The Most Comprehensive History of the Vietnam War*, ed. Marvin Gettleman et al., rev. and enlarged 2nd ed. New York: Grove.

Holloway, John, and Sol Picciotto. 1977. "Capital, Crisis and the State." *Capital and Class 2*.

———. 1978. "Introduction: Towards a Marxist Theory of the State." In *State and Capital: A Marxist Debate*, ed. John Holloway and Sol Picciotto. London: Arnold.

Huberman, Leo, and Paul Sweezy. 1961. *Cuba: Anatomy of a Revolution*. New York: Monthly Review Press.

Isaacs, Harold. 1961. *The Tragedy of the Chinese Revolution*. 2nd rev. ed. Stanford, Calif.: Stanford University Press.

Jamieson, Neil L. 1995. *Understanding Vietnam*. Berkeley: University of California Press.

Jessop, Bob. 1982. *The Capitalist State*. New York: New York University Press.

Johnson, Chalmers. 1962. *Peasant Nationalism and Communist Power*. Stanford, Calif.: Stanford University Press.

———. 1964. *Revolution and the Social System*. Stanford, Calif.: Hoover Institution, Stanford University.

Kagarlitsky, Boris. 2002. *Russia under Yeltsin and Putin*. London: Pluto.

Karnow, Stanley. 1991. *Vietnam: A History*. New York: Penguin Books.

Katz, Mark N. 1997. *Revolutions and Revolutionary Waves*. New York: St. Martin's.

———, ed. 2001. *Revolution: International Dimensions*. Washington, D.C.: Congressional Quarterly Press.

Kaufmann, Walter, ed. 1970. *Hegel's Political Philosophy*. New York: Atherton.

Keddie, Nikki R. 1981. *Roots of Revolution*. New Haven, Conn.: Yale University Press.

———, ed. 1995. *Debating Revolutions*. New York: New York University Press.

Kennedy, Paul. 1987. *The Rise and Fall of the Great Powers*. New York: Random House.

Kenner, Martin, and James Petras, eds. 1970. *Fidel Castro Speaks*. London: Lane.

Kolko, Gabriel. 1968. *The Politics of War*. New York: Random House.

Kolko, Gabriel, and Joyce Kolko. 1976. *The Limits of Power*. New York: Harper & Row.

Krader, Lawrence. 1975. *The Asiatic Mode of Production*. Assem: Van Gorcum.

Kramnick, Isaac. 1972. "Reflections on Revolution: Definition and Explanation in Recent Scholarship." *History and Theory* 11, no. 1: 26–63.

Kumar, Krishan. 1971. *Revolution: The Theory and Practice of a European Idea*. London: Weidenfeld & Nicholson.

———. 1992. "The Revolutions of 1989: Socialism, Capitalism, and Democracy." *Theory and Society* 21.

Le Duan. 1970. *The Vietnamese Revolution: Fundamental Problems, Essential Tasks*. Hanoi: Foreign Languages Publishing House.

Lenin, V. I. 1947. *Works*. Vol. 31. Moscow: Foreign Languages Publishing House.

———. 1971. *Selected Works*. New York: International Publishers.

———. 1971. "The Three Sources and Three Component Parts of Marxism." In V. I. Lenin, *Selected Works in One Volume*. New York: International Publishers.

———. 1974. *The State*. In Karl Marx, Frederick Engels, and V. I. Lenin, *On Historical Materialism*. New York: International Publishers.

———. 1975. *The State and Revolution*. In V. I. Lenin, *Selected Works in Three Volumes*. Vol. 2. Moscow: Progress.

Lewin, Moshe. 1968. *Russian Peasants and Soviet Power*. New York: Norton.

———. 1969. *Lenin's Last Struggle*. New York: Monthly Review Press.

Liebman, Marcel. 1975. *Leninism under Lenin*. London: Cape.

Li Fu-Chun. 1950. *Report on the First Five-Year Plan of Development*. Peking: Foreign Languages Press.

Magri, Lucio. 1970. "Problems of the Marxist Theory of the Revolutionary Party." *New Left Review* 60 (March–April).

Maitan, Livio. 1976. *Party, Army, and Masses in China*. Atlantic Highlands, N.J.: Humanities Press.

Mandel, Ernest. 1975. *Late Capitalism*. London: New Left Books.

———. 1977. "The Leninist Theory of Organization." In *Revolution and Class Struggle*, ed. Robin Blackburn. Atlantic Highlands, N.J.: Humanities Press.

———. 1979. *From Class Society to Communism*. London: Ink Links.

Mao Zedong. 1971. "On the Question of Agricultural Cooperatives." In *Selected Readings from the Works of Mao Tse-tung*. Peking: Foreign Languages Press.

——. 1971. "China's Path to Industrialization." Part 12 of "On the Correct Handling of Contradictions among the People." In *Selected Readings from the Works of Mao Tse-tung*. Peking: Foreign Languages Press.

Marcuse, Herbert. 1941. *Reason and Revolution: Hegel and the Rise of Social Theory*. New York: Oxford University Press.

Marger, Martin N. 1987. *Elites and Masses: An Introduction to Political Sociology*. 2nd ed. Belmont, Calif.: Wadsworth.

Markoff, John. 1996. *Waves of Democracy: Social Movements and Political Change*. Thousand Oaks, Calif.: Pine Forge.

Marquit, Erwin. 1968. *The Eighteenth Brumaire of Louis Bonaparte*. In Karl Marx and Frederick Engels, *Selected Works*. New York: International Publishers.

——. 1972. *The Civil War in France*. In Karl Marx and Frederick Engels, *Selected Works*. New York: International Publishers.

——. 1978. *The Socialist Countries*. Minneapolis: MEP Press.

Marx, Karl. 1965. *Pre-Capitalist Economic Formations*. New York: International Publishers.

——. 1972. *Critique of the Gotha Programme*. In Karl Marx and Frederick Engels, *Selected Works*. New York: International Publishers.

Marx, Karl, and Frederick Engels. 1972. "Manifesto of the Communist Party." In Karl Marx and Frederick Engels, *Selected Works*. New York: International Publishers.

McAlister, John T. 1969. *Vietnam: The Origins of Revolution*. New York: Knopf.

McDaniel, Tim. 2003. "The Russian Revolution of 1917: Autocracy and Modernization." In *Revolutions: Theoretical, Comparative, and Historical Studies*, ed. Jack A. Goldstone. Belmont, Calif.: Wadsworth/Thomson Learning.

McMichael, Philip. 2004. *Development and Social Change: A Global Perspective*. 3rd ed. Thousand Oaks, Calif.: Sage.

Medvedev, Roy. 1971. *Let History Judge*. New York: Knopf.

Michels, Robert. 1968. *Political Parties*. New York: Free Press.

Miliband, Ralph. 1969. *The State in Capitalist Society*. New York: Basic Books.

——. 1977. *Marxism and Politics*. London: Oxford University Press.

Miller, Norman, and Roderick Aya. 1971. *National Liberation: Revolution in the Third World*. New York: Free Press.

Moore, Barrington, Jr. 1950. *Soviet Politics: The Dilemma of Power*. Cambridge, Mass.: Harvard University Press.

——. 1966. *The Social Origins of Dictatorship and Democracy*. Boston: Beacon.

Morley, Morris H. 2002. *Washington, Somoza and the Sandinistas: State and Regime in U.S. Policy toward Nicaragua 1969–1981*. London: Cambridge University Press.

Mosca, Gaetano. 1939. *The Ruling Class*. New York: McGraw-Hill.

McNamara, Robert. 1995. *In Retrospect: The Tragedy and Lessons of Vietnam*. New York: Random House.

Nelson, Lowry. 1950. *Rural Cuba*. Minneapolis: University of Minnesota Press.

O'Connor, James. 1970. *The Origins of Socialism in Cuba*. Ithaca, N.Y.: Cornell University Press.

Offe, Claus. 1974. "Structural Problems of the Capitalist State." In *German Political Studies*, ed. K. Von Beyme. Vol. 1. London: Sage.

———. 1975. "The Theory of the Capitalist State and the Problem of Policy Formation." In *Stress and Contradiction in Modern Capitalism*, ed. L. Lindberg et al. Lexington, Mass.: Heath.

Olson, James S., and Randy Roberts. 1991. *Where the Domino Fell: America and Vietnam, 1945 to 1990*. New York: St. Martin's.

Page, Charles. 1952. "The Development of Organized Labor in Cuba." Ph.D. diss., University of California, Berkeley.

Parenti, Michael. 1994. *Democracy for the Few*. 6th ed. New York: St. Martin's.

Pareto, Vilfredo. 1935. *The Mind and Society*. 4 vols. London: Cape.

———. 1969. "Elites and Their Circulation." In *Structured Social Inequality*, ed. C. S. Heller. New York: Macmillan.

Parsons, Talcott. 1967. "On the Concept of Political Power." In T. Parsons, *Sociological Theory and Modern Society*. New York: Free Press.

Perez-Stable, Marifeli. 1999. *The Cuban Revolution: Origins, Course, and Legacy*. 2nd ed. New York: Oxford University Press.

Perry, Elizabeth, and Li Xun. 1997. *Poletarian Power: Shanghai in the Cultural Revolution*. Boulder, Colo.: Westview.

Petras, James. 1978. "Toward a Theory of Twentieth Century Socialist Revolutions." *Journal of Contemporary Asia* 3.

———. 1981. *Class, State, and Power in the Third World*. Montclair, N.J.: Allanheld Osmun.

———. 1983. *Capitalist and Socialist Crises in the Late Twentieth Century*. Montclair, N.J.: Allanheld Osmun.

Phang Thang Son. 1971. "Le Movement ouvrier vietnamien de 1920 à 1930." In *Tradition et révolution au Vietnam*, ed. Jean Chesneaux, Georges Boudarel, and Daniel Hémery. Paris: Anthropos.

Picciotto, Sol. 1979. "The Theory of the State, Class Struggle, and the Rule of Law." In *Capitalism and the Rule of Law*, ed. Ben Fine et al. London: Hutchinson.

Poggi, Gianfranco. 1978. *The Development of the Modern State*. Stanford, Calif.: Stanford University Press.

———. 1990. *The State: Its Nature, Development, and Prospects*. Stanford, Calif.: Stanford University Press.

Polanyi, Karl. 1944. *The Great Transformation: The Political and Economic Origins of Our Time*. Reprint 1957. Boston: Beacon.

Popper, Karl, R. 1950. *The Open Society and Its Enemies*. Princeton, N.J.: Princeton University Press.

Post, Ken. 1989. *Revolution, Socialism and Nationalism in Viet Nam*. Vol. 1: *An Interrupted Revolution*. Aldershot, U.K.: Dartmouth.

Poulantzas, Nicos. 1969. "The Problem of the Capitalist State." *New Left Review* 58.

———. 1973. *Political Power and Social Classes*. London: Verso.

———. 1978. *State, Power, Socialism*. London: Verso.

Quoc Viet, Hoang. 1960. *Short History of the Vietnamese Workers' and Trade Union Movement*. Hanoi: Foreign Languages Publishing House.

Rabinowitch, Alexander. 1976. *The Bolsheviks Come to Power*. New York: Norton.

Resell, Mertz. 1973. *Luchas obreras contra Machado*. Havana: n.p.

Rousset, Pierre. 1975. *Le Parti Communiste vietnamien*. 2nd ed. Paris: Maspero.

Ruiz, Ramon Eduardo. 1968. *Cuba: The Making of a Revolution*. New York: Norton.

Sacks, I. Milton. N.d. "Communism and Nationalism in Vietnam." Ph.D. diss., Yale University.

Salert, Barbara. 1976. *Revolutions and Revolutionaries: Four Theories.* New York: Elsevier.

Sanderson, Stephen K. 2005. *Revolutions: A Worldwide Introduction to Political and Social Change.* Boulder, Colo.: Paradigm.

Saville, John. 1995. *The Consolidation of the Capitalist State, 1800–1850.* London: Pluto.

Schrecker, John E. 2004. *The Chinese Revolution in Historical Perspective.* 2nd ed. Westport, Conn.: Praeger.

Schwartz, Benjamin. 1971. *Chinese Communism and the Rise of Mao.* Cambridge, Mass.: Harvard University Press.

Selbin, Eric. 1999. *Modern Latin American Revolutions.* 2nd ed. Boulder, Colo.: Westview.

Selden, Mark. 1974. *The Yenan Way in Revolutionary China.* Cambridge, Mass.: Harvard University Press.

——. 1979. *The People's Republic of China: A Documentary History of Revolutionary Change.* New York: Monthly Review Press.

——. 2003. "The Chinese Communist Revolution." In *Revolutions: Theoretical, Comparative, and Historical Studies,* ed. Jack A. Goldstone. Belmont, Calif.: Wadsworth/Thomson Learning.

Selznik, Philip. 1952. *The Organizational Weapon: A Study of Bolshevik Strategy and Tactics.* New York: McGraw-Hill.

Sheehan, Neil. 1988. *A Bright Shining Lie: John Paul Vann and America in Vietnam.* New York: Random House.

Sklar, Holly. 1988. *Washington's War on Nicaragua.* Boston: South End.

Skocpol, Theda. 1979. *States and Social Revolutions: A Comparative Analysis of France, Russia, and China.* New York: Cambridge University Press.

——. 1994. *Social Revolutions in the Modern World.* Cambridge: Cambridge University Press.

Skocpol, Theda, and Ellen Kay Trimberger. 1977–1978. "Revolutions and the World-Historical Development of Capitalism." *Berkeley Journal of Sociology* 22: 101–13.

Smith, Ralph. 1971. *Viet-Nam and the West.* Ithaca, N.Y.: Cornell University Press.

Snow, Edgar. 1944. *Red Star over China.* New York: Modern Library.

Sorokin, Pitirim A. 1925. *The Sociology of Revolution.* Philadelphia: Lippincott.

Soto, Lionel. 1977. *La Revoluoión del 33,* 3 vols. Havana: Editorial Ciencias Sociales.

Stalin, J. V. 1939. *Questions of Leninism.* Moscow: Foreign Languages Publishing House.

Stokes, Gale. 1993. *The Walls Came Tumbling Down: The Collapse of Communism in Eastern Europe.* New York: Oxford University Press.

Stone, Lawrence. 1966. "Theories of Revolution." *World Politics* 18, no.2 (January): 159–76.

Sweezy, Paul M., and Charles Bettelheim, eds. 1971. *On the Transition to Socialism.* New York: Monthly Review Press.

Szymanski, Albert. 1978. *The Capitalist State and the Politics of Class.* Cambridge, Mass.: Winthrop.

————. 1979. *Is the Red Flag Flying? The Political Economy of the Soviet Union.* London: Zed Books.

Tabares del Real, José. 1971. *La Revolución del 30: Sus dos ultimos anos.* Havana: n.p.

Tanter, Raymond, and Manus Midlarsky. 1967. "A Theory of Revolution." *Journal of Conflict Resolution* 11, no. 3 (September): 264–80.

Ta Thu Yhau. 1938. "Indochina: The Construction of the Revolutionary Party." *Fourth International* (November–December).

Taylor, A. J. P. 1980. *Revolutions and Revolutionaries.* London: Harnish Hamilton.

Telleria Toca, Evelio. 1973. *Los Congresos obreros en Cuba.* Havana: Editorial de Arte y Literatura, Instituto Cubano del Libro.

Terzani, Ti-ziano. 1976. *Giai Phong: The Fall and Liberation of Saigon.* New York: St. Martin's.

Therborn, Goran. 1978. *What Does the Ruling Class Do When It Rules?* London: New Left Books.

Tilly, Charles. 1978. *From Mobilization to Revolution.* New York: McGraw-Hill.

————. 1993. *European Revolutions, 1492–1992.* Oxford: Blackwell.

Tilly, Charles, Louise Tilly, and Richard Tilly. 1975. *The Rebellious Century, 1830–1930.* Cambridge, Mass.: Harvard University Press.

Trotsky, Leon. 1932. *The History of the Russian Revolution.* 3 vols. New York: Simon & Schuster.

————. 1959. *The Russian Revolution.* Selected and ed. F. W. Dupee; trans. Max Eastman. New York: Doubleday.

Wales, Nym. 1945. *The Chinese Labor Movement.* New York: Day.

Walker, Thomas. 1982. *Nicaragua in Revolution.* New York: Praeger.

————. 1985. *Nicaragua: Land of Sandino.* 2nd ed. Boulder, Colo.: Westview.

————. 1987. *Reagan versus the Sandinistas: The Undeclared War on Nicaragua.* Boulder, Colo.: Westview.

Wallerstein, Immanuel. 1971. "The State and Social Transformation: Will and Possibility." *Politics and Society* 1: 25–58.

Weber, Max. 1967. *From Max Weber: Essays in Sociology.* Trans., ed., and with an intro. by H. H. Gerth and C. Wright Mills. New York: Oxford University Press.

————. 1968. *Economy and Society*, 3 vols. ed. Guenther Roth and Claus Wittich. New York: Bedminister.

Wertheim, W. F. 1974. *Evolution and Revolution: The Rising Waves of Emancipation.* Baltimore, Md.: Penguin Books.

Wheelwright, E. L., and B. McFarlane. 1970. *The Chinese Road to Socialism.* New York: Monthly Review Press.

Wilber, Charles K. 1969. *The Soviet Model and Underdeveloped Countries.* Chapel Hill: University of North Carolina Press.

Wolf, Eric. 1969. *Peasant Wars of the Twentieth Century.* New York: Harper & Row.

Zeitlin, Irving M. 1997. *Ideology and the Development of Sociological Theory.* 6th ed. Upper Saddle River, N.J.: Prentice Hall.

Zeitlin, Maurice. 1967. *Revolutionary Politics and the Cuban Working Class.* Princeton, N.J.: Princeton University Press.

Index

About the Author

Berch Berberoglu is a professor of sociology and the director of graduate studies in the Department of Sociology at the University of Nevada, Reno. He received his Ph.D. from the University of Oregon in 1977. He has been teaching and conducting research at the University of Nevada, Reno, for the past twenty-nine years. His areas of specialization include political economy, globalization, class analysis, development, and comparative-historical sociology. Dr. Berberoglu has written and edited twenty-four books and many articles. His most recent books include *Labor and Capital in the Age of Globalization* (2002), *Globalization of Capital and the Nation-State* (2003), *Nationalism and Ethnic Conflict: Class, State, and Nation in the Age of Globalization* (2004), and *Globalization and Change: The Transformation of Global Capitalism* (2005).